Foreword

Rules may take various forms. Some are unwritten, some are enshrined in legislation, some in codes of practice and some are part of contractual relationships. Even when they are backed by law, they may not be uniformly enforced, monitoring may not be fully effective and sanctions may vary where failure occurs.

Those who write the rules vary according to the form they take but what is more important is who says what the rules should be.

Within Great Britain, the rules that form legislation for *farm* animal welfare are written by the Ministry of Agriculture, Fisheries and Food (MAFF), as are the MAFF Codes of Practice. But industry groupings also write their own Codes of Practice and the RSPCA has written standards for their 'Freedom Foods' scheme.

Fortunately, there is general agreement that there should be common standards and that deciding what the rules should be cannot be left to the whims of individuals or to interested parties. Different people and groups are bound to differ in their perceptions of what is needed and what is practicable; and there are fundamental differences of view as to what constitutes good welfare for any particular animal, even taking account of its species, size, sex, age and the environment in which it is kept.

The overwhelming need therefore is for an independent, authoritative body, whose membership reflects all relevant interests, to arrive at a consensus of what constitutes good welfare and the conditions required to provide it.

The Farm Animal Welfare Council (FAWC) has this responsibility and publishes its findings in reports on sectors of the farm livestock industry.

Many other countries — but not all — have similar arrangements and it makes increasing sense for all these bodies, within and beyond Europe, to liaise closely and to collaborate where this is appropriate. Trade occurs internationally and, ultimately, we shall need internationally agreed rules. It is an interesting question as to who will write those.

FAWC's advice to Ministers may not always result in legislation, even where that is the recommendation and, in many cases, this now has to be EU-wide. Agreement across so many countries inevitably takes time and is likely to be reduced to what can be agreed upon.

Even if the European Union takes a position on welfare, it cannot enforce it outside its boundaries and cannot operate in conflict with international trade agreements. Legislation is thus coming to be seen as somewhat weak and ineffective, difficult to agree upon and to enforce within Europe, unable to apply to imports from outside Europe.

Legislation is necessary to ensure minimum standards but there may be better ways of achieving real welfare improvements.

Ultimate power rests with the consumer. If the product is not purchased, because of the way it is produced, the method of production will change or the producer will go out of business. However, few consumers actually use this power and the economic realities may make it difficult for them to do so.

None the less, public opinion, peer pressure and pressure groups all play a part in bringing about change. The public is entitled to say that certain practices are unacceptable but they are rarely competent to say how things should be changed. That is a responsibility that must genuinely be accepted by those with the necessary knowledge and practical experience.

Increasingly, the major retailers are exerting their enormous power in the direction that they perceive their customers will ultimately want and are imposing welfare standards on their suppliers. They have enormous advantages compared with Government action.

They can work faster, they can impose standards on their sources world-wide, without regard to international trade agreements, they can more easily add welfare requirements to the existing audit trails (for food safety and quality) and they have available severe sanctions. Once having publicly committed themselves, they cannot afford to be caught out and must deal harshly with any supplier who does not conform. The supplier thus risks contract and very likely livelihood.

Fortunately, virtually all of the retailers wish to base their standards on FAWC recommendations, directly or indirectly but, of course, everything cannot be changed overnight. Even where production costs may not necessarily be much increased, some changes may incur large capital expenditure.

But it is surely better to achieve a broad programme of improvement than to weaken motivation by complaining that the ideal cannot be reached in one great leap.

Colin Spedding.

To organize this meeting the British Society of Animal Science (BSAS) has joined with the Scottish Centre for Animal Welfare Sciences (SCAWS).

BSAS wishes to thank the meeting organizers Dr Angus Russel, Dr Colin Morgan, Dr John Savory and Ms Joyce Kent, and to acknowledge support received from the Royal Society for the Prevention of Cruelty to Animals and the Universities Federation for Animal Welfare.

LIST OF DELEGATES

Aitken, Mrs Eileen	Advocates for Animals, Edinburgh
Angus, Ms Lucy	Intervet (UK) Ltd, Huntingdon, Cambridgeshire
Appleby, Dr Mike	University of Edinburgh
Ashley, Miss Doranne	Glasgow University Vet School
Avizienius, Mr John	RSPCA, Horsham, West Sussex
Barton Gade, Mrs Patricia	Danish Meat Research Institute, Roskilde, Denmark
Bayvel, Dr David	MAF, Wellington, New Zealand
Birnie, Dr Linda	University of Aberdeen
Black, Dr Murray	BSAS, Edinburgh
Blaney, Mr Ralph	University of Reading
Bornett, Miss Hannah	SAC, Edinburgh
Brooks, Mr N. G.	MAFF, Tolworth, Surbiton, Surrey
Burgess, Ms Diane	The Queen's University Belfast
Calvert, Sheena	SAC, Edinburgh
Carlisle, Ms Ailsa	Roslin Institute, Roslin, Midlothian
Cockram, Mr Michael	University of Edinburgh
Collins, Mrs Judith	SIGNET (c/o ABD, SAC, Edinburgh)
Craig, Mrs Lorna	Deans Farm Ltd, Tring, Hertfordshire
Cross, Miss Deborah	University of Aberdeen
Croston, Mr David	MLC, Milton Keynes
D'eath, Dr Ric	SAC, Edinburgh
Dandrea, Miss Jennifer	University of Nottingham
Darling, Mrs Joyce	BSAS, Edinburgh
Day, Dr John	ADAS Terrington, King's Lynn
Docksey, Miss Caroline	ADAS Terrington, King's Lynn
Don, Mr John	FAWC, Insch, Aberdeenshire
Dwyer, Dr Cathy	SAC, Edinburgh
Dyson, Mr Alan	PIC, Abingdon, Oxon
Edwards, Dr Sandra	SAC, Aberdeen
English, Prof. Peter	University of Aberdeen
Fallon, Dr Richard	Teagasc, Dunsany, Co. Meath, Ireland
Flynn, Mr Mike	SSPCA, Edinburgh
Ford, Ms Rebecca	Advocates for Animals, Edinburgh
Goddard, Dr Pete	MLURI, Aberdeen
Grant, Miss Sheona	University of Aberdeen
Guise, Dr Jane	Cambac JMA Research, Chippenham, Wiltshire
Guy, Dr Jonathan	University of Newcastle
Halls, Mr Lionel	Marshall Food Group Ltd, Newbridge, Midlothian
Harper, Mr Eddie	RHA, Bruton, Somerset
Harris, Dr David	MAFF, Carlisle, Cumbria
Harris, Mrs Judith	MAFF, Tolworth, Surbiton, Surrey
Harris, Mr Tim	Animal Transportation Association, Redhill, Surrey
Haskell, Dr Marie	Roslin Institute (Edinburgh), Midlothian

FARM ANIMAL WELFARE — WHO WRITES THE RULES?

Proceedings of an International Symposium organized by
THE BRITISH SOCIETY OF ANIMAL SCIENCE

BSAS OCCASIONAL PUBLICATION

Number 23

edited by A. J. F. Russel, C. A. Morgan, C. J. Savory, M. C. Appleby
and T. L. J. Lawrence

technical editors HILARY DAVIES and CAROL WOOLLIAMS

BSAS
EDINBURGH
1999

Occ. Publ. Br. Soc. Anim. Sci. No. 23

ISBN 0 906562 28 7
© 1999 THE BRITISH SOCIETY OF ANIMAL SCIENCE
Printed in Great Britain by D. & J. Croal Ltd., Haddington.

Hilton, Mrs Bridget	BSAS, Edinburgh
Hinchly, Mr Stuart	Premier Poultry Ltd, Scunthorpe, North Lincolnshire
Hocking, Dr Paul	Roslin Institute (Edinburgh), Midlothian
Hopley, Mr Philip	Grampian Country Food Group, Inverurie, Aberdeenshire
Hosie, Mr Brian	SAC, Edinburgh
Hunter, Mr Richard	Roslin Institute, Roslin, Midlothian
Jagger, Dr Steve	Dalgety Agriculture, Grantham
Jarvis, Susan	SAC, Edinburgh
Jorêt, Mr Andrew	Daylay Foods Ltd, Newark, Nottinghamshire
Kent, Miss Joyce	University of Edinburgh
Kirkwood, Dr James	UFAW, Wheathampstead, Hertfordshire
Layton, Ruth	Consultant, Salisbury, Wiltshire
Le Sueur, Miss Caroline	RSPCA, Horsham, West Sussex
Lewis, Miss Megan	Marks & Spencer, London
Lowman, Dr Basil	SAC, Edinburgh
Mann, Miss Jackie	SAC, Edinburgh
Margerison, Dr Jean	University of Plymouth
McGill, Miss Alison	Collier & Brock MSRCVS, Troon, Ayrshire
McPherson, Mr Owen	University of Aberdeen
Metheringham, Miss Jill	Humane Slaughter Association, Wheathampstead, Hertfordshire
Meyer, Ms Kathrin	University of Aberdeen
Milne, Mr Charles	SOAEFD, Edinburgh
Mitchell, Dr Malcolm	Roslin Institute, Roslin, Midlothian
Molony, Dr Vincent	University of Edinburgh
Morgan, Dr Colin	SAC, Edinburgh
Morris, Mr James	Scottish SPCA, Edinburgh
Mylne, Mrs Judith	Advocates for Animals, Edinburgh
Pack, Mr Brian	ANM Group Ltd, Inverurie
Parry, Dr Margaret	Harper Adams College, Newport, Shropshire
Pocknee, Dr Brian	ADAS, Lincoln
Radford, Mr Mike	University of East Anglia, Norwich
Randle, Dr Hayley	University of Plymouth (Seale-Hayne)
Roberts, Dr David	SAC, Crichton Royal Farm, Dumfriesshire
Roberts, Prof. Crad	University of Edinburgh
Roderick, Dr Stephen	University of Reading
Rose, Miss Sarah	Scottish Farm & Countryside, Educational Trust, Royal Highland Centre, Edinburgh
Russel, Dr Angus	SCAWS, Peebles, Peeblesshire
Russell, Miss Alison	BQP, Framlingham, Suffolk
Rutter, Dr Mark	IGER, North Wyke, Okehampton
Savory, Dr John	SAC, Auchincruive
Selwyn-Williams, Mr Nigel	Deans Farm Ltd, Tring, Hertfordshire
Sharp, Mr Malcolm	SAC, Aberdeen
Simpson, Mr Brian	SQBLA, Newbridge, Midlothian
Spedding, Prof. Sir Colin	Chairman FAWC Reading, Berkshire
Speed, Mr Brian	SSPCA, Edinburgh
Speers, Ms Anne	Daylay Foods Ltd, Thornton, Fife
Sprigge, Prof. Timothy	Advocates for Animals, Edinburgh

Contents

Farm animal welfare — who writes the rules?
Occasional Publication No. 23 — British Society of Animal Science 1999
edited by A. J. F. Russel, C. A. Morgan, C. J. Savory, M. C. Appleby and T. L. J. Lawrence

The pig producer's perspective

J. Guise

Cambac Research, Manor Farm, Draycot Cerne, Nr Chippenham SN15 5LD

Abstract

This paper is designed to demonstrate that practical, applied research, which is popular with the farming community, is an important part of the decision-making process. Three recent or current projects are described in areas where strategic and basic science has made an important contribution to the debate but has not provided solutions. Confinement at farrowing, tail biting and fully slatted finishing systems are all areas of concern to producers and legislators alike and these concerns are not confined to the UK. The results of surveys of industrial practice have suggested that: (a) non-confined systems may perform as well as farrowing crates, (b) tail-docking appears an effective control measure for tail biting but more importantly, the relative influence of different management practices is measurable using the techniques described and could provide solutions to the tail-biting problem, and (c) experimental studies of finishing systems have produced ambivalent results and a new approach may be of value. The recent Scientific Veterinary Committee Report of the European Union is used extensively as the basis for the discussion.

Introduction

One of the most influential documents in framing future legislation is the Report of the Scientific Veterinary Committee (Animal Welfare section) entitled 'The Welfare of Intensively Kept Pigs' which was adopted on the 30 September 1997. The members of the expert working group were invited on the basis of their scientific expertise and not as representatives of their country. However, the UK contributed 25% of the expertise to this committee, which perhaps reflects the level of interest and expertise in this subject. My knowledge of the bureaucratic processes in the European Union is strictly limited but I assume that this report will eventually form the basis for upgrading directives on the welfare of pigs, which member states will then be

required to introduce into national law. The stages take some time and I learn from colleagues in the Ministry of Agriculture, Fisheries and Food of the somewhat tortuous negotiations which are necessary before there is pan-European agreement on improvements in welfare regulations. The only advantage in these delays is that there is time for the pig industry to study what is being proposed and if it does not agree, or does not feel that there has been enough work to provide a proper, balanced view, there is opportunity to rectify the situation. This all sounds very easy but with severely restricted budgets and a wide range of cultures within the scientific community, it is not always easy to make sure the appropriate balance of basic, strategic and applied science is in place before national regulations are formed. There is insufficient money right across the scientific spectrum but, as I operate in the very near-market end of applied science, I am going to take some of the important messages from the Scientific Veterinary Committee (SVC) report (1997) and hopefully demonstrate how practical science can help and how producers and allied industries can help to support our legislators to ensure that informed decisions are made.

The farrowing crate

The SVC reports extensively on farrowing and lactation accommodation. The concluding recommendation is that the further development of farrowing systems in which the sow can be kept loose and carry out normal nest-building, without the systems compromising piglet survival, should be strongly encouraged. The general tone of the discussion appears to be one of concern about the restriction of sow movement and lack of rooting substrate and bedding material in farrowing crates but accepts that the available science, on balance, shows that piglet mortality is likely to be higher if the sows are not restrained at farrowing.

An extensive and detailed programme of work to develop an alternative farrowing system (Baxter, 1991) did not result in a dramatic change in industrial practice. This was not particularly a fault of the system or of the science behind it. A number of the resulting 'freedom farrowing' units were installed and some continue to exist today. However, when they were installed at the pig unit of the National Agricultural Centre it was very quickly found that the piglet mortality rates were unacceptably high, mostly due to a proportion of the sows choosing to farrow in the passages and not in the pen, (Hales, 1989). Farmers have traditionally been reluctant to make radical changes in their approach to various production issues and these results were greeted with some relief. To a degree, the issue of restraint at farrowing was shelved for a period in the UK but continued to be of interest in other European countries (Burke, 1996). However, a recent survey of free-farrowing systems has highlighted some interesting developments in the UK industry (Mayland and Guise, 1997). It appears that non-restraint systems in which the sow is kept separate from other sows may work better than 'community' systems. It also shows that a small number of forward-looking producers have developed systems which appear to perform as well as the traditional crates, although confounding within and between farms means that firm conclusions cannot be drawn at this stage. Some 'freedom' crates are now being used as individual pens and not as a community system, with apparent success.

While the strategic science examines the impact of restraint at farrowing and during lactation on sow and piglet welfare (Lawrence et al., 1994), pressure to find ways of keeping pigs in non-confinement systems grows. Family pens, where pigs are kept in small stable groups of sows remain together throughout the breeding cycle and young pigs are not removed until they reach market weight (Arey and Sancha, 1996), have been a subject of scrutiny for many years. This approach may be appropriate in years to come but a move towards such family pens involves a radical alteration in practice not only for breeding systems but also for rearing and finishing

systems, which will take much longer to be taken up if it is appropriate to do so.

The fact that there are non-confinement farrowing systems in operation on UK farms which appear to be working, provides the industry with an opportunity to take an active part in writing the rules. Figure 1 shows mortality rates for crated (confined) and pen (free) systems on one 800-sow farm over a period of more than a year. There is no significant difference between the production performance in terms of piglet loss between the confined and the non-confined system ($P > 0.05$). The Y axis is not labelled for reasons of commercial sensitivity.

This is an indication that non-confined but *individual* farrowing arrangements may work in practice. However, there are features other than the degree of confinement which vary between the two systems, in this case the physical nature of the food. It is not possible to draw any firm conclusions from these observations, the results merely provide a strong lead. What is now needed and what was missing from the 'freedom farrowing system' programme, is a large scale commercial testing programme, which eliminates, as far as is practicable, the confounding factors on the farms where the systems are present. It is very difficult to find funding for work of this nature, owing to the unpopularity of very applied, practical science with the statutory funding bodies. It is perhaps an indication of the concern within the industry about the future of the farrowing crate that a number of companies have formed a consortium to fund work at this level. We are currently in the process of developing the facilities for this testing programme but within 3 years there should be some very soundly based comparative information on the production, mortality and economics of a range of farrowing systems.

Tail-docking and tail-biting
Tail-docking is a radical and unpleasant means used to control tail-biting in pigs. Tail-biting has been reported in the literature for over 100 years (Coburn, 1883) and the use of tail-docking as a management tool has increased dramatically during the last 20 years, from 34% in 1974 (Penny and Hill, 1974) to at least 80·9% in 1997 (Hunter et al., 1998). Recent reports that methods other than docking are effective in controlling tail-biting (Fraser and Broom, 1990) and that docking does not eliminate tail-biting (Robertson, 1997) have heightened the debate on the acceptability of docking as a management procedure.

It is widely recognized that tail-biting is usually the result of a number of factors and a range of opinions

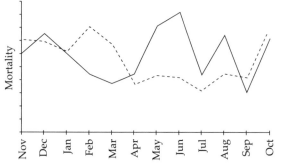

Figure 1 The effects of confinement on pre-weaning piglet mortality: ——— free; - - - - confined.

exist on the relative importance of each of these. Early reports of a study which was aimed at increasing our understanding of the aetiology of tail-biting (Guise and Penny, 1998) were criticized (Webster and Day, 1998) but this was one of the first attempts to understand tail-biting using a clinical approach. Most of the earlier studies were experimental and aimed at identifying trigger factors by inducing tail-biting, e.g. Ewbank (1973). Other surveys have not been carried out on a sufficient scale, as confining observations to one abattoir may not provide a full picture (Robertson, 1997). Our study was also limited, being conducted during a 2-month period. It was, however, only designed to be a pilot exercise and, although the tail-biting frequencies between categories (i.e. docked or long-tails) are robust, we can draw no firm conclusions about the relative influences of farm management system. The pointers the work has provided are useful but, more importantly, the work has served to demonstrate that if a study were to be conducted to a suitable scale and design, the solutions to tail-biting lie within information gleaned from the industry and are more likely to yield solutions than more expensive, strategic studies. The scrutiny of an independent statistician and the addition of the results from a sixth abattoir (total number of tails examined 62 971) have shown that the odds of a docked pig not being bitten were 2·73 times better than the odds of a long-tailed pig being bitten (95% confidence interval 2·509 to 2·978 (Figure 2).

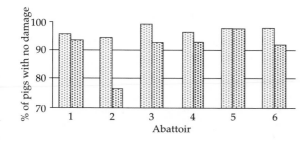

Figure 2 Tail biting damage in docked (▦) and long-tailed (▨) pigs.

I hope sincerely that as a result of this work the techniques employed will be used on a less modest scale over more seasons to provide a firmer picture of the relative effects of the various factors which are thought to be involved. Once again, the answers which are urgently needed to allow tail-docking to cease, are available within the industry. This is the second opportunity for farmers and allied trades to help write the rules by supplying practical facts.

Fully slatted floor systems

A key recommendation of the SVC is that 'all pigs should be provided with a lying surface which is physically and thermally comfortable and which does not result in injuries. Materials for investigation and manipulation, which may be bedding or earth floors but need not be, must be provided whenever possible for pigs.'

There has been concern from producers about the welfare image of fully slatted systems and this key recommendation does little to dispel those fears. Fully slatted systems are used for 36% of finished pigs (Sheppard, 1996) because of their ease of management, their reported economic performance and because pigs are physically separated from their own urine and faces, which theoretically should lead to a microbiologically cleaner product. This proportion is reported by the agricultural buildings manufacturers to be growing, as most new buildings being erected feature fully slatted floors. The main areas of concern for these systems are the effects of flooring on foot and leg injuries, air quality and its impact on respiratory disease and the barrenness of the pig environment which may be associated with vice.

The science regarding both production and welfare in such systems compared with their slatted counterparts is not clear-cut. In welfare terms thermal comfort may be more easy to achieve because a fully controlled environment is part of the fully slatted 'system'. Commercial pressures to maximize growth and food efficiency performance are factors which have encouraged producers to use these systems. On the other hand, pressure from the welfare lobby encourages the use of straw-bedded systems which many producers perceive as uneconomic and in some areas of the country the supply of straw may be a limiting factor.

Whether there is adequate and appropriate science to support any decision to be made about the relative merits of fully slatted systems compared with those which are straw-based is questionable. Work with weaned pigs suggests that they will work harder for thermal comfort than they will for physical comfort (Fraser, 1985). This would tend to support the use of fully slatted accommodation as behavioural thermoregulation is difficult in straw-based systems in hot weather. However, extrapolation of these results to heavier-weight pigs is a doubtful practice, as any degree of discomfort may increase with body weight. There have been many reports of a higher prevalence of bursitis, lameness and swollen joints in fully slatted systems compared with bedded systems (e.g. Jakob and Etter, 1980) but there are recent reports of lesions which are more likely to be associated with straw-based systems than with others (Smith and Morgan, 1998a). The quality of the concrete, the width of the slat, the solid:void area and the sharpness of the slat edges have a strong influence on the prevalence of foot and leg injuries (Smith and Morgan, 1998b) but whether improving these features can reduce the overall levels of injury and provide adequate comfort to those of straw-bedded systems is unclear. It seems that it is possible to meet the behavioural need for a rooting substrate by means other than straw bedding (Pearce and Patterson, 1993; Sneddon and Beattie, 1995), so if floor design can be improved to avoid the potential injuries caused in non-bedded systems they may be supportable on welfare grounds.

The currently available production science further complicates the argument, as many producers perceive fully slatted systems to perform better than straw-based ones. However several studies have not supported this view and results are often contradictory (Lyons et al., 1995). A recent study concluded that straw yards would perform better than slatted ones in production terms, as described in the Table 1.

On the basis of these results and in view of the welfare issues associated with fully slatted systems, it is surprising that slatted systems remain popular. However, the production parameters reported are not representative of commercial experience, where growth rates of 1000 g/day are achievable in fully slatted systems. There is clearly room for more work on this subject, both on improving floor design and establishing the relative economic merits of different systems. Other issues, such as microbial cleanliness should also be taken into account to provide an accurate, balanced view of finishing systems for the future, to protect the pig's welfare, the economics of production and the safety of the product. There is a lack of research and development facilities where these studies can take place on an adequate scale but there are plenty of commercial farms where both systems are represented on one site. As long as there

is sufficient replication a multi-site study could provide some useful support to decision makers both in the production sector and regulatory bodies.

Conclusion

There is a wide range of cultures within the scientific community and practical, applied research lies very close to the near-market end of the research spectrum. Research conducted within the industry has some advantages and three examples have been described where such work can contribute to the decision-making process. It undoubtedly cannot exist without the support of other scientific sectors but often does not sit comfortably with more traditional scientific principles. Basic or strategic science which shows, for instance, that the farrowing crate compromises sow welfare, that tail-docking is an insult or that the use of fully slatted accommodation is questionable, is an important part of the debate. However this is only part of the whole picture. The conclusion of the Scientific Veterinary Committee on this subject is strongly recommended.

'Conclusions about welfare should always be based on all available evidence properly weighted and should not rely only on, for example, preference or other trials in experimental conditions, or epidemiological surveys. When recommendations about modified practices are produced the relevance of experimental studies where effects of only one or a few factors have been varied must be carefully considered. On practically operating farms, effects of such single variables may be exaggerated or compensated by other factors and the stockman factor is central in the effective functioning of a particular system. It is therefore normally desirable that on-farm surveys are carried out before definite recommendations are issued'.

References

Arey, D. S. and Sancha, E. S. 1996. Behaviour and productivity of sows and piglets in a family system and in farrowing crates. *Applied Animal Behaviour Science* **50:** 135-145.

Baxter, M. R. 1991. The freedom farrowing system. *Farm Building Progress* **104:** 9.

Burke, J. 1996. *An investigation of experimental and commercial non-confinement and group farrowing systems in the Netherlands, Germany, Denmark, Sweden and Norway.* Seale Hayne Faculty of Agriculture, Food and Land Use, Newton Abbot.

Coburn, F. D. 1882. *Swine husbandry: a practical manual.* Orang Judd Co., New York.

Jakob, P. and Etter, H. 1980. Evaluation of economic and technical parameters of the open-front, deep-litter system for pigs. In *Aktuelle Arbeiten zur artgemassen Tierhaltung 1980.* Vortrage anlasslich der tagung 'Kriterien artgemasser Tierhaltung' der Deutschen Veterinarmodizinischen

Table 1 *Key production parameters for different finishing systems*†

	Straw yards	Slatted pens
Daily food intake (kg)	1·9	1·7
Average daily gain (g)	750	670
Food conversion ratio	2·55	2·77

† From Guy *et al.* (1995).

Gesellschaft c.V. Fachgruppe Verhaltensforschung vom 19-22 November 1980. darmstadt-Kranichstein, German Federal republic, Kuratorium fur Technik und Bauwesen in der Landwirtschaft eV, pp. 133-141.

Ewbank, R. 1973. Abnormal behaviour and pig nutrition. An unsuccessful attempt to induce tail-biting by feeding a high energy, low fibre vegetable protein diet. *British Veterinary Journal* 129: 366-369.

Fraser, D. 1985. Selection of bedded and unbedded areas by pigs in relation to environmental temperature and behaviour. *Applied Animal Behaviour Science* 14: 117-126.

Fraser, A. and Broom, D. 1990. *Farm animal welfare and behaviour*. Bailliere Tindall, London.

Guise, H. J. and Penny, R. H. C. 1998. Tail biting and tail docking in pigs. *Veterinary Record* 142: 46.

Guy, J. H., Rowlinson, P. and Chadwick, J. P. 1995. A comparison of two genotypes of finishing pig housed in outdoor paddocks, straw yards and fully slatted pens. 1. Performance. *Animal Science* 60: 518 (abstr.).

Hales, P. 1989. An analysis of piglet mortality on the new unit. *Pig Unit Newsletter 29*. National Agricultural Centre, Stoneleigh, Kenilworth, Warwickshire.

Lawrence, A. B., Petherick, J. C., McLean, K. A., Deans, L. A., Chirnside, J., Vaughan, A., Clutton, E. and Terlouw, E. M. C. 1994. The effect of environment on behaviour, plasma cortisol and prolactin in parturient sows. *Applied Animal Behaviour Science* 39: 313 - 330.

Lyons, C. A. P., Bruce, J. M., Fowler, V. R. and English, P. R. 1995. A comparison of the productivity and welfare of growing pigs in four intensive systems. *Livestock Production Science* 43: 265-274.

Mayland, A. P. and Guise, H. J. 1997. *A survey of units with unconfined farrowing systems*. Report to Sponsors. Cambac Research, Manor Farm, Draycot Cerne, Nr Chippenham.

Pearce, G. P. and Paterson, A. M. 1993. The effect of space restriction and provision of toys during rearing on the behaviour, productivity and physiology of male pigs. *Applied Animal Behaviour Science* 36: 11-28.

Penny, R. H. C. and Hill, F. W. G. 1974. Observations of some conditions in pigs at the abattoir with particular reference to tail-biting. *Veterinary Record* 94: 174-180.

Robertson, J. F. 1997. *Management of tail-biting — a farm guide for the Scottish Pig Industry Initiative*. SPII, Rural Centre, West Mains, Ingliston, Newbridge.

Scientific Veterinary Committee. 1997. *The welfare of intensively kept pigs*. DocXXIV/B3/ScVC/0005/1997 (Final) prepared in accordance with Article 6 of Council Directive 91/630/EEC.

Sheppard, A. 1996. *The structure of pig production in England and Wales*. Report 33, Agricultural Economic Unit, University of Exeter.

Smith, W. J. and Morgan, M. 1998a. Claw lesions: their relationship with the floor surface: finishing pigs — part 1. *Proceedings of the 15th International Pig Veterinary Society Congress, Birmingham, England*.

Smith, W. J., and Morgan, M. 1998b. Claw lesions: their relationship with the floor surface: finishing pigs — part II. *Proceedings of the 15th International Pig Veterinary Society Congress, Birmingham, England*.

Sneddon, I. A. and Beattie, V. E. 1995. Improving the welfare of pigs. *Irish Journal of Psychology* 16: 419-426.

Webster, S. D. and Day, J. E. L. 1998. Tail biting and tail docking in pigs. *Veterinary Record* 142: 375.

Farm animal welfare — who writes the rules?
Occasional Publication No. 23 — British Society of Animal Science 1999
edited by A. J. F. Russel, C. A. Morgan, C. J. Savory, M. C. Appleby and T. L. J. Lawrence

Walking the animal welfare tight-rope: an egg industry view

A. D. Jorêt

Daylay Foods Limited, The Moor, Bilsthorpe, Newark, Nottinghamshire NG22 8TS

Abstract

There is a wealth of animal welfare legislation affecting the egg industry. Legislation can be over-prescriptive and can be a barrier to progress even where welfare benefits would result. Codes of practice (e.g. Freedom Food; The Lion) present a more flexible way forward, but to be effective they have to be both understood and credible in the eyes of the consumer.

With the increasing globalization of trade, welfare legislation must be framed to protect domestic industry from unfair competition.

In the context of the theme of this conference — Farm animal welfare — who writes the rules? — it is first appropriate to ascertain what are the rules as far as the egg industry is concerned. I can find four pieces of legislation on animal welfare directly affecting all or parts of the egg industry, namely: the Agriculture (Miscellaneous Provisions) Act 1968; the Welfare of Livestock Regulations 1994; the Welfare of Animals (Transport) Order 1997; and the Welfare of Animals (Slaughter or Killing) Regulations 1995.

Legislation provides the basic framework in which we operate but, following that, we also have the Government's 'Codes of Recommendations for the Welfare of Livestock — Domestic Fowls'. These are not laws in themselves but failure to abide by them will be taken as tending to establish guilt when accused of offences under the above specific legislation.

When you then add the legislation and codes of practice on poultry health, environment, employment and so on and so on, you begin to wonder why any sane minded person is in business at all, particularly given the ease with which you can fall foul of the multitude of legislation affecting our industry.

What is certainly essential from a producer's point of view is that one belongs to a sound trade association such as the British Egg Association or National Farmers' Union, so that one is kept aware of one's current obligations and advised of impending ones. As a plea at the very start of my paper I would ask for less, not more, legislation, since legislation is generally a very blunt tool.

One of its failings is that it can be pointlessly over-prescriptive. I give here the example of the laying cage floor angle from the 1994 Welfare of Livestock Regulations: 'the slope of the floor shall not exceed 14% or 8 degrees, when made of rectangular wire mesh, and 21·3% or 12 degrees for other floor types'. The 1994 regulations actually implement the European Union (EU) Directive 88/166 laying down minimum standards for the protection of laying hens kept in battery cages. We shall return to the influence of Brussels later but, as is now so often the case, the wording in our legislation was lifted directly from the original Directive. The problem with this particular detail is that no-one determined in legislation how one should measure such a complicated thing as cage floor angle. Was it with birds in or not? Is it an average over the whole floor area or not? At the margins what is the difference in animal welfare terms between 7, 8, or 9 degrees? And again, was there any scientific justification for specifying one floor angle for wire mesh floors and another for other floor types? What this all does is to trivialize the law, but it has also made many egg producers incur unnecessary expenditure in order to comply with a highly arbitrary point.

A second and probably more important failing of welfare legislation is that it fossilizes systems. It can stymie development even if it were to give positive welfare benefits since the prospect of changing legislation, particularly at the European level, is negligible and would in any event be many years in the process.

Given my dislike of legislation — what should take its place, if anything? Let us imagine a situation where no animal welfare legislation exists. In those circumstances what would influence what producers did and how they did it? In principle I think you would agree that decisions would be driven by economic factors although altruistic factors could influence individuals' actions. Those economic factors could, of course, include the use of higher-cost, perceived more welfare friendly systems, producing a premium market product. In this situation you really would find out both how much and how many are prepared to pay above the economic minimum for an animal product with perceived welfare benefits. We all know of those surveys telling us how almost everyone would pay more for this or that benefit, but we also know the reality of how many actually do it.

The point I am coming to is that, in my view, animal welfare is not a producer issue but a consumer one. However, that does imply that the consumer is actually in a position to determine what the differences are and then to make a judgement on them.

Clear and accurate labelling is essential to this and is an area where the egg industry has not always been as open as it now is. As an aside you may wonder why there has been a change by the industry on labelling. Criticism of the industry by consumer groups and animal welfare organizations has had an effect here. Incidentally, you can also add to my list of poultry welfare legislation the need to comply with the Egg Marketing Regulations which includes the issue of labelling and the use of the 'special marketing terms' and thus has an indirect welfare implication.

A very good example of consumer choice on laying-hen welfare is the success of the RSPCA's Freedom Food scheme which includes two egg products — 'barn eggs' and 'free range' eggs. Nearly all the major retailers in this country now sell Freedom Food eggs with the Freedom Food logo on the pack as well as the special marketing term descriptor — free range or barn — and those who do not have introduced their own in-house specification which mirrors the Freedom Food one.

The Freedom Food specification for laying hens was set up some 4 years ago. This was not done in isolation by the RSPCA but in conjunction with producer representatives, creating a specification

that was much more stringent than the basic minimum for free range or barn, as set out in the European Egg Marketing Regulations but which was still achievable and practical. Changes to the specification are ultimately approved by the RSPCA Council, acting on the recommendations of a working group which is composed of RSPCA officials, Freedom Food officials, poultry veterinarians and egg industry members. I am pleased to be one of those industry members.

As you can imagine, at the outset there was a need for several amendments to the specification as a result of the experience of its use. Now, however, the specification changes are infrequent, if at all. The ability to change the specification is a major advance compared with the inflexibility of legislation. Of course, for any code of practice to be credible it has to be effectively policed and there has to be a structured way in which alterations to the code are made. I have already described how alterations are made and for the policing there is the annual inspection of registered premises as well as random monitoring by the RSPCA. Note that I said *premises* and not just farms, as far as inspection is concerned. This is vitally important as far as the credibility of the scheme is concerned. If there is cheating going on it is not often a failure on farm but usually a case of switching of product at, or on the way to, the packing centre. The ability to demonstrate full traceability of product is here the critical point.

The success of the scheme is undoubtedly due to the esteem with which the RSPCA is held by the general public. I don't suppose for one minute that many people will have any idea what the details of the laying hen specifications are but they trust that the RSPCA will have ensured that anything they put their name to will be a genuine welfare advance.

From a welfare standpoint there are, of course, some problems with the alternative systems, in particular the need to beak trim and, despite this, a much greater incidence of cannibalism than any of us would like to see. A great deal of research effort is currently being spent on these subjects. The primary breeding companies are also now generally including selection against aggressive tendencies in their programmes. I suspect that this latter point will eventually be the most fruitful of all the approaches to the problem, but it will take many years before we can see significant changes in flocks at commercial level.

The non-cage sector in the United Kingdom (UK) is now the largest in Europe. At four million hens, we have half of all the free range hens in Europe. This has been achieved by market demand, not legislation. This has been led by various bodies, especially the retailers, but the important thing is that it actually sells — if it didn't the product would not be given the shelf space in store.

The egg industry also has its own code of practice, allowing producers who comply with it to use the 'Lion' quality mark. This code covers both food safety and welfare issues and covers all types of production:- cage, barn and free range. In animal welfare terms it mirrors the Freedom Food specification for barn and free range. For the consumer it is another scheme and could, therefore, lead to confusion, but this is being addressed by industry-funded advertising. The aim of the advertising is to get across the simple message that buying Lion eggs ensures you are buying a safe product which has been produced to welfare standards that exceed those set out in basic legislation.

All the provisos, as far as credible codes of practice are concerned, also apply here, with independent monitoring, full product traceability, clear labelling and an advertising campaign to spread the message.

The Lion could be a very valuable tool to protect our industry from the worst effects of the proposed new EU Directive on the keeping of laying hens. This Directive should win the prize for being the most ill-thought-out and badly drafted document ever to emerge from Brussels. In the context of the theme of the conference 'Who writes the rules' it would appear in this case it is a Brussels bureaucrat. The only fair thing to emerge in the first draft is that it would make illegal virtually every current system of keeping hens used in Europe, both cage and alternatives.

Our UK Farm Animal Welfare Council (FAWC) is a very influential body and has a big bearing on the position that the UK Government will adopt on forthcoming welfare legislation such as this proposed new Directive. It is a body almost without parallel in other member states of the EU and its influence extends across Europe. In July 1997 FAWC published a report on the welfare of laying hens. Their main conclusions were: 600 cm^2 per bird in

new cage installations immediately and within 5 years in existing ones; cages in their *present* form to be phased out as a longer term aim if additional features such as nests, perches and dust bathing can be provided *without* an increase in injurious pecking; UK industry *must* be protected from unfair competition from elsewhere within the EU; phasing out throughout the EU *must* take place simultaneously; imports of shell eggs and egg products into the EU must be *banned* from those countries in which conventional cages are still used. GATT/WTO arrangements should *not* be allowed to prevent these measures and, if necessary, the UK Government should seek an amendment in order to protect the welfare of animals; there are signs that genetic selection for reduced injurious pecking behaviour may remove an obstacle to the widespread use of non-cage systems. The phasing out of battery cages should *not* be effected until after the elimination or successful control of injurious pecking and cannibalism through genetic progress or improvements in management techniques.

Unfortunately the draft Directive appears to have ignored this report, as it has also ignored the opinion of its own Scientific Veterinary Committee. In particular it offers absolutely no protection against third country imports — the very point that the FAWC said was essential in any new measure. What has emerged is a document which betrays the prejudices of whoever drafted it and which seems to ignore both rational science and common sense. Let us hope that the final form of the Directive is very different from the current one. If it does not change then all that will happen is that the egg industry in Europe will be a lot smaller — particularly in the northern member states which tend to apply EU Directives firmly. There will be a large influx of egg and egg products from third countries whose welfare standards are below those which *currently* apply in Europe, let alone any further changes which the proposals will finally produce.

The minimum cage stocking density in Europe is currently 450 cm^2 per bird and the draft Directive proposes 800 cm^2 with additional cage height. In the United States of America (USA) there is no legislation on cage stocking density; the typical figure in use in the USA is 350 cm^2 per hen.

The new Directive, whatever its final form, will undoubtedly increase the costs of production of cage eggs in Europe. Whilst it would be difficult for third country imports to penetrate our retail shell egg market, particularly if we have by then a really effective Lion mark, this is not the case for the products market. The threat from this Directive to our industry is a real one; it is not just a case of

Table 1 *Egg production costs at different stocking densities*

Stocking density (cm² per bird)	Birds per standard cage	Capital cost (£ per bird)	Running costs (£ per dozen eggs)
350	7	£10·00	£0·42
450/500	5	£14·00	£0·45
550/600	4	£17·50	£0·48
750/800	3	£23·33	£0·54
750/800 + 50 cm high	3	£26·66	£0·56

'crying wolf'. The egg products market takes around 25% of European egg production. This is a growing market fuelled by our lifestyle changes which demand more and more ready prepared food and less and less food preparation at home. If we follow the trends in the USA we would expect this to be 40% by the year 2010. Egg products are the 'invisible eggs'. When you buy a cake, do you even think about it containing eggs, never mind the system in which those eggs were produced? Already eggs have come to Europe from the USA for processing. This is an area where economics is all. The costs of production at various cage stocking densities are presented in Table 1. European animal food costs are used in the calculations. The reality of the present situation is that European food costs are still significantly above world prices and are likely ever to remain so, Agenda 2000 notwithstanding.

As can be seen, the additional cost burden from the new proposals will rule out the use of domestically produced eggs in egg products. What welfare benefit does this proposal produce when examined in this global context?

Conclusion

In conclusion, I would urge that we have less legislation, not more, and that instead we have effective codes of practice coupled with clear labelling so that welfare becomes the consumers' choice that it always should have been. However, if welfare legislation is inevitable, then it should be framed in such a way that our domestic industry is not put at risk from unfair competition either from within the EU or from the rest of the world. There is no welfare gain in legislating our own industry out of existence only to turn round and import the product from those very same systems, but operated to lower standards, that were formerly in use in this country.

Farm animal welfare — who writes the rules?
Occasional Publication No. 23 — British Society of Animal Science 1999
edited by A. J. F. Russel, C. A. Morgan, C. J. Savory, M. C. Appleby and T. L. J. Lawrence

Striking the balance: a chicken meat producer's view

P. T. Hopley

Grampian Country Food Group Ltd, Blackhall Road, Inverurie, Aberdeenshire AB51 3NA

Abstract

We are now trading in a world market and it is vital we are aware of the chicken meat production systems and ethics employed in other European and third world countries. All these countries have generally a lower cost of production than the United Kingdom. The strength of the United Kingdom industry is the level of efficiency and biological performance and we must be careful not to load excessive additional cost onto our industry by the introduction of onerous welfare legislation. One of the major points of difference between the United Kingdom and the rest of the world is that of stocking density. In the United Kingdom stocking density is laid down in the 'Codes of Recommendations for the Welfare of Livestock — Domestic Fowls'. The pace of change within the industry has made this single figure approach obsolete. Industry bodies, such as the British Poultry Meat Federation and the National Farmers' Union, have an important rôle in representing producers' views to Government and consumers. We need more concentration and funding on research and finding solutions, and less on ever more ways of measuring problems.

The rules that already exist in the chicken meat industry are very similar to those mentioned in the previous paper on laying hens, which I will not repeat, except to say that we do not have to contend with the complexities of the cages regulations. We will also probably be seeing new requirements on farming under the new European Union (EU) framework directive agreed in June.

When writing animal welfare rules there are basically three interested parties: producers, scientists and consumers, the Government (four if you count the birds themselves). Legislators are in effect the coordinating force.

When considering legislation for the chicken industry it is worthy of note that we are now trading in a world market and it is vital we are aware of the production systems and ethics employed in other European and third world countries. I only make reference to this as I am not suggesting for one moment we should adopt the practices of the lowest common denominator. It is a fact that under current World Trade Organization (WTO) rules we cannot limit or prevent the importation of such produce on the grounds of poor welfare or because a therapeutic or prophylactic substance is used elsewhere in the world. Therefore we must be careful not to export our industry to less welfare and health conscious countries. An example of this was where the Government took a unilateral decision to ban the use of veal crates in the United Kingdom (UK) (a principle with which I agree). The result was in effect a deterioration of welfare due to 1-week-old calves being transported on lorries and ferries and subjected to the largely unregulated continental veal crate system. Perhaps in hindsight it would have been better if industry, scientists and consumers had got together and accepted the existence of veal production but worked on developing a more welfare-friendly system and thereby keeping the industry at home where better welfare could be exercised and controlled. We must learn the lesson from this.

As I have indicated above, we are trading in an international commodity, the volume exporters being predominantly France, Denmark, and Holland within Europe, and the United States of America, Brazil and Thailand. It is fair to say that eastern Europe is now expanding its production, predominantly Hungary and Poland. All of these countries have generally a lower cost of production than the UK, either in terms of labour cost or raw material food cost. For example, in Thailand, a poultry worker is paid 5 US dollars per day (£3·00); our own staff are paid in excess of this per hour. The food raw material cost is, however, comparable with that of the United Kingdom. At the other extreme is the United States where labour costs are almost comparable to ours but the food raw material cost is much less. The strength of the UK industry is the level of efficiency and biological performance from our stock and management systems but we must be careful not to load excessive additional cost on to our industry by the introduction of onerous welfare legislation.

One of the major points of difference between the UK and the rest of the world is that of stocking density. In the UK stocking density is laid down in the Ministry of Agriculture's publication 'Codes of Recommendations for the Welfare of Livestock — Domestic Fowls'. This was first published 30 years ago in 1968 and revised in 1987. I believe that the pace of change within the industry in terms of technology in our housing systems, nutritional fine tuning of suitable raw materials, veterinary science and genetic selection have made this single figure approach obsolete. However, it is true to say that some of the production facilities that were in existence in 1968 are still there today, which is why the industry would support a more flexible approach to welfare codes in terms of adopting a variable stocking density standard, comparable with the quality of the growing facility and management. It is accepted, in some cases, this density may well be less than the current limit of 34 kg/m^2 but experience confirms significantly higher densities are achievable in high-quality properly equipped houses.

I believe the variable approach is important to convey the right message to producers and consumers in terms of encouraging investment in modern houses and better facilities to drive in better welfare standards. The previous paper makes reference to the Farm Animal Welfare Council as being the UK's leading force behind good welfare, an organization that we in the industry whole-heartedly support, being made up of farmers, scientists, veterinarians and academics. However, I feel, and I am sure they do at times, that their rôle is not fully understood by consumers and producers. Their main rôle in life is to identify issues within the farming industry and recommend to Government suitable legislation where appropriate.

It is a sad day for us all when we need legislation to drive good welfare. We obtain better and more sustainable results from industry collaboration with science and balanced consumer groups who deal with real welfare issues and not perceived welfare. A prime example of this dates back to 1992, when the Farm Animal Welfare Council identified that the chicken industry had a serious welfare situation pertaining to leg abnormalities in growing birds. The Council wrote in its report that 'the current level of leg problems in broilers is unacceptable' and went on to say 'the Council intends to look at this aspect of broiler production in five years time when significant improvements should be apparent! If no reduction in leg problems is found we may recommend the introduction of legislation to ensure the required improvements'.

The report on the 5-year study is still awaited but during this period the industry worked actively to improve this situation in terms of genetic selection, improved nutrition and veterinary science, along with improved and more controlled husbandry practices. Not wishing to pre-empt the Council's findings, those of us directly involved in the industry have seen a dramatic improvement in the situation over this period of time. This example of recognition, consultation and recommendation is, I believe, achieving a far better and lasting result than any 'take it or leave it' approach that by its very nature legislation adopts.

Industry bodies, such as the British Poultry Meat Federation and the National Farmers' Union, to name but two, also have an important rôle to play, both in representing producers' views to Government and consumers and also in giving balance to the debate. The UK retailers also have a part to play in representing their consumers' views on welfare and food safety issues. But caution should be exercised in adopting the moral high ground on welfare to score a competitive advantage over the opposition and therefore detracting from the real issue of genuine welfare improvements.

The same goes for research. We need more concentration and funding on finding solutions and less on ever more ways of measuring problems. We have to refrain from thinking that all facets of poultry management systems that have evolved with a little science and a lot of experience have to be 'legitimized' by scientists. Knowledge from field experience is relevant and has a valid rôle in forming policy.

Other less front-end sectors of our industry are also open to scrutiny, namely, our breeding and hatching businesses. All of these are under the watchful eye of the Farm Animal Welfare Council and the Humane Slaughter Association and I believe the degree of cooperation between industry and these bodies is significant. As long as this level of cooperation continues, the need for 'rules' or legislation is limited. Good welfare is good business. It is in the industry's interest as much as that of any one else. Some of the issues that are currently being addressed in this sector include controlling appetite of broiler parents and the now limited number of mutilations to male breeding chicks. The parent-stock market is an important part of the UK export economy and therefore we need to maintain pressure on well controlled welfare in the UK rather than exporting the sector to other countries. Continuous efforts are being made to maintain the natural mating process by getting the balance right between weight gain, body conformation and reproductive ability. All these issues are being addressed in the awaited report from the Farm Animal Welfare Council on broiler breeders.

In conclusion I believe we have one of the best poultry industries is the world, in terms of health and welfare controls, all of which have a cost which I feel is covered by our enhanced levels of biological performance, but this balance is a fine one. One cannot legislate good welfare into a company. Welfare must be part of the company ethos; it must be strongly endorsed at the top and run through everything the company does. Welfare is about attitudes, education, and understanding. I believe that in the UK we have the right balance of cooperation and understanding between the industry, scientists and the consumers to drive in good, genuine, welfare without the need for onerous legislation.

Farm animal welfare — who writes the rules?
Occasional Publication No. 23 — British Society of Animal Science 1999
edited by A. J. F. Russel, C. A. Morgan, C. J. Savory, M. C. Appleby and T. L. J. Lawrence

The producer's view — ruminants

B. Lowman

Animal Biology Division, Scottish Agricultural College, Bush Estate, Penicuik, Midlothian EH26 0PH

Abstract

Ruminant producers blame almost equally supermarkets and Government for welfare legislation for many reasons but mainly because legislation incurs additional administrative and policing costs. All of these are eventually paid for by the producer, increasing their production costs but not those of their overseas competitors. There is little doubt that the final responsibility for legislation lies with each of us as individual consumers. A significant factor influencing our view of animal welfare is our upbringing, associating 'nice animals' with similar feelings to ourselves. However, such instinctive principles are generally forgotten when we are asked to pay a premium for them in the supermarket. Hence the main activators of welfare legislation are the 'evangelical few'. Supermarkets claim that the demands they impose on their suppliers are simply a reflection of their customers' demands. However another reason is to allow supermarkets clearly to differentiate their ruminant products to encourage consumers through the door but it has been difficult for them to pass on a premium to their suppliers for meeting tighter specifications for which the consumer will not pay a premium. This dilemma has recently reached breaking point in the pig industry with the ending of the Malton pig contract. To move farm animal welfare forward requires a firm basis of 'systems' welfare research which would also act as an effective vehicle for technology transfer to producers. Nevertheless, the main dilemma, our reluctance as consumers to pay for high welfare products, will continue to restrict progress. If, however, high welfare systems could be shown to improve product eating quality for which consumers will pay a premium, developments in animal welfare will be rapidly and willingly accepted by producers.

Introduction

When asked the question 'Who writes the rules?' beef, sheep and dairy producers are equally split between blaming the supermarkets and government, both the United Kingdom (UK) Government and the European Community (EC). However, when asked perhaps the more pertinent question 'Who initiates this legislation?' the replies are almost unanimous in accusing a few verbose (a polite interpretation of the phrases actually used) individuals with little or no knowledge of practical livestock production.

The initial attitude of nearly all producers when asked such questions is one of concerned anger, so that the reply is normally preceded with the remark 'well I blame . . . .'. There are several different concerns resulting in this common attitude to increased welfare legislation.

Repetition. Including farm assurance schemes under the broad welfare legislation heading clearly demonstrates the problem — most assurance schemes simply restate current welfare legislation.

Legislation on what is already standard practice. An example of this would be the milk hygiene legislation which dairy producers are forced to adhere to in order to market their product regardless of the legal requirements. While it is perhaps fair to suggest that such legislation is simply legalizing current good practice, producers see it as unnecessary administration creating 'jobs for the boys' who, due to their lack of practical knowledge, are unaware that meeting the rules is already an essential requirement for each and every dairy producer.

Jobs for the boys (and girls) paid for by the agricultural industry. All legislation has to be enforced, involving additional costs to the industry. For a mixed upland farm this could currently mean up to six different inspections per year involving different organizations and personnel each time. Of even greater concern is that the number of inspections enforced on producers is rapidly increasing.

Impractical legislation. The major frustration to producers is legislation which they believe is detrimental rather than beneficial to welfare during the lifetime of the animal. An example of this would be the recent legislation on the welfare of calves prohibiting calves to be tethered for more than 2 hours. However, in Orkney where many beef cows are still overwintered in byres it is standard practice to tether young calves behind their mothers, both to control suckling and hence the risk of scour but also to train heifer calves for when they eventually enter the herd and will themselves be tethered in the byre. Outlawing this practice greatly magnifies the stress to the first-calved heifer when she eventually finds herself restricted in the byre situation — with the greatly added risk of injury to the stockpersons.

Increased production costs — unfair competition. Undoubtedly the main concern of producers is the increased production cost UK legislation can force on them which overseas competitors do not face. Classic examples of this would be the legislation on battery cages and tethering of pregnant sows. While to date ruminant producers have not had to face such major capital investment due to purely welfare legislation, cattle producers have had to absorb additional costs to meet the recent cattle identification and movement legislation. While the additional cost of double-tagging is almost acceptable to producers, the cost of the corresponding paperwork, both in terms of the farmers' own time and the central administrative overheads, is much less acceptable. Finally, for a few units where the large official plastic tags are ripped out of young calves' ears on deer fences etc, obeying one set of legislation results in animal welfare being compromised and additional production costs imposed on the producer.

Who initiates the rules?

There is little doubt that final responsibility for legislation lies with each of us as individuals. In terms of farm animal welfare legislation, it is largely the way we each behave as a consumer in what we buy which has the long-term effect. For example, if the market for RSPCA Freedom Foods expands rapidly, there is no doubt that their standards will quickly be seen as normal and eventually enter into legislation.

However, how we react in the marketplace does not initially explain some of the more contentious welfare legislation such as some of the recent regulations on transport of ruminants. Nevertheless even this legislation is influenced by each of us and how we contribute to the overall understanding of animal welfare of the whole population. This became obvious to me recently when I became a grandparent. Currently, my 3-month-old grandson is surrounded by cuddly, soft cows, sheep, rabbits, bears etc. — with not one cuddly spider or rat in sight! Already he is associating such animals with his own feelings in the warmth and safety of his cot.

Obviously if he follows his father's footsteps in agriculture he will quickly realize that a mature Holstein bull is not the cuddly soft animal that shared his cot. Increasingly, however, the majority of the general public do not come into close contact with real farm animals and carry this early imprint of nice or nasty species throughout the remainder of their life. Obviously 'nice species' have a right to the same welfare standards as us humans — after all, they shared my cot — whereas for the 'nasty species'! Such early imprints from our youth are reinforced throughout our lifetime as can clearly be seen with the current $3\frac{1}{2}$ hours of prime television time per week allocated to the welfare of our pets. One consequence of this is that we begin to assume that the same level of animal welfare applies to farm animals as we provide for our pets. These childhood images determine our response when faced with a welfare issue relating to farm animals, be it from the television or when questioned in the street by yet another pollster. Interestingly, however, such instinctive principles are generally forgotten when we are asked to pay a premium for them in the supermarket! This conflict between words and action highlights the well known importance of how questions are worded for polls. Who in their right mind would admit publicly that they have no interest in the welfare of animals?

The evangelical few

If the general environment in which we are raised encourages high standards of animal welfare (for some species) that is not reflected in our purchasing habits, why is legislation on the welfare of farm animals such a growth industry? The answer is undoubtedly due to the dedicated vocal few often in conjunction with a lack of technical knowledge of the production system as a whole. An example of this would be a common debate I have with dedicated, well meaning people on the need to underfeed spring-calving suckler cows during the winter. To them, underfeeding is apparently in direct conflict with one of the five freedoms — 'freedom from hunger'. As we all know, underfeeding pregnant spring-calving cows is essential to avoid them becoming overfat and having more calving difficulties and metabolic disorders — i.e. it is in the welfare interests of the animal, over its whole production cycle that we underfeed it. Pointing out to such people that the basic physiology of cattle is still very similar to their wild ancestors, who in a normal UK winter, would suffer a much higher degree of underfeeding than is imposed in UK farming systems helps alleviate their concerns. However, how many people would answer 'yes' to the question 'do you agree that pregnant cows should be underfed?'.

The rôle of the supermarkets

Supermarkets have traditionally claimed that the demands they impose on their suppliers are simply a reflection of their customers' demands and that the consumer is king. Undoubtedly this is partly true, although it does raise the question of how supermarkets monitor consumer demand. If demand is monitored through questionnaires, listening to the vocal few, etc., then their claims are obviously questionable. If, however, it is monitored in actual sales, then their claims should be fully justified although, as stated previously, sales records indicate few if any consumers being prepared to pay a premium for a high welfare product.

The other reason for supermarkets increasingly tightening the specifications to their suppliers is the intense competition that exists between the supermarkets themselves. Ruminant products and in particular meat, are one of a few commodities where supermarkets can present a clearly different product compared with their rivals, unlike the majority of the products they stock such as soap powders, where the identical product is available in every store. Hence the major objective of supermarkets in tightening the specifications to their suppliers is not a response to consumer demand but simply a method to differentiate one company from another, e.g. 'all our beef comes from Lowman inspected farms', in order to attract the consumer into the store for this unique product when she will then do all her week's shopping. In this situation supermarkets are pandering, for their own financial benefit, to the instinctive welfare concerns of the consumer and not responding directly to consumer's concerns which they are prepared to pay for. The importance of ruminant products in achieving a clearly distinctive high welfare product compared with rival supermarkets has made it difficult for them to pass on a premium to their suppliers for meeting the tighter specification as the consumer herself does not pay any premium.

As we as consumers are reluctant to pay any premium for a high welfare product, supermarkets are in a dilemma. To make their beef unique by demanding higher welfare standards of their producers may not be as effective in attracting customers into the store as simply reducing the price of the product. This dilemma has recently reached breaking point in the pig industry with the ending of the Malton pig contract, under which a forward contract price was agreed with UK pig producers meeting high welfare specifications. The collapse of this contract was simply due to the low cost of imported pig meat, the majority of which fell below UK welfare standards. Nevertheless the attraction to the supermarkets is that as their customers are not prepared to pay a premium for welfare they can now attract more customers into their stores by having the lowest price for pig meat compared with rival stores. As a consequence of the collapse of the Malton pig contract agreement, it is not surprising that the whole agricultural industry now views retailer assurance schemes and the associated welfare legislation on which they are all based, with extreme distrust.

The rôle of Government

The rôle of the Government is simply to respond with legislation when apparent public concern reaches the state at which it is politically expedient to do so. In this context, the continuing decline in personnel involved in agriculture as a percentage of the voting population increasingly weights the system in favour of the general public.

The other important rôle of Government in animal welfare is to produce the eventual legislation. Like the majority of legal documents, animal welfare legislation is generally incomprehensible to those to whom it applies — the producers. Certainly producing an 'idiot's guide' (which even I could understand) would go a long way to reduce concerns of producers who often have little or no idea exactly what the legislation means for their businesses.

Responsibilities of scientists and advisers

Like welfare legislation, welfare and behavioural research has been a major growth area in recent years. As for other sciences, it is rapidly developing its own 'jargon' and moving towards increasingly fundamental studies. As a result the data produced are increasingly less correctly understood, or even not understood at all, by personnel deciding on whether legislation is or is not required, let alone by the end user — the producer. Furthermore, the continued fragmentation of research to a more and more basic level runs the increasing risk of positive welfare findings from one specific experiment actually turning into a net welfare cost when considered in the whole lifetime of the animal. To avoid this and to act as a demonstration of putting good science into practice it is essential that holistic research continues to be a major area of future welfare and behavioural research.

Traditionally the rôle of advisers has been to link together scientists with producers, often by simply translating one set of jargon into another and *vice versa*. The end objective has been to facilitate the transfer of new scientific findings into practice, where appropriate and to take back to the scientists new problems, ideas encountered by producers. To a large extent this communication rôle no longer exists in the structure of British agriculture. The few production advisers remaining, myself included, find it increasingly difficult to maintain close contact with real production systems on the farm and increasingly find fewer scientific publications which we can first understand let alone transfer to our farmer clients.

As has been stated in the press recently, while much excellent scientific work is being undertaken in the UK, the marketing of that research is abysmal. Perhaps both our societies should learn the lesson from our supermarket colleagues that marketing is, in the long term, everything and each employ an ex-supermarket salesman.

The rôle of producers

The rôle of producers is obviously critical to the success of any developments in farm animal welfare. Producers are no different from people in other professions and businesses — they do respond rapidly to market forces. Many of my scientific colleagues do not believe this to be the case but if every farmer responded immediately to each new experimental finding few, if any, would still be in business today. For producers willingly to implement welfare legislation, they need simple information in a form they can understand, on: the underlying scientific principles of the legislation; the legislation itself; how the legislation will affect the overall system of production they run; the financial implications of the legislation on the profitability of their business; the implications of the legislation on their market.

Unfortunately the rescinding of the Malton pig contract has meant that members of both our societies will face an even greater challenge in the future if we are to have the full support of producers for any future legislation in animal welfare.

The future?

For future animal welfare research and legislation to be effective in improving the overall welfare of the animal throughout its life and to be enthusiastically implemented by producers will require the following. Basic research on the underlying principle of animal behaviour to be matched by lifetime systems studies, as it is the systems themselves which arguably give rise to the welfare problems. Such systems studies would also act as an effective focus for technology transfer to producers as well as clearly identifying the financial consequences to researchers and legislators. The whole area from basic research to legislation to be simply 'translated' for producers, to enable them to justify and fully understand the impact any new legislation will have on their business.

However such changes will still not be effective as long as we, as consumers, do not financially support high welfare products in the marketplace. One possible way of overcoming this dilemma would be to investigate relationships between animal welfare and product quality, particularly eating quality, positive correlations being indicated in some of the scientific literature. If such a positive relationship can be identified, then consumers will pay a premium for high welfare animal products, not specifically because they are a high welfare product but rather because they have a higher eating quality.

Farm animal welfare — who writes the rules?
Occasional Publication No. 23 — British Society of Animal Science 1999
edited by A. J. F. Russel, C. A. Morgan, C. J. Savory, M. C. Appleby and T. L. J. Lawrence

Transport from farm to slaughter

T. Harris

Crab Hill Farm, South Nutfield, Redhill, Surrey RH15NR

Abstract

Live animal transport has a long history, dating back to biblical times. Today, the national and international transport of live animal is governed principally by a number of European Union Directives. In the UK these have been distilled into the welfare of Animals (Transport) Order 1997. This is primarily the responsibility of the Ministry of Agriculture, Fisheries and Food but in practice the day-to-day administration of the regulations is devolved to local authorities. It is feared that this may lead to regional differences in interpretation. The situation is made more complex by the addition of further layers of bureaucracy from, for example, the Road Haulage Association, supermarkets and the multiplicity of quality assurance schemes. The responsibility for the lawful transport of live animals from farm to market or abattoir lies with the supplier who, under recent legislation, must satisfy himself or herself that the carrier is competent to transport the particular class of livestock. Similarly, the insurance of the animals during transit is the supplier's responsibility. The multiplicity of rules and regulations governing stocking densities, journey times, lairage, the cleaning and disinfection of vehicles and vehicle construction standards is resulting in many carriers deciding not to continue in the business of live animal transport.

Historical background

The first rules for animal transport are of Biblical origin and specified for Noah's ark: a very large vessel with three decks, having a total floor area of 4500 square cubits, which converts to 9406 m^2 available to livestock. Whilst the stocking density was not specified, the Designer obviously knew that there was sufficient floor area for the whole animal kingdom in breeding pairs. Sufficient by today's standards for about 40 000 sheep at 40 kg. Whilst it is popularly assumed that these were all breeding animals, several were in fact destined for slaughter, either during the journey of nearly a year, or on disembarkation:

'Of every clean beast thou shalt take to thee by sevens, the male and his female; and of beasts that are not clean by two, the male and his female (Genesis, Ch.7, v. 2).'

'Every beast . . . went forth out of the Ark. And Noah builded an altar . . . and took every clean beast . . . and offered burnt offerings (Genesis, Ch. 8, v. 19-20).'

It seems as though the Meat Hygiene Service was at work even in those days!

There must have been some remarkable stories to tell of wild animals being captured in Africa and elsewhere to be brought to Rome and other amphitheatres for popular entertainment. Whilst the slaughter was more likely to involve the unfortunate humans they were set upon, I imagine that the conditions under which they were transported were the best available to the technology at the time because of their potential value. But we learn that these demoralizing amusements did in fact encounter severe censure. The Roman government in 486 AD managed to procure a decree of the people prohibiting the importation of foreign animals to Rome.

Until the advent of the railways, all slaughter animals were in fact driven on foot to their place of slaughter. My cousins, C&T Harris of Calne, Wiltshire, had the good sense to stop the drovers on the long road from the West Country to London. They offered to slaughter the animals so that they could continue their journey as meat. It saved a lot of walking for the drovers and for the animals. I am sure this principle was repeated in many different parts of the country in conjunction with livestock markets. Some are extremely ancient. Ashford Market claims to be the oldest registered business in the UK dating from about 1250 AD.

The point of this history lesson is simply to show that there was very little change from Biblical times until about 150 years ago. Sea transport would still have been reserved for breeding stock. The exceptions, perhaps, being the movement of slaughter cattle from North America to the UK. Some of the descriptions of the dreadful journeys at the time gave rise to the first legislation on welfare of animals in transit.

As an aside, I must mention the first known case of transporting a racehorse to a race occurred in 1816. (Eclipse was earlier transported to stud in 1771 due to laminitis or poor condition of his hooves.) I paraphrase from *Spirit of the Times*, June 1838.

'Sovereign, a race horse belonging to John Terret, was conveyed to Newmarket racecourse in a 'caravan' previously used to transport bullocks to agricultural shows. It seems to have been Terret's trainer, John Doe, who suggested that the horse be vanned, probably — as in the case of the bullock — to spare the animal the wear and tear of self-propulsion The caravan for the conveyance of the bullocks was fixed on the axle tree without springs; but on Doe's recommendation the bottom was removed, and a new one substituted with springs underneath. The inside was also padded, to prevent the horse from being bruised by an accidental jolt. The caravan thus fitted up, was drawn by three strong heavy horses, two at wheel and one in front, after the manner of what is called a 'unicorn team'; and it travelled at the rate of forty miles a day, about twice the distance usually performed by a racehorse when on a journey.'

It was again trainer John Doe who advised his latest employer, Lord Lichfield, to van the latter's horse Elis to the Doncaster races in 1836. Elis was stabled so far from Doncaster that Lichfield's colleague, Lord George Bentinck, had wanted to withdraw the horse from the prestigious St Leger stakes. But the odds against Elis were so high that Lichfield and Bentinck decided to confound the bookmakers by having the London coachbuilder, Herring, construct an enormous wagon. It was backed up to a high bank and Elis and another Lichfield horse, the Drummer, were led in. This amazing vehicle covered 80 miles a day; it got Elis well rested to Doncaster, where he won the big race.

Following Elis' win, Lord Chesterfield, the Marquis of Exeter and trainer John Day had caravans constructed upon the Elis model. The axles of Elis's van were about 18 inches in height and, I think, a wheel from the van is in the UK Jockey Club. Dr Sharon tells me she has a photo of it in her book, courtesy of Roger Mortimer, the photographer. Newer vans built by Herrings used a crank down axle and added a tailgate. Vanning gave a great impetus to competition and enhanced stud fees, but was enormously expensive. The innovation was also resisted by conservative horsemen who argued against it as damaging to the feet and legs and 'unnatural'.

Two major changes then occurred. The first was the introduction of the railways from about 1840. I mention this because rail travel is an excellent medium for livestock, but sadly no longer available in UK. The second, and quite the most important development, was the invention of the internal combustion engine. This has been a mixed blessing, but the decline of the railways for livestock transportation was inevitable when animals could be loaded at the farm gate and delivered to the door of the market or abattoir without any transhipment. Road transport now represents the single most important method of delivery, for not only animals but for all goods. There is not one item in your own home that was not delivered to you by road.

In my experience, the majority of road transporters take the greatest care over their animals, but, as in any walk of life, there is always a careless, thoughtless, individual or even a criminal element who make the most unwelcome headlines. As in any other walk of life it is largely for this small element that legislation has had to be written.

Present-day legislation

When I first joined the Farm Animal Welfare Council (FAWC) and suggested that stocking densities would be required on livestock vehicles, I was told that it would probably be impossible: 'too many variations by species, time of the year, state of pregnancy, length of wool, horned or unhorned, unsocial groups or gender, etc., etc.' Whilst I never claimed it would be easy, I had to calculate on a daily basis exactly how many animals could be loaded into an aircraft hold and had indeed developed my own tables for doing so. For commercial reasons I was not too happy to share this valuable information with others. If you think about it, every carrier, whether by road, rail, sea or air had his own sets of tables and criteria, so you can see how the myriad stocking densities have developed.

Although we have our minds much concentrated by Directives from Brussels, it must be remembered that their precursor was the Council of Europe's *European Convention for the Protection of Animals during International Transport* signed 13 December 1968. The original signatories were Belgium, Denmark, France, Germany, Greece, Iceland, Norway and Switzerland. This is presently being redrafted and updated and there is a general desire to apply its principles to movements within countries, not just to international movements.

In addition to this Convention, certain Recommendations were also developed by the Committee of Ministers at later dates which have a bearing, *viz*:
● Recommendation no. R(87) 17 on the transport of horses, 17 September 1987;
● Recommendation no. R(88) 15 on the transport of pigs, 22 September 1988;
● Recommendation no. R(90) 1 on the transport of cattle, 15 January 1990;
● Recommendation no. R(90) 6 on the transport of poultry, 21 February 1990;
● Recommendation no. R(90) 5 on the transport of sheep and goats, 21 February 1990.
These recommendations incorporate a lot of detail, in particular recommended stocking densities for these classes of livestock.

It will be seen that the Council of Europe predates the formation of the European Economic Community, now referred to as the European Union (EU) and their stocking densities predate the EU Directives. Since all members of the EU are also members of the Council of Europe, they have naturally introduced the principles of the Convention into EU Directives. They have, however, taken the recommended stocking densities referred to above and made them the *legal maximum* for any journey over 50 km. Only now are questions being asked regarding the suitability of these figures and there are likely to be some amendments in the light of research. On top of this there are new specific rules for travel times, rest periods, feeding and watering.

This of course implies that rules also have to be written and imposed for the throughput and cleanliness of lairages, staging posts or markets. This has now appeared as the Welfare of Animals (Staging Posts) Order 1998 (WASPO98). Whilst it may seem easy to write down the requirements, the interpretation and implementation is quite another matter.

In general, all carriers of livestock will be bound by national legislation that protects the welfare and health of animals. This will include anyone involved, especially the consignor, the driver, the transport undertaking the movement and any intermediate handlers or staging posts. Animals shall be loaded only into transport which has been thoroughly cleansed and, where appropriate, disinfected.

Now I come to the most important current EU legislation relating to transport of animals within Europe and within individual Member States:
● Directive 90/425/EEC (26 June 1990) — concerning veterinary and zoological checks applicable in intra-Community trade in live animals and products with a view to completion of the internal market;
● Directive 91/628/EEC (19 November 1991) — on the protection of animals during transport amending 90/425/EEC & 91/496/EEC;
● Directive 95/29/EC (29 June 1995) amending Directive 91/628/EEC concerning the protection of animals during transport.

Most legislation is generally directed towards 'commercial movements', although the principles of good welfare naturally relate to all animals. To try to clarify this problem, there is an attempt to define a 'transporter' as any natural or legal person transporting animals on his own account, or for the account of a third party, or by providing a third party with a means of transport of animals.

It is generally assumed that any movement of live animals is carried out as a commercial operation, unless all of the following conditions can be met: the animals belong to the carrier; they are being transported in the owner's own vehicle; and the journey does not exceed 50 km.

All live animals for movement through, into, or out of, the EU must be transported in accordance with Council Directive 91/628/EEC plus its amendment 95/29/EC on the protection of animals during transport.

For movements of animals within an EU state, the following is a general schedule of documents that may be required: accompanying certificate; health certificate (if 'unfit'); list of unique identification numbers; movement licence (especially for pigs); passport (for cattle); and movement register.

For a long time we have had legislation requiring the correct cleansing and disinfection of vehicles and containers. It has to be said that whilst many farmers and hauliers are aware of the need for this, I do not believe that enough of them receive from the Ministry of Agriculture, Fisheries and Food (MAFF) the listing of approved disinfectants and their required dilutions for effective use.

The EU Directives in UK have been distilled into the Welfare of Animals (Transport) Order 1997, abbreviated as WATO97. MAFF are to be congratulated in the work they have done on this but they cannot be blamed for the messy wording of the dreadful Directives from which they had to draw their inspiration. No other country has been quite as thorough, or communicated so widely with its transport industry as has MAFF and I want to thank them for that.

Application of this legislation is under the overall responsibility of MAFF, but the day to day administration is farmed out to the Local Authorities. Although MAFF have carried out a major operation in addressing authorities around the country about evenness of approach and the elusive 'level playing field', we are fearful that there will be a degree of varied local interpretation even within our own country. We already know that this interpretation varies widely elsewhere.

If this is not all complicated enough, several other groups have added their own layers of interpretation with the result that we are approaching a chimera of chameleon-like controls that change colour depending on the circumstances or environment.

To explain what I mean, let me start with the Road Haulage Association (RHA) conditions of carriage. If you read these, you will find, perhaps with some relief, that 'farm animals' are excluded. But there is no definition. With the present vogue for diversification, are llamas, deer or ostriches 'farm' animals? How about Vietnamese pot-bellied pigs? I farmed crickets (*Acheta domestica*) for some years and was selling up to 80 000 per week. All left the farm by road.

The RSPCA have done some pioneering work in setting up their standards for 'Freedom Foods'. I congratulate them on their persistence and indeed, courage, in the face of opposition from within their own ranks. Above all, it shows that animals have to be farmed, traded, transported and *eaten* if they are to survive as part of the farming scene. This is a vital element often lost on 'conservationists' who seem to think that conservation means letting animals follow their own inclinations unhindered. It doesn't conserve anything.

Next, we get the major buyers such as the supermarket chains setting up their own standards. Whilst they all start from a similar base line of wishing to trace animals from source, and to illustrate their concerns for welfare and quality throughout the food chain, we inevitably get into slight variations between one scheme and another as a result of commercial pressures and the wish to have the 'best' code of practice. This means that we actually have hauliers having to bring all sorts of new parameters into their transport planning.

● 'Can I go that distance from farm to slaughterhouse with those animals?' — 'No, but I could go to this alternative location.'
● 'Can I load animals at this stocking density for that slaughterhouse?' — 'No, but I could go to this other outlet.'

I was involved with one major commercial concern where they had put 18 months' work into their draft contract with producers in order to trace from stable to table but all reference to transport of the live animal was surprisingly absent. When I asked them why, their response was that this was not their concern but the responsibility of the slaughterhouse. I had to correct them. The supplier not only finds and instructs the carrier but under new legislation must satisfy himself that the carrier is competent for that species of animal. It should also be remembered that animal transport is quite the most visible aspect of livestock production. In spite of school visits to farms, very few members of the public have actually entered a so-called intensive livestock facility. Even fewer, if any, have ever entered a slaughterhouse but *everyone* has seen livestock wagons on the road and often have their own self-conceived opinions about stocking densities or even the very ethics of transport.

Insurance of livestock in transit

I often ask groups of farmers at what point 'title' to their livestock passes from them to the next person be it buyer, market or slaughterhouse. Therefore at what point their risk of loss passes to someone else. Many fondly imagine that this point is passed when the tailgate slams shut on their animals. If not then they imagine that the transporter's own insurance will cover any losses. Sadly they do not discover the truth until a loss occurs. A transporter is only insured against third party or negligence. If you seek insurance in transit, the broker may not impose any rules but may ask a lot of questions about the detail of the load, suitability of the vehicle, state of pregnancy, ages, weights, distance, experience of the drivers, species, source and destination.

Training and certification

These are two very distinct disciplines. Whereas the RHA has had a training course for livestock drivers since the 1970s, *nobody* has ever attended a course. Training is now beginning to be available from various different sources (LANTRA — formerly ATB-Landbase, agricultural colleges, in-house company training etc.). From this it follows that certification is required both for the training course and for the students that emerge (National Proficiency Test Council (NPTC), RHA assessors, etc.).

Air transport

For the sake of completeness, I must digress a little. This conference is concerned mainly with slaughter animals, primarily within these shores. This is probably about 98% of all animals produced. Very few of these are transported by air for slaughter but if they are, as often they are for breeding, their conditions of packing and transport are laid down by the International Air Transportation Association (IATA) Live Animal Regulations which change slightly every year. I may be the only person in this room who has exported pigs for slaughter to Japan. This required a specific licence from MAFF, if only because they were castrates and I could not smuggle them out as breeding animals.

In parallel with this, my own Association, the Animal Air Transportation Association (AATA), is developing training and assessment programmes for grooms in aircraft. This sounds simple enough, until you realize that they are distributed all over the world and not all speak English. Very few are to be found in the UK, though all will require a Certificate of Competence when they depart these shores.

Sea transport

Sea transport for slaughter has developed into an important issue. Whilst the numbers of animals may represent only a small percentage of the total, we are supposed to be part of a borderless trading group called Europe and it has already been demonstrated that access to mainland markets for our sheep can have a powerful influence on our local prices. In the absence of sea transport on the regular roll on-roll off carriers, it is therefore quite natural for farmers to seek their own ships. I am now aware that welfare groups in Europe are seeking specifically to include sea transport of live animals into the International Maritime Union legislation.

Livestock carriers and the Meat Hygiene Service

If a carrier is careless enough to accept dirty animals onto his vehicle he needs to know the risks he runs. The most likely will be the requirement to return them to source. Not only will this increase the contamination of the carrier's vehicle that he will have to clean, but it will mess up the rest of the day's schedule and the driver's hours. Naturally, the transporter must not become a source of contamination, especially from upper decks contaminating those below.

Vehicle construction standards

One of the more recent developments in legislation is the proposal for vehicle construction standards. Our industry finds it very hard to understand how legislators located in temperate central Europe (or even comfortable air conditioned offices) can envisage or impose a standard set of design criteria for livestock vehicles from the Arctic Circle to Athens or from Madrid to Moscow. Short of a fully air-conditioned vehicle, it cannot be done. In this area, perhaps more than any other we will have local design and interpretation.

Conclusions

So, having mentioned all these different influences and authorities, and I am sure I have still omitted someone, you begin to get a flavour of the new diversity of disciplines that are being imposed upon us. We really begin to wonder how we did it at all for so long! What have we been doing all these years? Sadly, many carriers have simply decided that transporting animals is just too much trouble. It is the simplest commercial decision just to say 'no'. And I don't just mean the carriers who were of dubious quality, whom we would like to see disappear, but longstanding carriers of good repute, be they road, sea or air carriers, which makes our task as professionals in seeking suitable carriers just all the more difficult.

With this forest of new rules, rule writers and regulators we have found it hard to adapt to everyone's requirements. But, as professionals we can adapt to any disciplines, however onerous, provided the reasons are well explained to us and above all that the same rules are evenly applied and policed for all.

Farm animal welfare — who writes the rules?
Occasional Publication No. 23 — British Society of Animal Science 1999
edited by A. J. F. Russel, C. A. Morgan, C. J. Savory, M. C. Appleby and T. L. J. Lawrence

Welfare in livestock markets

B. S. Pack

ANM Group Ltd, Thainstone Centre, Inverurie ABS1 5XZ

Abstract

Livestock markets are under constant pressure from a variety of sources as regards animal welfare. Their openness to the public helps to ensure that only acceptable welfare practices are operated. These practices are set out in the Welfare of Animals at Markets Order 1990, supplemented by a Code of Practice for the Welfare of Animals in Livestock Markets. These 'rules' represent minimum standards and there is a continuing pressure to further improve welfare in auction marts. This comes from the market operators themselves, from consumers via the large retail outlets, and from a small but vociferous minority who oppose the production of livestock for food. All concerned with any part of the food chain have a rôle to play in ensuring a continuing improvement in animal welfare.

Introduction

Livestock markets, like many bodies involved in commercial livestock production, are continually pressurized about animal welfare from many sources some of which have constructive objectives and some with only destructive ends.

An auction market's greatest benefit as regards animal welfare is that it is a very public place, with all practices highly visible. Such a setting ensures that only acceptable animal welfare practices are followed. The question, however, is 'acceptable to whom?'

As regards the 'rules', livestock auction marts again are at a definite advantage compared with many involved in commercial livestock production, in that there exists an up to date statutory instrument, the Welfare of Animals at Markets Order 1990. This order, with its very clear description of what is and is not acceptable, has been supplemented by a Code of Practice for the Welfare of Animals in Livestock Markets, which was revised last year.

The above Order and Code of Practice are issued by Government Ministers, advised by the civil service and numerous other bodies and thus we can say that society 'writes the rules'. The same Order and Code of Practice lay down what are, in effect, minimum standards but we are entitled to ask 'is this enough?'

The answer must be 'no', for the following reasons.

Market operators

Any company in the 1990s is striving for continuous improvement in all that it does and therefore forward-looking auction companies are seeking to improve their standards and effectiveness. To them, codes of practice on animal welfare can be only the minimum standard required. Improvements in animal welfare will result from strong leadership and through investment in staff training and development.

Equally, as outdated facilities are replaced with modern state-of-the-art livestock auction centres, there is opportunity to use current knowledge to ease greatly the task of moving stock; thus an improvement in animal welfare is possible.

Those companies not embracing modern thinking and practices will not deliver improved animal welfare but neither will they survive in business.

Concerned consumers

As businesses fit for the 1990s have a different attitude, so do consumers. Many consumers are concerned about the whole food chain from primary production to the retail outlets. They require assurances that all processes in the chain are acceptable and safe. These concerns are voiced mainly by the large retailers on behalf of their customers .

In recognition of this, schemes such as Scottish Quality Beef and Lamb Assurance (SQBLA) exists to provide an independent verification that prescribed standards are achieved. As an essential part of the food chain, livestock auction markets are subject to inspection and certification for farm assurance.

Anti-livestock production

A small sector of society is totally against the production of livestock for food. They start with the premise that livestock production for this purpose is wrong; and thus any standards based on common sense and good practice will not be sufficient. Accordingly, the views of this minority cannot be incorporated in sensible guidelines for the operation of markets.

Conclusion

In conclusion, livestock markets constitute a very necessary part of the food chain and are subject to many pressures as regards animal welfare, They are closely regulated, but all with an interest in livestock for food have a rôle to play in ensuring continuous improvements in animal welfare but none more so than the auction company with a hundred year vision.

Farm animal welfare — who writes the rules?
Occasional Publication No. 23 — British Society of Animal Science 1999
edited by A. J. F. Russel, C. A. Morgan, C. J. Savory, M. C. Appleby and T. L. J. Lawrence

Welfare in abattoirs

E. Murray

Reivers Veterinary Services, Housebyres, Melrose, Roxburghshire TD6 9BW

Abstract

The Meat Hygiene Service (MHS) is responsible for the enforcement of the welfare legislation governing the slaughter of a wide range of food animal species. The principal legislation is contained in the Welfare of Animals (Slaughter or Killing) Regulations 1995 (WASK) which give effect to the Provisions of Council Directive 93/119/EC on the Protection of Animals at Time of Slaughter or Killing, as contained in the EU Official Journal No. 340, 31/12/93. Codes of practice, prepared and issued by the Ministry of Agriculture, Fisheries and Food after consultation with all interested parties, provide guidance in respect of these welfare regulations. The legislation governing animal transit are contained in the Welfare of Animals (Transport) Order 1997 (WATO) which is enforced by local authorities, although MHS officers at abattoirs monitor the unloading of livestock and carry out ante-mortem inspections. Animal welfare standards, which must never be compromised, should be continually improved and based on sound science rather than on uninformed opinion and anthropomorphism. There is a need for more high quality research on animal welfare, for clear concise user-friendly codes of practice for the industry, and for continued education of all parties involved, including consumers.

Introduction

As a Principal Official Veterinary Surgeon (POVS) contracted to the Meat Hygiene Service (MHS) in Scotland and Cumbria I provide advice and guidance for veterinarians, inspectors and the industry. As I prepared to write this paper my mobile phone rang. The call was from an OVS, seeking reassurance that slaughtering a sheep immediately at the start of production had been correct, as at *ante-mortem* inspection it appeared distressed, but was damp and slightly dirty, having been down in the lairage pen. 'Animal welfare comes first', was my immediate response and I agreed that this had been the correct decision.

Recently hygiene has taken centre stage in the media, with food safety scares in abundance. While hygiene is of immense importance, profit is not; welfare is paramount. Even if an animal is too unhygienic to dress for human consumption, humane destruction on welfare grounds must be carried out and the carcass disposed of as waste. In my experience, the majority of the farming and abattoir industries take active steps to ensure that this is the case.

I remember a recent occasion when I was urgently called to attend the lairage to examine a 'downer' (moribund) lamb. Collecting a humane killer *en route*, I attended the lairage and on inspection concurred that the lamb should be duly dispatched. A small lorry drew up at the loading bay and I went to inspect the livestock and noted that some lambs had dry dung clags on the breech area. I pointed this out to the farmer and explained that livestock must be presented in a hygienic state and that these lambs required dagging. He very readily and enthusiastically agreed to do this straight away. I left him in a lairage pen avidly clipping and, on passing the man in charge of the lairage, commented on how keen the farmer was to comply with my request. 'No wonder' he said. 'You've got a gun hanging out of your coat pocket!' It was *not* loaded!

In this paper I will deal with the main welfare regulations applying in abattoirs, the bodies which enforce them and ensure that they are adhered to and, finally, who makes these regulations.

Abattoirs

Abattoirs are excellent collection points to monitor the general standard of welfare of food animal species, although unfortunately they are now fewer in number, but with increased throughputs. In fulfilling my remit as a POVS with the MHS I am responsible for monitoring and advising on the welfare of a broad spectrum of food animal species: cattle, sheep, goats, pigs, all categories of poultry (including turkeys and ostriches), farmed deer and farmed game birds, coming from a wide area.

Increasingly greater distances are unfortunately travelled by livestock and myself as the industry is rationalized.

The MHS took over in 1995 as the government agency responsible to the ministers for safeguarding public health and animal welfare by ensuring fair, consistent and effective enforcement of hygiene, inspection and welfare regulations. One of its primary functions is the enforcement of welfare at slaughter, including legislative requirements in licensed red, poultry and farmed game meat slaughterhouses. In 1995/96 the MHS carried out an animal welfare audit throughout Great Britain, reinforcing the importance of animal welfare practices at all licensed premises. This was repeated in 1997/98 and in 1997 all MHS operational staff were provided with additional animal welfare training by the University of Bristol, and using the Humane Slaughter Association's material.

The main piece of legislation is the Welfare of Animals (Slaughter or Killing) Regulations (WASK) which came into force on 1 April 1995. These regulations extend to Great Britain as a whole and give effect to the provisions of Council of the European Community Directive 93/119/EC on The Protection of Animals at Time of Slaughter or Killing (OJ No. 340, 31.12.93, p. 21). This legislation repealed, amended and revoked a considerable number of separate pieces of complex legislation providing a much more 'user friendly' and updated set of requirements: it concerns an animal awaiting slaughter or killing and applies until that animal is dead.

The ministers may from time to time, and do, after consultation with such organizations as appear to them to represent the interests concerned, prepare and issue codes of practice for the purpose of providing guidance in respect of welfare regulations, and revoke, vary, amend or add to the provisions of the codes. A code is prepared in pursuance of this regulation and any alterations proposed to be made on a revision of such a code are laid before both Houses of Parliament. It is also a requirement that ministers shall not issue the code or revised code, as the case may be, until after 40 days, beginning on the day on which the code, or the proposed alterations to it, were so laid. If, within the period mentioned, either House resolves that the code should not be issued or the proposed alterations made, the minister shall not issue the code or revised code (without prejudice to their power under that paragraph to lay further codes or proposed alterations before Parliament).

The legislation also requires that ministers shall

cause any code issued or revised under this regulation to be printed and distributed and to make such arrangements as they think fit for its distribution, including causing copies of it to be put on sale to the public at such reasonable price as the ministers may determine.

A failure on the part of any person to follow any guidance contained in a code issued under this regulation shall not of itself render that person liable to proceedings of any kind.

If, in proceedings against any person for an offence consisting of the contravention of any provision of these regulations, it is shown that at any material time, he or she failed to follow any guidance contained in a code issued under these regulations, being guidance which was relevant to the provision concerned, that failure may be relied upon by the prosecution as tending to establish his or her guilt.

WASK covers the licensing of slaughtermen, the construction and maintenance of slaughterhouses, the equipment used, the requirements of animals awaiting slaughter, restraint of animals pre-stunning, slaughter or killing, the bleeding and pithing of animals, the killing of pigs and birds by exposure to gas mixtures, additional provisions for the slaughter or killing of horses in slaughterhouses and additional provisions for slaughter by a religious method.

Execution offences and penalties are also contained within WASK.

As indicated above, abattoirs are excellent centres for monitoring animal welfare standards and the unloading bays are useful for monitoring the welfare of animals in transit and on-farm welfare.

Animal transit

The regulations governing animal transit are contained in the Welfare of Animals (Transport) Order 1997 (WATO) which came into force on 1 July 1997. This Order is executed and enforced by local authorities and implements the European Directives 95/29/EC in UK legislation.

It is decreed that no person shall transport any animal unless it is fit for the intended journey and that suitable provision has been made for its care during the journey and on its arrival at its destination. Without prejudice to the generality of this decree, and for the purposes of this paper, an animal shall not be considered fit for its intended journey if it is ill, injured, infirm or fatigued, unless it is only slightly injured, ill, infirm or fatigued and the intended journey is not likely to cause it unnecessary suffering.

Thus, the MHS officers present at the unloading of livestock and during the *ante-mortem* inspections can monitor compliance with WATO and, if they suspect that it is not being complied with, can then notify the competent local authority officer. If it is considered that there may be an on-farm welfare problem, they would also notify the relevant MAFF Divisional Veterinary Manager as the enforcing officer who would conduct an investigation.

Regulation policy

It is therefore clear that the regulations or rules are made by the Minister of Agriculture, Fisheries and Food and the Secretaries of State, being ministers designated under the European Communities Act 1972 in relation to the Common Agricultural Policy of the European Community and the Animal Health Act 1981, to implement European Union Directives into UK legislation.

Clearly these ministers may not necessarily be experts in animal welfare and thus the EU and the Government are advised by many experts, including the European Standing Veterinary Committee, Ministry civil servants, the Farm Animal Welfare Council, MAFF officials, scientific and legal experts, industry representatives, etc. How then can producers, research scientists, consumers and those in all stages of production and consumption have any influence or input into 'the rules'?

All interested parties are consulted and given opportunity to comment on draft regulations. These parties include organizations such as the Farm Animal Welfare Council, local authorities, the National Farmers' Unions, the SSPCA and RSPCA, Compassion in World Farming, the State Veterinary Service, the Road Haulage Association, relevant meat trading associations, landowners' federations, local and national animal welfare groups, etc. All interested parties may make their points of view and recommendations to the Ministers responsible.

I sought the views on animal welfare and its legislation of a respected member of industry, who is both a farmer and the owner of a fresh meat business, and who voluntarily undertook animal welfare training. His opinion was that more science should underpin the formulation of welfare legislation and that there should be more research into animal behaviour and less 'knee jerk' reaction to the opinions of the general public which, he felt, lacked understanding and are anthropomorphic. He considered that there is a heightened awareness of welfare needs throughout the industry and cited plant veterinary supervision and consumer demand as forcing up welfare standards. He also made the point that good welfare ensured better quality stock and an improved level of profitability.

As regards the EU, this person considered that EU legislation diluted UK standards; unified EU rules are not as effective as UK legislation, especially with regard to climatic differences. Legislation was required, he felt, to ensure continued improvements but it was important that the public should be made aware of the considerable financial implications involved for the industry.

As a committed veterinary surgeon I will not compromise on animal welfare. I believe that it is my duty to continue to improve animal welfare standards and that the way forward requires an increase in the level of high quality relevant research, clear concise user-friendly codes of practice for the industry as a whole and continued education of the separate industries involved, the enforcing authorities and the general public.

Good communication and consultation among all interested parties is essential for the sake of what is of paramount importance: maintaining high standards of animal welfare throughout the country and beyond.

References

Council of the European Community. 1991. Directive on the protection of animal during transport. *Official Journal of the European Community* **L340:** 17-38.

Great Britain Parliament. 1995. *The Welfare of Animals (Slaughter or Killing) Regulations.* Her Majesty's Stationery Office, London.

Great Britain Parliament. 1997. *The Welfare of Animals (Transport) Order.* Her Majesty's Stationery Office, London.

Farm animal welfare — who writes the rules?
Occasional Publication No. 23 — British Society of Animal Science 1999
edited by A. J. F. Russel, C. A. Morgan, C. J. Savory, M. C. Appleby and T. L. J. Lawrence

Quality assurance

B. M. Simpson

Scotch Quality Beef and Lamb Association, Rural Centre, West Mains, Ingliston, Newbridge, Midlothian EH28 8NZ

Abstract

A description is provided of the development of quality assurance in the Scottish beef and lamb industry during the period 1988-98. The contributions of many organizations and individuals are explained and three essential development phases are identified: setting the standards, gaining commitment from the industry and establishing independent credible assessment procedures. While Scotland has achieved some economic advantage, the author acknowledges that much has still to be done to reward all participating sectors.

Quality assurance (QA) involves a range of agreed standards which are implemented by food producers on a voluntary basis and assessed by a wide range of bodies. Animal welfare is often a component part of these schemes.

Up until the late 1980s there was little or no interest in animal welfare from the British consumer and certainly not from consumers in mainland Europe. Post war, the priorities had been to obtain sufficient food at an affordable price no matter where it came from or what process had been involved in its production .

In the last 10 years this situation has altered dramatically for a number of reasons. First, we had the development of food surpluses in the European Community and downward pressure on prices for all food commodities. Suddenly food was plentiful, available all the year round and presented in a wide range of styles and packaging. Secondly, the consumer had increasing levels of disposable income and time to consider how best to spend money. Thirdly, the media, and television in particular, took an interest in consumer affairs and provided an insight into food production methods. The phrase 'food scare' was about to enter our vocabulary.

Important changes were occurring at trade level which were to influence the development of quality assurance. The size of farming enterprise had grown substantially as had downstream processors and, most significantly, the multiple retail sector. This sector became dominant in the supply chain and had the power to determine prices as well as defining product quality.

The Scottish meat industry was not slow to see possible commercial advantage in this changing situation. In 1988 the Guild of Scotch Quality Meat Suppliers was established initially involving eight of the leading abattoir companies. The voluntary standards were mostly concerned with carcass conformation maturation for eating quality and hygienic standards for shelf life. This latter factor undoubtedly attracted the attention of the UK multiple meat buyers who were most concerned to minimize wastage due to failure to sell before sell-by dates. But what were the animal welfare implications? Not many. Lairage standards were included and stunning techniques detailed. The emphasis was on reducing animal stress to ensure good meat qualities but at least animal welfare standards improved indirectly. These standards were drawn up by meat plant operators, the Meat and Livestock Commission (MLC) specialists and Food from Britain. The Scotch Quality Beef and Lamb Association (SQBLA) became the scheme managers and contracted the MLC to carry out inspections on a 2-monthly basis. Reports were made to a technical committee and action taken against members who failed to meet the standards.

It was not until 1990 that animal welfare from farm to meat plant became a major feature of quality assurance. The Scottish Pig Industry Initiative (SPII) and SQBLA Farm Assured Beef and Lamb became leaders in this field. The agreement of professional standards for these schemes was a major piece of painstaking work requiring inputs from a wide range of bodies with relevant experience. These included the MLC, the Scottish Agricultural College (SAC), the Agricultural Training Board (ATB), the National Farmers' Union Scotland, the Institute of Auctioneers and Appraisers in Scotland, the Scottish Association of Meat Wholesalers, the Scottish

Consumers Council, the British Retail Consortium and many other individuals and organizations. This work became the industry benchmark and was effectively copied by many other countries and retail groups who claimed to have developed their own schemes.

Having agreed the industry standards, a much more difficult task began the recruitment of farmers into the schemes. Inevitably there was a cost involved for participation and inevitably the question was asked how these costs might be recouped by higher prices. If these standards were being demanded by trade and consumers then why were they not prepared to pay the price of delivering them?

The argument from the trade and consumer organizations was that producers were only being asked to do what was expected of them any way, and they should therefore pay the costs. Farmers argued that if this was expected of them then the same standards and costs should apply to all meats including imported products. It became increasingly clear to SQBLA that farm assurance with high animal welfare standards had little commercial advantage and that the only way forward was to integrate the farm assurance message with the standards set by the Guild of Scotch Quality Meat Suppliers.

In 1997 the Board of SQBLA agreed to develop a truly farm to plate scheme involving farms, auction markets, road hauliers, animal food suppliers, meat plants, wholesalers, retailers and caterers. The simplified consumer message was embodied in the brands *Specially Selected Scotch Beef* and *Specially Selected Scotch Lamb*. This simplification had a major advantage of assisting the various trade sectors to see how their efforts and investment fitted with the whole consumer message. The results were spectacular as shown by the levels of participation detailed in Table 1.

This commitment by the Scottish meat industry is without parallel and undoubtedly has considerably

Table 1 *Numbers of participants in SQBLA quality assurance scheme, 1990-1998*

Sector	1990	1995	1998
Farms	500	2000	6700
Animal food suppliers	0	0	60
Auction markets	0	0	30
Livestock hauliers	0	0	0
Meat plants	15	20	25
Retailers	0	0	3500
Restaurants	0	40	170

enhanced the already high reputation of Scottish meats. But further issues had to be addressed. The standards were accepted by trade and consumers but questions were being raised about the independence and credibility of the inspection process. The Scottish Office now played a vital rôle in establishing a new body Scottish Food Quality Certification Ltd which was specifically given the task of representing consumer interests and ensuring that QA schemes met European standards EN45011. This is a rigorous process and has so far been achieved by the SPII scheme and the Guild of Scotch Quality Meat Suppliers. The other SQBLA schemes are in the process of attaining this new standard.

High standards, high levels of commitment and high levels of integrity are key elements of the SQBLA schemes. It is also essential that the schemes make economic sense, particularly against a background of the worst crisis faced by the British livestock industry. It is essential that the people who write the rules fully understand that every tightening of standards inevitably raises costs and that someone has to pay for this.

The commitment of Scottish producers to quality assurance has certainly paid off in the price of finished cattle. This is highly encouraging but similar incentives have still to be obtained for store cattle and sheep producers.

Farm animal welfare — who writes the rules?
Occasional Publication No. 23 — British Society of Animal Science 1999
edited by A. J. F. Russel, C. A. Morgan, C. J. Savory, M. C. Appleby and T. L. J. Lawrence

Food production — the price being paid by farm animals

L. G. Ward

Director, Advocates for Animals, 10 Queensferry Street, Edinburgh EH2 4PG

Abstract

There is varying understanding about life for farm animals. The majority of farm animals have gone from the land, only to be caged, crammed and confined behind the closed doors of the factory farm — battery hens sentenced to remain for life in wire cages, broiler chickens reared in overcrowded conditions and pigs tethered and confined in narrow stalls or in equally narrow farrowing crates. Other farm animals are sent abroad to the cruel veal crate system of continental Europe or to abattoirs where welfare standards, both during transportation and at the time of slaughter, are often appallingly low. Many of the animals slaughtered in Britain, or for the live export trade, are processed through live auction markets. A recent investigation revealed many instances of infringements of the regulations governing the treatment and welfare of animals at markets. The controversy over BSE and the cloning and genetic engineering of farm animals have all resulted in close scrutiny and inquisitions by the public into the conditions in which our farm animals are reared, treated and slaughtered. Those involved in the food industry and also those who care about the welfare of animals and recognize their sentiency must take action to ensure that the animals are reared with due thought to their behavioural needs and well being and, when the time comes, granted a quiet and humane death. For far too long in food production programmes farm animals have paid a heavy price in suffering. From birth to death, farm animals must be treated humanely and with respect.

Introduction

Believe it or not but there are still some for whom the mention of the words 'down on the farm' always conjure up images of a farmhouse, barn and sheds, haystacks, cows and sheep grazing in rich green fields, hens, overseen by a strutting cockerel scratching around the farmyard and pigs rooting around in the orchard with piglets running excitedly in all directions. Farms are viewed as congenial places far removed from their own bustling lives.

There are others who claim to know about life 'down on the farm' but who, in fact, know very little about modern methods of animal production. They simply have no idea of the real cost of the food they eat. For them they are happy to accept that the final purchase in the shop, in a neat plastic package, is the culmination of a long process in which all but the end product has been delicately and conveniently screened from their eyes. It hardly bleeds. There is no reason for them to associate this package with a once living, breathing, suffering animal.

Of course, such comfortable images of farms and their animals held by these two minority groupings bear little resemblance to modern-day farming. Since the Second World War, the western world has seen intensive farming increase and with it one of the greatest disappearing acts of our time. The majority of farm animals have gone from the land, only to be caged, crammed and confined behind the closed doors of the factory farm. Here they are treated like animal machines. They are reduced to the level of mere commodities, goods, agricultural products.

The status of animals seems to have been relegated to the level of cogs in a machine in the quest for what some call efficiency and in the interests of commerce. But what is efficient about a system which causes great environmental damage, outrageous spectacular public health disasters such as BSE or immense suffering on the part of farm animals? It is a definition of efficiency based on the acceptance that someone or something else will pay the real cost.

As far as 'commerce' is concerned, factory farming is in the main driven by big business. Farming is competitive and the methods which are adopted are those which cut costs and increase production. Animals are treated like machines that convert low price fodder into high price flesh and any innovation which results in a cheaper conversion ratio is liable to be adopted. In the introduction to her now world-renowned book, *Animal machines* the author, Ruth Harrison, wrote:

> 'If one person is unkind to an animal it is considered to be cruelty but when a lot of people are unkind to a lot of animals, especially in the name of commerce, the cruelty is condoned and,

once large sums of money are at stake, will be defended to the last by otherwise intelligent people' (Harrison, 1964).

The book when published prompted an immediate government inquiry into factory farming.

When the inquiry under the chairmanship of Sir Rogers Brambell released its findings one year later, (Brambell Committee, 1965) it made a number of recommendations, many of which are still to be implemented. The most important recommendation stated:
> 'An animal should at least have sufficient freedom of movement to be able without difficulty to turn round, groom itself, get up, lie down and stretch its limbs.'

More recently the government's advisory committee, the Farm Animal Welfare Council (FAWC, 1992), produced its own extension of what has become known as the 'five freedoms': (1) freedom from hunger, thirst and malnutrition; (2) provision of appropriate comfort and shelter; (3) prevention (or diagnosis and treatment) of injury, disease or infestation; (4) freedom to display most normal patterns of behaviour; (5) freedom from fear. Despite these clear statements by the Brambell Committee (1965) and FAWC (1992), on factory farms very few of these basic and fundamental rights are granted.

Poultry
Egg-laying birds
There are currently 34 million egg laying hens in the UK. About 86% of these are kept in battery cages, with the rest in loose house alternative systems such as free-range (11%) or barn/perchery (3%). As for the 30 million battery hens their lives are spent incarcerated in large windowless, dimly lit, evil-smelling battery houses each containing between 10 000 and 70 000 hapless hens, sentenced to remain for life in wire cages which are piled in long rows of up to six tiers high. These cages, each containing four or five birds, have a floor space for each bird of 450 cm^2 — less than a sheet of A4 paper.

A hen's instinct is to keep busy throughout the day scratching with her feet to find food, walking, running, nesting and, occasionally, flying. Dust-bathing is an important activity to the hen to rid her feathers of mites and dirt. The instinct to dust-bathe is so strong that battery hens frequently make futile and pathetic attempts to perform this activity on the bare metal of the caged floor. As a result of being deprived of the opportunity to carry out so many of their natural behaviours, the hens out of frustration tend to peck at each other instead. This goes a long way to explaining why so many battery hens are

virtually featherless when taken for slaughter after about a year in the cage. To control severe feather pecking and cannibalism amongst the confined cage mates, 50% of battery hens suffer the mutilation of being debeaked by having up to a third of their beaks sliced off with a red hot blade.

The lack of exercise also causes bone weakness in caged hens. A recent study found bone fragility to the point where birds were experiencing bone breakages whilst still in their cages. This condition was also responsible for more than a third of all mortalities in the caged layers studied (McCoy et al., 1996). Up to 30% of battery hens suffer broken bones by the time they reach the slaughterhouse (Gregory and Wilkins, 1989).

Battery cages have been widely condemned on welfare grounds by a succession of official bodies as well as by scientists. Professor Mike Baxter, Head of the School of Design, Ravensbourne College and a member of the government's FAWC, reviewed this scientific evidence and his conclusions included:
> 'Cages failed to provide for hens' welfare needs. Deprived of litter, caged hens are prevented from dust-bathing and foraging. Without access to a nest site, nesting motivation is frustrated and without a perch, roosting is prevented. Restrictions of movement within a cage cause frustration and prevent normal bone maintenance, particularly in the legs and wings. Confinement in a battery cage is concluded to cause suffering to laying hens in several different ways' (Baxter, 1994).

The battery cage system of egg production has been cited as being cruel in courts of law in Australia and Germany. In Switzerland, where the keeping of laying hens in cages has been banned since 1992, the Swiss Society for the Protection of Animals, in its report (Poultry Working Group, 1994) on the alternatives available stated:
> 'The keeping of laying hens in cages is one of the most monstrous forms of cruelty to living creatures in the service of man'.

On a related issue, before moving on from battery hens — how many battery eggs are packaged in boxes labelled 'Fresh' or 'Farm Fresh'? These labels often mislead consumers into believing the eggs that they are buying come from free-range hens or, at least, from hens kept in high welfare conditions. However, sadly, the reality is that the birds that laid those 'fresh' or 'farm fresh' eggs will, in nearly all cases, have spent their lives in battery cages. Some supermarkets have responded to consumer concerns over potentially misleading labelling by using the term 'Eggs from Caged Hens' on battery egg boxes. One notable case, Marks & Spencer, has gone one step further by selling only free-range eggs. It is interesting to note that in Oslo, Norway, a court ruled that an egg carton depicting happy hens wandering around a farmyard was illegal because it was far from the reality of industrial egg production. Criticizing the decision, a spokesman for the egg companies declared:

'You don't show pictures from a slaughterhouse when you are trying to sell meat'!! (The Independent, 1996).

I believe this short statement speaks volumes about the battery hen system of egg production.

Broilers

Again, in long evil-smelling, windowless sheds, annually around 750 million broiler chickens are reared for their meat. They are kept in such overcrowded conditions that, as the birds get bigger, one can barely see the floor so thickly is it carpeted with chickens. The modern broilers are creatures so manipulated by genetic selection and stimulated by growth-promoting antibiotics that only 20% get to slaughter weight at 6 weeks of age without developing leg problems which are sometimes painful and crippling. It is known that the more severely affected birds soon become unable to get to food and water and are likely to starve to death amongst their multi-thousand companions — unless some merciful and alert stockperson puts them out of their misery first. Many broilers develop painful hock burns and foot sores from the ammonia-ridden floors in their sheds.

As a result of growing too quickly, the birds' hearts and lungs are also affected. Around 7 million birds a year die from congestive heart failure. Another 2·8 million die from heart failure during the journey from the farm to the slaughterhouse and more die from injuries such as dislocated hips, ruptured livers and crushed heads. There is no doubt that in its husbandry, transport and slaughter practices, the broiler industry imposes massive suffering on hundreds of millions of animals. Broiler production as it now stands is wholly unacceptable and should not be permitted to continue.

In the foreword to a report by Stevenson (1995) for the Compassion in World Farming Trust, which discusses the chronic pain which the broiler chicken endures, John Webster, Professor of Animal Husbandry at the Department of Veterinary Science at the University of Bristol and a former member of FAWC, wrote:

'This must constitute the single most extreme example of man's inhumanity to another sentient creature'.

Pigs

More than 13 million pigs are reared and slaughtered annually in Britain. The breeding herd comprises some 800 000 sows. In the most intensive units in Britain and Europe, sows are to be found tethered and confined in narrow stalls throughout their 16 week pregnancies. They are kept in rows like breeding machines, able only to stand up or lie down, take a pace forward and a pace backward. Exercise is rendered impossible by the metal bars or chains that restrain them. Thankfully, due to long and hard campaigning by the animal welfare movement and others, these sow stalls and tether systems are being phased out in the UK and will be banned at the end of this year, 1998. However, this is not the case in the rest of the European Union (EU) where tethers will not be banned until the year 2006.

Whilst most British sows can now look forward to relative freedom when pregnant, the same cannot be said at farrowing time. Often referred to as 'motherhood behind bars', about 80% of sows are confined in the farrowing crate before giving birth and whilst mothering. This crude, metal barred contraption is so narrow that the sow cannot walk or even turn round. Her strong instinct to build a nest for her piglets is completely frustrated. She will remain trapped like this until her piglets are taken away at 3 to 4 weeks of age. Many intensive farmers argue that farrowing crates are necessary to prevent the sow from lying on and crushing her piglets. This deliberately overlooks the drawbacks of the modern system. Selective breeding has again produced a large sow which has larger litters than her wild ancestor. In addition, increasing intensive production has resulted in sows being allocated much smaller pens and the removal of most, if not all, straw bedding.

The stress of being separated from their mother at 3 or 4 weeks of age causes the piglets to redirect their natural sucking behaviours towards pen mates and pen fixtures. The effects of current early weaning practice can be exacerbated by the barren and crowded conditions under which many weaner pigs are kept. Densely stocked flat-decked cages with slatted or perforated floors devoid of bedding, are still commonly used. The subsequent fattening pens used in intensive farms provide an equally harsh and overcrowded environment.

Given the chance, pigs will generally spend much of their time chewing, rooting and exploring in bedding material. It has other potential benefits too. For example, it provides a source of relative comfort. It is not surprising, then, that an absence of straw can lead to increased problems with so-called 'vices' such as tail-biting and chewing of pen mates. To control these behavioural problems, brought on by impoverished and densely stocked housing and early weaning, tail-docking is practised — cutting off half the tail with pliers or a hot iron when the animal is a few days old. This mutilation is still inflicted on around 70% of piglets each year, despite the fact that the *Welfare of Livestock Regulations 1994* banned routine tail-docking. A farmer has a defence under the law if he can show that not to tail-dock might lead to tail biting.

Veal production

Were it not for the EU ban on the export of British beef in response to the controversy over BSE, then annually some 500 000 calves would have been packed into lorries and sent across the Channel, the majority ending up in the appalling veal crates in France and Holland, a system of animal production which has been illegal in Britain since 1990 because it is considered cruel. Dairy farmers have already made it clear that they intend to resume this trade as soon as the beef ban is lifted. I consider it indefensible to send calves into systems abroad which in this country we have banned for reasons of cruelty.

It is worth noting that the campaign which helped bring about an end to the veal crate system in Britain probably sparked off one of the most successful consumer boycotts this country has ever known. Watching their television sets, reading their newspapers, listening to their radios, people were horrified to find that young calves were kept in solid-sided wooden boxes, so narrow that they could not even turn round. The public was so shocked that these young animals were being fed an all-liquid, iron-deficient diet in order to make them anaemic and thus produce white veal that when they went out shopping they avoided this cruelly produced product. The boycott proved so successful that by the time the government acted in 1987 to phase-out this system, there were only eight veal-crate farms left in Britain. The others had either switched to a more humane system or had gone out of business. This is a clear example of how consumer power can bring about real change. It also demonstrates how public opinion, expressed through consumer action and political progress, are so often inextricably linked.

Export of live animals

Whilst the BSE scare ensures that the restrictions over the export of British cattle remain, the trade in other animals continues apace. Recent figures show that over 1 million lambs, sheep and pigs were sent abroad, the majority destined for slaughter in continental abattoirs. Once these animals arrive on the continent of Europe they enter a world where welfare standards, both during the journey and at slaughter, are often appallingly low. Many of the animals exported from Britain are sent to Spain, Italy and Greece, countries notorious for the brutality of their slaughter methods.

Animals are frequently deprived of food and water, even during journeys of 30 h or more. For example, sheep have been trailed going for 28 h without food and water on a journey from the south of England to southern France. Pigs have been sent on a 37-h journey — again without food or water — from Britain to Portugal.

Of course, it is not only the journeys which cause British animals so much suffering but also the practices and conditions which face them at the slaughterhouses when they arrive. Unloading can be a brutal process with animals being beaten and kicked and the use of the electric goad being commonplace. In France sheep are often to be seen being dragged from the truck to the slaughterhouse by one front leg. In Holland animals were filmed being dragged off trucks, often by their ears or by chains attached to a rear leg. The stunning equipment used to kill them is often inadequate and sometimes they are not stunned before having their throats cut and being left to bleed to death. In Spain, RSPCA inspectors filmed sheep being stabbed in the neck with a blunt screw-driver and another animal being repeatedly stabbed behind the head with a short-bladed knife in order to sever its spinal chord to paralyse it prior to throat-slitting.

As a result of the concern over the live export trade, a coalition of animal welfare organizations has now been formed called the European Committee for Improvements in the Transport of Farm Animals. At the Committee's launch, one of the founding members, Prince Sadruddin Aga Khan (Agscene, 1993) of the Bellerive Foundation, commented:

> 'The cruelties currently associated with the transport of live farm animals across Europe are scandalous. How can the perpetration of such atrocities continue to be tolerated in a society which considers itself to be civilised?'

Although the *Welfare of Animals (Transport) Order 1997* has now come into force, implementing the 1995 *EU Transport Directive 95/29/EC* it will, in my opinion do nothing to reduce the length of animal journey times. The Order imposes an 8-h journey limit. However, in practice, no exporter is ever likely to be caught by the 8-h rule as this applies only to animals transported in lower-quality vehicles. Exporters who comply with some minimal rules on vehicle standards escape the 8-h regime altogether. They can transport sheep for 30 h, with a derisory 1-h mid-journey break, give them 1 day of rest and then transport the animals for another 30 h. I regret to say that the new rules are akin to giving a quick lick of paint to a house whose foundations are rotten.

The export of live animals for slaughter places the welfare of our farm animals at considerable risk and I question why it is ever necessary to subject animals to such journeys when there are slaughterhouses in this country and refrigerated lorries to carry the meat abroad. We should therefore insist that they are slaughtered as close to the point of production as possible and, when transport is unavoidable, that journey times between resting, feeding and watering should not exceed 8 h.

Markets and slaughterhouses

Many of the animals destined for slaughter in Britain or for the live export trade are processed through livestock auction markets. During the period July to November 1995 I, personally, visited eleven livestock markets in Scotland and one in England filming all that I saw. By coincidence, shortly after the Advocates for Animals' investigation had ended, the then President of the Institute of Auctioneers and Appraisers in Scotland, William Blair, held a press briefing during which he challenged 'any animal welfare campaigner to visit any Scottish market at any time'. He went on to say:

'It is in no-one's interest to treat stock badly. As far as our markets are concerned, we are under constant scrutiny from the Scottish Offices' veterinary service and the public. The fact that not one single complaint or prosecution has resulted from that scrutiny gives us, I think, a clean bill of health.' (The Scotsman, 1994).

When I released the evidence which I had gathered I got the feeling that Mr Blair had begun to regret that he had issued such a challenge or made such a bold statement. The investigation revealed 34 instances where there had been infringements of the regulations governing the treatment and welfare of animals at markets. These included: pigs being kicked in the face, head and other parts of the body; pigs being beaten with sticks or the broken and rough edges of pig boards; calves, barely able to walk, being hit about the face and other parts of the body; calves being picked up and thrown into the back of pick-up trucks; cattle being hit violently with sticks about the face, head and other parts of the body; pigs when loaded onto lorries being punched, kicked, stamped on and pulled by the ears and tails; spent dairy cattle being viciously kicked in the udder.

After being shown the filmed evidence, Sir Colin Spedding the Chairman of FAWC stated:

'The level of violence, particularly the beating with sticks was extremely disappointing. It was almost as though people enjoyed using sticks violently. The behaviour of these operators was really in violation of all the Ministry's codes.' (The Scotsman, 1995).

As a result of the investigation, one individual was prosecuted and a number of others lost their jobs. What struck me most forcibly about this investigation was that while all this violence towards animals was going on around them, no auctioneer, buyer, farmer, drover or visiting members of the public did anything to stop it. They seemed to be totally unconcerned as if it was just another ordinary day at the livestock auction market.

Origin of animal food and disease

An investigation like the one I have just mentioned will usually result in short-term press interest in that particular subject. However, the controversy over bovine spongiform encephalopathy (BSE) or so-called 'mad cow disease' and the link with Creutzfeldt-Jakob disease (CJD), the human equivalent of BSE, has never been far from the headlines during the last 3 years. It is an absolute disgrace that food containing meat and bone meal from sheep believed to be infected with scrapie should have been manufactured, supplied and given to other animals. Anyone with a sense of responsibility or an ounce of commonsense would have known that turning vegetarian animals into meat eaters was asking for trouble. I trust that those responsible will be made to account for their scandalous actions. You also would have thought that the animal food and livestock industry would have learned a lesson as a result of the crisis over BSE. Seemingly not. Although animal-derived cattle food is now banned, pig slaughterhouse waste is still being given as swill to pigs and chickens are still being given poultry and feather waste (The Herald, 1998).

What this long-lasting BSE affair has achieved is further close scrutiny and inquisitions into the conditions in which our farm animals, which provide the bulk of our food, are reared, treated and slaughtered. For example, an editorial in one of Scotland's leading national newspapers commented:

'Beyond the immediate beef issue, however, this affair raises wider questions about the way in which food — and particularly meat and fish — is produced. In the quest for maximum quantities at minimum cost animals are subjected to treatment which can only be described as a perversion. Factory farming has little to do with animal welfare and everything to do with profit. BSE, the result of feeding sheep offal to an animal which by no stretch of the imagination can be described as carnivorous, is the latest state in the development which began with battery hens and broiler chickens. Such a cavalier disregard for animal welfare and such grotesque treatment of livestock is now coming home to roost . . . the whole way in which animals are factory farmed for meat is symptomatic of the way in which the culture of industrialised societies has lost any sense of what is appropriate in a natural environment. The next step on the road is the controversy surrounding genetic engineering. What, precisely, is the advantage of a cloned sheep for us, the consumers, over one produced by more natural methods? (The Scotsman, 1996).

Cloning and genetic engineering

Cloning and the genetic engineering of farm animals, the manipulation of life at its very source, deserves more attention than the space allows. But I have to say that this technology poses real animal welfare concerns. Cloning procedures involve surgical interference to harvest egg cells and the killing of the surrogate mother. A higher than average death rate has been recorded and many of the animals have been born with congenital abnormalities in their kidneys and cardiovascular systems. The production of herds of cloned animals would make them vulnerable to disease because of the reduced gene pool from which they were drawn; manipulating animals so that they grow more quickly and convert food to muscle more efficiently; designing animals with high milk yield or tender meat; inserting growth hormone genes into animals to increase their size; the possibility of featherless chickens.

Summary

At the beginning of this paper I referred to those with their comfortable images of farms and their animals which bore little resemblance to modern-day farming. Thankfully, now in the minority, they have been replaced by an ever-growing majority of people who are much more aware of what is happening 'down on the farm' and who are becoming increasingly concerned about how farm animals are being reared, transported and slaughtered and the subsequent health implications for them as consumers in the food that they and their families eat.

Pressure groups like Advocates for Animals build on this public awareness and concern and, indeed, may have been responsible for raising it in the first place. It is when this power of public feeling is roused to a stage where it can no longer be ignored that politicians are forced to sit up and take notice. At this point new legislation can be influenced and introduced.

I remember years ago the front cover of *Private Eye* showing our then Prime Minister, John Major, saying to the American President, George Bush: "Is it time to act?" to which Bush replied: "Yeah — act concerned."

I trust that those directly involved with farm animals, those involved in the food industry and also those who care about the welfare of farm animals and recognize their sentiency will in future do more than just 'act concerned' but will take action to ensure that the animals which provide the bulk of our food are reared with due thought to their behavioural needs and well-being and, when the time comes, granted a quiet and humane death. For far too long in the area of food production farm animals have paid a heavy price in suffering. In a so-called 'civilized society', economics, free trade and the profit motive must no longer be allowed to reign supreme over the welfare needs of animals thus preventing action from being taken to halt cruelty and suffering. From birth to death farm animals must be treated humanely and with respect. As someone who has seen farm animals suffer all too often, I have no doubt that they deserve nothing less.

References

Anonymous. 1993. New transport coalition formed by Aga Khan. *Agscene* **113**: 8-9.

Anonymous. 1994. Scab of more concern than journey length. *The Scotsman* 15 December, Edinburgh.

Anonymous. 1995. Secret film shows animals being mistreated. *The Scotsman* 9 February, Edinburgh.

Anonymous. 1996. The human way with animals. *The Scotsman* 25 March, Edinburgh.

Anonymous. 1996. Bad day for chickens. *The Independent* 17 October, London.

Anonymous. 1998. New food chain fears over BSE. *The Herald* 23 April, Glasgow.

Baxter, M. R. 1994. The welfare problems of laying hens in battery cages. *Veterinary Record* **23**: 614-619.

Brambell Committee. 1965. *Report of the Technical Committee to Enquire into the Welfare of Animals Kept under Livestock Husbandry Systems.* Her Majesty's Stationery Office.

Farm Animal Welfare Council. 1992. *The extension of the Five Freedoms.* 7 October, press release.

Gregory, N. G. and Wilkins L. J. 1989. Broken bones in domestic fowl: handling and processing damage in end-of-lay battery hens. *British Poultry Science* **30**: 555-562.

Harrison, R. 1964. *Animal machines.* Vincent Stewart, London.

McCoy, M. A., Reilly, G. A. C. and Kilpatrick, D. J. 1996. Density and breaking strength of bones of mortalities among cage layers. *Research in Veterinary Science* **60**: 185-186.

Poultry Working Group of the Productive Livestock Committee. 1994. *Laying hens: twelve years of experience with new husbandry systems in Switzerland.* Swiss Society for the Protection of Animals, Basel.

Stevenson, P. 1995. *The welfare of broiler chickens.* Compassion in World Farming Trust.

Farm animal welfare — who writes the rules?
Occasional Publication No. 23 — British Society of Animal Science 1999
edited by A. J. F. Russel, C. A. Morgan, C. J. Savory, M. C. Appleby and T. L. J. Lawrence

The consumer, the citizen and animal welfare

R. Layton and R. Bonney

Apple Trees, Grims Lodge Farm, Coombe Bissett, Salisbury SP5 4LP

Abstract

In answer to the question 'who writes the rules?' relative to animal welfare the only accurate answer there can be is that the animal writes the rules. However in deciding the current animal welfare standards adopted by society the consumer plays a key rôle as the retail market is constantly working to meet the consumer's concerns. The consumer has a real, if often uninformed, concern regarding animal welfare. Animal welfare science clearly demonstrates that current systems are often at odds with the needs of animals. Ethical sectors of the food chain will put in place systems which reflect knowledge of animal welfare science as far as is currently possible and not merely the consumer perception in this area. The ability to deliver good animal welfare depends upon the willingness of the food chain to provide and the consumer to pay. The development of assurance schemes which truly address animal welfare science, translated into accurate labelling and backed by an awareness programme will make it easy for consumers to take the responsibility which, as citizens, they wish to do. We will then have an accurate picture of society's concerns to which the food chain can respond.

Introduction

There can only be one accurate answer to the question 'Who writes the rules?' and that is, the animal writes the rules. As we are unable to ask animals 'how is it for you?' by speaking to them, many of us revert to our personal observations and perspectives when trying to make a judgement. However, with the rapidly developing science of animal welfare, which is the science of finding out from animals 'what do *you* want?', those up to date with the current knowledge are more likely to know what does and does not matter to the animal. This subject is reflected in the aim of the British Society of Animal Science (BSAS) itself which is 'to enhance the understanding of animal science'. Animal welfare

science is not to be confused with animal welfare ethics which is 'what are we (society) going to do with the knowledge we gain from the science?' In other words, when and how do we instigate change in the light of this information. This subject is also reflected in the aim of the BSAS 'to integrate animal sciences into animal production'.

Animal welfare science and ethics

Amongst some farmers, veterinarians, retailers, consumers and others there is a growing desire to gain knowledge which is able to help us make judgements about good or poor welfare of food animals through recognized techniques. These are partly measurements of physiological and biochemical parameters such as heart rate, blood pressure and levels of substances in the body known to change under stressful circumstances. There are also more easily accessible measurements which can be used on a regular and practical basis relating to behaviour and production. A behavioural example might be the fact that we often get the odd cow lying in the dunging passage when we know the majority of cows choose a soft, dry lying area. Instead of calling her rude names perhaps we should consider whether she really wants to do this or is it the best option for her under the conditions we have provided, i.e. she wants a dry bed but the only cubicle available is next to a dominant cow? In the case of production we might consider that the life of a dairy cow at around three lactations for the national average is ridiculously short in terms of farmer effort and commercial soundness as well as animal welfare. If the shortness of life is due to a change in breeding policy or some other factor under the control of the management then this is perhaps justifiable in terms of animal welfare. However, if the high cull rate is as a result of disease or injury then we have to look to improving our systems.

The knowledge derived from animal welfare science may then be used within the ethical debate when deciding where we draw the line between acceptable and unacceptable practice. Ethical frameworks such as the 'five freedoms' have been developed to help us, but ultimately we, having dominion over animals, draw this line and this is where the consumer plays a vital rôle.

Consumers and citizens

Research has shown us that the positive interest consumers show to questions on animal welfare are not reflected in their decisions at the point of purchase. This is often interpreted as a sign that most consumers do not really care about animal welfare. There are other factors which come into play to complicate this issue and several examples are given here in an attempt by the authors to suggest what is really happening.

When the consumer can differentiate at the point of purchase between products which are produced under systems with good animal welfare many will choose those systems even when the price is significantly higher. For example, where the idea, if not the reality, is closely linked with good animal welfare, as with free range eggs, this is clearly demonstrated by the increase in sales of this product.

There is currently limited uptake by the consumers of high welfare animal produce and this may again be interpreted as a lack of interest but the authors ask you to consider the following argument. When questioned as members of the public regarding such ethical issues, many of us perhaps give answers which we feel are politically correct, in that they reflect an area about which we or others have concern. We could say that in this instance we are acting as *citizens*. At the point of purchase, however, it is easy to be just a *consumer* and forget such concerns, buying merely on price and other more easily recognizable quality issues such as appearance.

Thus to expand on these definitions we might describe the citizen as someone who acts for the greater good, which in this case means animals as well as themselves. Consumers on the other hand are acting in the interest of themselves and their immediate family and have to balance requests for expensive clothing, computers, etc. with the need to feed a family on what may be a very limited budget. However, the vast majority of us also think as citizens and there is therefore an obvious need to enable our actions to mirror our desires.

If we put ourselves in the position of someone selling food we will not merely provide what the consumer of today demands, but will look towards addressing their underlying concerns which will influence buying patterns in the future. In a relatively stable society, which we currently have in the west, the citizen of today *is* the consumer of tomorrow. Thus, forward-looking business is striving to put in place systems which will meet these requirements. These cannot be put in place overnight and thus the current interest in assurance schemes within the food industry seems premature to many, particularly those furthest removed from the customer. The facts are that it is in the commercial interest of farmers and others in the food chain, just as much as retailers, to put in place systems that benefit the animals and therefore enable the consumer to buy with confidence. The debate needs to centre around how this should be managed rather than whether it needs to happen at all.

The way forward

It is currently made easier for the public than for the producer to expound an ethical perspective as they are allowed the luxury of a detached position, i.e. poor animal welfare is nothing to do with me. Change will happen more effectively if all those involved in the food industry, including retailers and consumers are enabled to take this responsibility by having the necessary systems in place. The following are positive actions underway which need assistance. A relevant example is given in each case.

1. Development of our knowledge of animal welfare science and ethics in order that all those in the food chain from the farmer to the consumer make decisions which are *relevant* to animal welfare.

An example here is the great confusion which surrounds the humane slaughter of animals. In many cases an effective stun of an animal is accompanied by exaggerated movements of the body. These movements, however, occur precisely *because* the animal is unconscious and if we really are interested in animal welfare we have to understand the science, do what is right for the animal and overcome the feeling of aversion we may have.

2. Support and understanding of the concept of assurance schemes.

Assurance schemes are becoming increasingly regulated under the United Kingdom Accreditation Services (UKAS) which, although at first sight they can seem onerous, will be beneficial to those with robust schemes provided they are administered with care. All interested parties have a route by which their concerns have to be taken into consideration under this system, and thus in theory at least the consensus of opinion will be reflected. Thus, for example, if society decides that the majority wish to purchase pork from systems with a rich environment then this will be reflected in the standards and the price of pork. This will put the responsibility for the decision into the hands of society and remove the current situation where the responsibility is being placed largely in the hands of the farmer alone.

3. Understanding of the legal requirements for the labelling of food and ensuring that these are communicated simply and unambiguously to the consumer. The encouragement of voluntary labelling of foods by the retail market where this assists decision making on animal welfare.

The labelling of food in relation to animal welfare is often currently ambiguous and misleading. To revisit the example of free range eggs; the free range label does not *assure* good welfare, as it is merely a regulation stipulating requirements such as access to range and stocking densities in order for the words free range to be used on the package. However, the words free range have become synonymous with good welfare and the consumer is increasingly buying this product and the words free range are now attached to a variety of other products which may or may not have good welfare. This is the simplistic attitude that everything outdoors must be good while everything indoors is bad which is blatantly not the case. To assure good welfare the consumer needs to be educated in this respect and encouraged to ask for products which are produced under labels seriously addressing these issues such as the Freedom Food Label.

4. Working alongside experts in other areas of ethical concern for the food industry, such as food safety, the environment and the welfare of those persons involved in the industry. Animal welfare cannot be considered in isolation.

There are many areas where there is conflict between areas of ethical concern. An example is the treatment of animals for external parasites and the damage some of these products do to the environment. Experts need to agree a compromise in the best interest of all concerned, i.e. animals, man and the environment.

Conclusion
In response to the question posed by this conference we propose that the consumer has a key rôle in the writing of animal welfare rules as the retail market is constantly working to meet the concerns of the consumer. The consumer has a real, if often uninformed, concern regarding animal welfare. The ethical sectors of the food chain will put in place systems which reflect the current knowledge of animal welfare science as far as is possible and not merely the consumer perception in this area. The provision of assurance schemes, which address animal welfare science translated into accurate labelling and backed by an awareness programme will make it easy for consumers to take the responsibility which, as citizens, they wish to do. We will then have a true reflection of society's concerns and the market can respond.

Further reading
Broom, D. M. and Johnson, K. G. 1993. *Stress and animal welfare.* Chapman and Hall, London.

Singer, P. 1975. *Animal liberation.* Jonathon Cape Ltd.

Spedding, C. R. W. 1996. *Agriculture and the citizen.* Chapman and Hall, London.

Webster, A. J. F. 1995. *Animal welfare: a cool eye towards Eden.* Blackwell Science Ltd, Oxford.

Webster, A. J. F. 1997. *Animals and husbandry. Seventh annual lecture of The Royal Agricultural Society of England.* RASE, Stoneleigh.

Farm animal welfare — who writes the rules?
Occasional Publication No. 23 — British Society of Animal Science 1999
edited by A. J. F. Russel, C. A. Morgan, C. J. Savory, M. C. Appleby and T. L. J. Lawrence

Rôle of research in the formulation of 'rules' to protect the welfare of farm animals during road transportation

M. S. Cockram[1] and M. A. Mitchell[2]

[1]*Department of Veterinary Clinical Studies, Royal (Dick) School of Veterinary Studies, University of Edinburgh, Easter Bush Veterinary Centre, Roslin, Midlothian EH25 9RG*
[2]*Division of Environment and Welfare, Roslin Institute (Edinburgh), Roslin, Midlothian EH25 9PS*

Abstract

This paper explains how research can contribute to an understanding of the welfare issues associated with transportation and the value of basing legislation to protect the welfare of animals on scientific evidence. However, it also indicates the limitations of existing research methodology and identifies where research can make a clear contribution to the amendment of existing legislation. The research should accurately reflect commercial practice and should focus upon the provision of readily transferable technological improvements and relevant legislation that will optimize both welfare and productivity. Research into the effects of transport on the welfare of animals involves the investigation of a multi-component process which can potentially affect the welfare of animals in many ways. The research should identify and quantify those components of transport environments and practices which constitute a major risk to the welfare of animals and determine the optimum conditions for transportation based upon matching the conditions and procedures to the animals' biological requirements. A range of different measurements have been made to evaluate the responses of farm animals to transportation. Physiological and biochemical variables should be selected to reflect responses or disturbances in the major homeostatic systems influenced by transport environments and practices. The value of the different measurements is strengthened by an understanding of the action and functional significance of the responses. Animal welfare legislation should be based upon sound scientific evidence relating to the animals' physiological and behavioural requirements and their interaction with their immediate environment. Nowhere is this more important than in animal transportation.

Introduction

Regardless of the identity or composition of the regulatory body which ultimately composes and implements welfare legislation, the 'rules' should be based upon sound scientific evidence relating to the animals' physiological and behavioural requirements and their interaction with their immediate environment. Nowhere is this more important than in animal transportation.

Animal welfare is currently high on the agricultural and political agendas of many nations, particularly within the European Union and the transportation of live animals is subject to close scrutiny. Public concern has been prompted by media attention and political lobbying by welfare organizations. Attention has been focused on specific aspects of transport practices by extensive reporting of public protests and by high profile articles in popular scientific journals (e.g. Birchall, 1990; Bonner, 1995). In the United Kingdom (UK), the Welfare of Animals (Transport) Order 1997 (WATO 1997) (Great Britain Parliament, 1997), implements European Directive 91/628/EEC (European Council, 1991) as amended by Directive 95/29/EC (European Council, 1995) and represents a standardization of animal transport practices in line with improved welfare. Elsewhere in Europe there has been extensive debate concerning the application and local adoption of this Directive and in practice standards may still differ considerably between nations. The complex nature of the regulations and of the animals' responses and behaviours coupled to the demands of efficient commercial animal production make standardization difficult. All concerned can only benefit from receipt of as much information as possible, supporting suggested improvements in procedures, practices or legislative requirements.

There are many facets to and influences upon the development, implementation and enforcement of 'rules' relating to animal transport. Animal welfare legislation is a consequence of the assimilation of expert opinion based upon practical experience, professional judgement and research evidence and is influenced by commercial consequences, lobbying by welfare groups and is formulated within a legal framework. In recent years there has been increased research activity into the welfare of animals during transportation. This present paper explains how research can contribute to an understanding of the welfare issues associated with transportation and the value of basing legislation to protect the welfare of animals on scientific evidence. However, it also indicates the limitations of existing research methodology and identifies where research can make a clear contribution to the amendment of existing legislation.

Before examining progress in animal transport research in more detail, it is perhaps pertinent to identify the precise rôles and objectives of these activities in improving the welfare of animals in-transit. It may be proposed that research should provide the sound scientific basis for:
- (a) improvements in transporter design and function,
- (b) improvements in transport practices,
- (c) informed policy, legislation and codes of practice, and
- (d) education of:-
    - (i) those responsible for animals in-transit,
    - (ii) those responsible for policing legislation,
    - (iii) policy makers and welfare organizations,
    - (iv) the agricultural and retail sectors, and
    - (v) the public.

To achieve these aims research must:

(a) Identify and quantify those components of transport environments and practices which constitute the major risk to the welfare and survival of animals during journeys. This will involve the characterisation of the physiological and behavioural responses to transport.

(b) Determine the optimum conditions for transportation and identify 'best practice' based upon matching the conditions and procedures to the animals' biological requirements.

The research should accurately reflect commercial practice and should focus upon the provision of readily transferable technological improvements and relevant legislation that will optimize both welfare and productivity. Animal transport research should provide *'practicable solutions to practical problems!'*

A study of the transport of animals involves many aspects. This paper deals only with road transportation, although many of the principles outlined can also be applied to air and sea transport. When evaluating the consequences of transportation on the welfare of farm animals it is important to consider all stages of transportation and not just the time that the animals are 'in-transit'. In general, these stages consist of (1) assembly, handling and management of the animals before transport, (2) loading, (3) transport/motion, (4) unloading, and (5) handling, re-grouping and post-transport management. When animals are transported they are potentially exposed to a number of factors that could result in animal welfare problems either on their own or in combination. In addition to the novelty of many aspects of transportation, the animals can be exposed to a variety of changes in their physical and social environment. The main potential effects of transport on the welfare of animals can be considered within the framework of the Farm Animal Welfare Council's five freedoms (Farm Animal Welfare Council, 1993), namely: (1) *freedom from thirst, hunger and malnutrition* (associated with water and food restriction); (2) *freedom from discomfort* (arising from thermal and physical discomfort due to inadequate ventilation and space, and vehicle vibration, acceleration and motion); (3) *freedom from pain, injury and disease* (following handling, impacts associated with motion, interactions between animals, and infection); (4) *freedom to express normal behaviour* (behavioural restriction due to confinement, vehicle motion and social disruption); (5) *freedom from fear and distress* (following handling, confinement and exposure to novel stimuli e.g. vehicle noise and motion).

All of the Farm Animal Welfare Council's freedoms could be impaired during transportation. Whether this occurs will depend upon the quality of the journey and the associated handling and management of the animals. As indicated within the existing legislation (WATO 1997), there are several important factors that can influence the effects of a given journey on the welfare of the animals, namely: pre- and post- transport handling; the environmental conditions during transport, journey duration; intervals between periods for resting, feeding and watering; and the duration and conditions provided for rest during and after a journey. In addition to the difficulties in investigating the numerous components of transportation, the responses of the animals are likely to vary widely. The ability of the different farm animals, e.g. cattle compared with pigs, to cope with each aspect of transportation differs and there are important differences in the way that each type of animal is transported. The emphasis in this paper is on cattle, sheep, pigs and poultry, (and on sheep and broilers in particular as we have carried out most of our transport research on these). The principles, however, will also apply to the other farmed animals.

Transport cannot be considered as a single factor and

the responses of the animal cannot be assimilated into the uninformative phrase 'transport stress'. Due to the complex nature of transport, research is required to identify the main factors that are likely to affect the welfare of the animals and to provide information on which to base recommendations on how to either reduce or avoid these potential problems. However, the multi-factorial nature of transport presents difficulties in both the approach to transport research and the writing of legislation. The results of research and the wording of legislation must be applicable in a wide variety of circumstances. This means that legislation written to protect animals during transport has to be general and somewhat vague in places so that sufficient leeway is available for interpretation of the legislation by relevant professionals in specific circumstances.

Research into the effects of transportation can be approached in several ways and in different stages. The difficulty is that the welfare problems arising from transportation are in many cases likely to be the consequence of the interaction of several factors. A study of the effects of individual components of transportation on animals will result in the identification of some of the main factors likely to influence welfare. However, these studies then have to be followed by further experiments to investigate the interaction between each of the components of transportation. This approach will succeed only if (a) the components of commercial transportation have been correctly identified, (b) these factors are successfully simulated under controlled conditions and (c) sufficient time, money and resources are available to examine all relevant interactions. An applied approach that has to be used when limited funding is available and answers to practical questions are required within a working lifetime, is to monitor the responses of animals to specified treatments within either commercial or simulated commercial situations. This has the advantage that the responses of the animals should represent their responses to the combined influence of the numerous components of transportation. If no adverse responses are found during or after a particular transport treatment, then either the method of welfare assessment requires further development or those set of transport conditions do not present a serious welfare problem to those animals, and further research into these component elements of transportation cannot be justified. If, however, adverse responses are found during commercial or simulated commercial transport it is likely that the nature of the responses will provide an indication of the principal factors that require more detailed investigation. This can be performed by either a modification of the transport conditions to vary that factor or by investigation of that factor under controlled conditions. Although the results of monitoring commercial or semi-commercial transport can provide useful results that are likely to have a general application, the results do need to be viewed in relation to the particular circumstances of the trial.

Measurements used in research to evaluate the effects of transport on welfare

Although there is no consensus on what the term animal welfare means, two practical approaches can be readily used to identify welfare problems in farm animals. First, the ability of animals to 'cope' with transport can be assessed and secondly the subjective experiences of animals in response to transport conditions can be evaluated (Duncan and Fraser, 1997). If welfare is viewed as a multi-component concept, a comprehensive monitoring of a variety of different types of response is required to ensure that each individual component that could affect welfare is assessed. Judgements can then be made on the relative importance of each component to the well being of the animals. This results in a more transparent approach to welfare assessment as the scientific collection of data and its analysis is separated from the ethical and consequential subjective interpretation of the research.

Whilst physiologists and behaviourists may accept the measurement of physiological and behavioural responses as indicative of disturbances in the predictability and controllability of an animals environment, it is also acknowledged that change per se in biological variables need not reflect reduced welfare (Moberg, 1985; Cashman et al., 1989; Barnett and Hemsworth, 1990). The highly dynamic patterns of homeostatic response observed during stress make it difficult to deduce any simple relationship between stress and welfare (Wiepkema and Koolhaas, 1993). The concept of a specific 'cut-off' point in a stress response or physiological variable at which welfare is deemed to be at risk has been criticized (Mendl, 1991). The use of a range of different measurements may represent a more effective approach which is further strengthened by a complete understanding of the action and functional significance of the physiological and behavioural responses and other measurements that are quantified (Mason and Mendl, 1993).

A whole range of different measurements have been made to evaluate the responses of farm animals to transportation, including: behavioural, physiological, immunological, pathological, and production and meat quality measurements. Physiological and biochemical variables should be selected to reflect responses or disturbances in the major homeostatic systems influenced by transport environments and practices. A range of different measurements is required in transport research as transport can affect several body systems and the interpretation of each measurement is difficult, as a response could be found as a result of more than one type of stimuli, i.e. most measurements used cannot be regarded as absolute markers for a particular condition. Although there are major problems in the interpretation of measurements, acceptance of the cognitive capacities and sentience of animals has lead to the argument that 'if there is uncertainty, even if only slight, about an animal's ability to feel pain or suffer, then the individuals should be given the benefit of the doubt' (Bekoff, 1994).

Mortality and morbidity
One important way of evaluating the effects of transport conditions on animals is to record the number and proportion of the total number of animals transported that die either during or shortly after a particular set of transport conditions. On the assumption that death in each case is not instantaneous, mortality rates can provide basic information on the relative effects of transport on the welfare of different types of animals and show where the transport conditions are so inappropriate that a significant proportion of the animals cannot survive the process. The quality of this information can be improved if the dead animals are subjected to post-mortem examination to determine the likely cause of death (Gregory and Austin, 1992). Surveys of animals either arriving dead at a slaughterhouse or dying in the lairage has shown that poultry (Bayliss and Hinton, 1990; Warriss *et al.*, 1992) are at the greatest risk of dying during transport, followed by pigs (Warriss and Brown, 1994) and that deaths involving sheep (Knowles *et al.*, 1994a) and cattle and are not common. Important risk factors for mortality in broilers have been identified by Bayliss and Hinton (1990) as health status, thermal environment, injury and journey duration. In pigs, a major risk factor affecting mortality is high temperature (Warriss and Brown, 1994). Knowles *et al.* (1994a) identified the influence of markets and pre-existing pathology on the risk of mortality in lambs during or after transport.

Morbidity following transport can arise for several reasons: the animals might be immunologically compromised by either transportation or movement to a novel environment (Murata and Hirose, 1991) or they may become exposed to pathogens either by mixing with animals from several sources before, during or after transport (Ribble *et al.*, 1995) and/or by inadequate cleansing and disinfection of vehicles (Wray *et al.*, 1991).

Injury
Injury associated with transportation can be most clearly identified *post mortem* by recording the occurrence of bone fractures, joint dislocations (Gregory and Austin, 1992), carcass bruising (Jarvis and Cockram, 1994; Jarvis *et al.*, 1995) and skin lesions (Sather *et al.*, 1995). However, any effects of transport must be separated from those occurring during the slaughtering and dressing procedures. Identification of injury in live animals is more difficult, unless there is an obvious effect on the posture and/or gait of the animal, or there is an obvious skin wound, such as bite wounds in pigs. Potentially traumatic events, e.g. wool-pulls by a handler or falls can be observed during handling (Jarvis and Cockram, 1995b) and transport and impacts monitored using sensors on the animal that record changes in acceleration (Cockram *et al.*, 1996), but it is not always clear which events result in injury. The activity of plasma creatine kinase and other plasma enzymes are often used as biochemical markers of injury (Lefebvre *et al.*, 1995). These enzymes are normally contained within the cells of tissues and they leak across cellular membranes and into the circulation following tissue damage. The response is not immediate and it can take several hours before a maximum plasma activity of creatine kinase is recorded, making it difficult to relate a specific potentially traumatic event to the response. In addition, work in poultry and pigs has shown that plasma creatine kinase activity can be influenced by factors other than injury, including heat (Mitchell and Sandercock, 1995) and hormones associated with a 'stress' response (Thoren-Tolling, 1991). As these factors are also often associated with transportation, the interpretation of plasma enzyme activity can be difficult.

Stress and fear responses
Stress responses during transportation can be assessed using the plasma concentrations of cortisol (Cockram *et al.*, 1996) (or corticosterone in poultry) and catecholamines (Dalin *et al.*, 1993). To obtain meaningful results the blood sample must be obtained without the sampling procedure affecting the plasma cortisol concentration and sufficient samples obtained before, during and after transportation to obtain a profile of the response. The effects of the sampling procedure on the plasma concentration of cortisol can be reduced by either the use of animals habituated to sampling, the use of indwelling venous cannulae or, if necessary, the use of automatic sampling devices that do not involve close proximity of humans during sampling (Cockram *et al.*, 1996). Stressors will change cardiovascular variables, such as heart rate and blood pressure, through the activity of adrenergic stimulation. These responses

are rapid and often reflect the imposition of acute, but potent stressors, the sum of which may be regarded as reducing the welfare of the subject. If unbiased recordings of variables such as heart rate can be made in transit then these can be usefully correlated with journey events or challenges. The value of heart rate recordings can be improved by taking into account the increase in heart rate due to increased exercise (Baldock and Sibly, 1990) and by recording the electrocardiogram (Ville *et al.*, 1993). Measurement of such sensitive physiological parameters is complicated by the fact that the procedures involved often affect the variable being recorded. This has led to the development of packages which can be either attached to the animal or implanted such that recordings can be made remotely. Parrott *et al.* (1998) used external heart rate monitors and subcutaneous electrodes to study heart rate in transported sheep and demonstrated that loading induced the biggest changes in heart rate. Doherty *et al.* (1997) showed close correlations between heart rate (measured by external monitors) and metabolic energy expenditure in transported ponies. A fully implantable radiotelemetry system has been developed which will continuously transmit electrocardiogram wave forms, heart rate and deep body temperature in poultry (Kettlewell *et al.*, 1997) and is being applied to the transportation of this species whilst undergoing further modification for application to large mammals. The advantages of this approach are numerous, including the use of unrestrained animals, freedom of movement and behaviour and remote location of human observers, in addition to long-term automated data collection.

Heart rate and endocrine responses produce relatively short-term responses and therefore the value of assessing the effect of stressors on the immunological competence (Artursson *et al.*, 1989) and reproductive performance (Nanda *et al.*, 1990) of animals following transport has been evaluated. Measurements of meat quality have been used to make judgements on the welfare of animals transported to slaughter. However, their use in this respect requires careful interpretation as, contrary to that frequently stated, the main factor affecting the occurrence of dark-firm-dry meat in cattle is exercise associated in the main with agonistic or mounting interactions and not psychological stress (Franc *et al.*, 1988). The occurrence of pale-soft-exudative (PSE) meat in pigs and measurements of post-mortem muscle pH (Lambooy and Engel, 1991) can provide some useful information on the effect of transport conditions. However, the occurrence of PSE is strongly influenced by genotype, carcass temperature at slaughter and method of slaughter (Tarrant, 1989).

Fear responses associated with transport have been evaluated using tonic immobility (Sherwin *et al.*, 1993) and by relating 'stress' responses with avoidance behaviour. Psychological testing can also be used to determine the relative aversiveness of different components of transportation (Stephens *et al.*, 1985; Nicol *et al.*, 1991; Grigor *et al.*, 1998).

Biochemical, clinical and behavioural responses to food and water restriction
When farm animals are transported, food and water are not normally available while the animals are in transit. Even when water drinkers are provided (in accordance with WATO 1997) for long journeys involving pigs, there is some evidence that the pigs do not drink while the vehicle is in motion (Lambooy *et al.*, 1985). Therefore an important welfare issue during a long journey is the interval at which the animals should be offered water and food. Animals can develop thirst and are at risk from dehydration if drinking water is not readily available on long journeys. The risk of dehydration is further increased if the animal increases insensible water loss in response to a hot environment. The degree of dehydration experienced by animals during transport can be evaluated by recording (a) the loss of body weight (i.e. respiratory and cutaneous water losses together with tissue, faecal and urinary losses) (Cockram *et al.*, 1996), (b) clinical evaluation e.g. skin elasticity and sunken eyes (Atkinson, 1992), (c) the loss of water from the circulation can be indirectly assessed by packed cell volume (relative volume of plasma to that of cells; the packed cell volume can, however, also be affected by changes in the numbers of circulating blood cells) and the concentrations of proteins that remain in the plasma when water and smaller molecules leave the circulation when plasma volume decreases, (d) the increase in plasma concentration as reflected by plasma osmolality and electrolytes (mainly sodium) and (e) the initiation of homeostatic mechanisms by the animal to conserve water such as the release of plasma vasopressin (Cockram *et al.*, 1996) (however, some workers believe that the release of vasopressin is also associated with motion sickness (Bradshaw *et al.*, 1996a)). Although drinking behaviour is an obvious consequence of thirst, increased post-transport drinking behaviour may not always be a consequence of thirst developed during transportation, as most drinking does not occur as a consequence of a water deficit. Drinking occurs mostly in association with feeding and in anticipation of a possible water deficit (Fitzsimmons, 1972). Also, drinking might be impaired if the animal is either in a novel environment, is not familiar with the type of drinkers, or is influenced by social factors, e.g. aggression or dominance. Therefore post-transport drinking behaviour requires careful

interpretation when determining the maximal intervals before animals should be provided with water.

Similarly post-transport eating behaviour can provide useful information on the effect of food restriction associated with transportation. However, eating can also be influenced by the animal's social environment, the novelty of the food and environment, time of day and type of food offered. If rapid feeding is preceded by metabolic changes that indicated that the animal had to use body energy reserves during the period of food restriction associated with transport, then a clear consequence of the period of food restriction on the animal has been demonstrated. However, this may not in itself indicate a welfare problem as there is no evidence of suffering. By human analogy monogastric animals could be said to be hungry in these circumstances, but in ruminants perception of an empty stomach and a fall in blood glucose concentration do not occur as a consequence of food restriction during transportation and the mechanisms for hunger perception are not as clear. The clearest and first indication of a mobilization of body reserves in response to an energy deficit is a reduction in liver glycogen concentration. During fasting, the plasma concentration of glucose may eventually fall in some animals but it is maintained as long as possible by utilization of body energy reserves and can be raised as part of a stress response to transport. An increase in the plasma concentration of free fatty acids could indicate a mobilization of body fat reserves in response to food restriction but an increase in circulating catecholamines, as part of a stress response to transport, can also increase the plasma concentration of free fatty acids. Particularly in ruminants, an increase in the plasma concentration of β-hydroxybutyrate indicates the accumulation of ketone bodies as a result of a mobilization of fat reserves. In ruminants, this is a reliable indicator of the effects of food restriction as the plasma concentration of β-hydroxybutyrate is not influenced by exercise or blood sampling (Warriss et al., 1989).

Physiological and behavioural responses to thermal conditions
Exposure to a thermal challenge induces a range of physiological and behavioural responses, the purpose of which is the maintenance of body temperature within a discrete range, by maximizing heat exchange in hot conditions and minimizing heat loss in the cold. Behavioural thermoregulation is generally the first strategy employed (Ingram and Dauncey, 1985) which may include attempts to seek a more comfortable environment (a response that may not be possible under transport conditions), and changes in posture which may alter surface area,

insulation and the exposure of 'thermal windows' e.g. bare skin areas. In groups of animals, huddling may also be employed under cool conditions. Behavioural thermoregulation is often not considered in the framework of commercial animal transportation but it is important. If livestock are unable to exhibit these behaviours the effective temperatures experienced in the vehicle may be much more detrimental to the animals' welfare than might be predicted from the temperature alone. Thus, if under hot external conditions an animal is unable to increase its heat loss by postural responses due to inappropriate stocking density, excessive vehicle motion or slippery floors, then the demands upon physiological thermoregulation will be increased and may become excessive. In other circumstances on open or semi-open vehicles, animals would exploit high speed air movements to enhance convective heat loss during hot conditions but would attempt to avoid the air movement in the cold. Quantification of thermoregulatory responses along with estimates of body temperature is an ideal technique for assessing the responses of the animals to their thermal environment. This might be summarized as: (1) measurement of thermoregulatory effort, and (2) measurement of thermoregulatory success, which indicates how hard an animal is working to maintain body temperature and how well it is achieving this objective. This approach has provided a sound basis for physiological modelling (Mitchell and Kettlewell, 1998). The precise parameters for measurement are dependent upon the nature of the environment. In the cold, animals will attempt to increase metabolic rate by shivering (Thompson, 1977) and the extent of this response can be assessed by electromyography (EMG) as described by George (1984). The animals will also exhibit piloerection (fluffing of the coat or feather cover) and peripheral vasoconstriction to decrease heat loss through the skin and this can be evaluated by surface temperature measurements using thermography. During heat stress, animals will increase heat transfer to the periphery by regional vasodilation and will increase evaporative heat loss via the respiratory tract through thermal polypnea or panting or open mouthed breathing (e.g. sheep and poultry) or by sweating (e.g. cattle and horses). Panting can be quantified by measurement of respiratory rate or respiratory volumes (Mitchell, 1986) or by the measurement of blood gas disturbances. Panting often results in overventilation of the gas exchange surfaces of the lung and reductions in blood carbon dioxide (pCO_2). The extent of the induced hypocapnic alkalosis is proportional to the degree of polypnea. In all these situations continuous or spot measurements of deep body temperature in the rectum of the animal will estimate thermoregulatory success but it should be remembered that the major purpose of thermal homeostatic control is the maintenance of brain or central nervous system temperature (Bligh, 1985) and that this may differ from 'core' temperature under some circumstances. Continuous measurements of deep body temperature can be made by the use of implanted recording or telemetry devices as used in poultry (Kettlewell et al., 1997; Mitchell et al., 1997) and pigs (Parrott et al., 1998) and yield important minute to minute alterations relating to the changing thermal environment. All thermoregulatory responses will involve changes in other physiological and metabolic systems. For example, in cold induced thermogenesis, energy substrate depletion will be enhanced. In heat stress, the evaporation of water may result in dehydration and the acid-base disturbances may eventually prove harmful to the individual. It is therefore necessary to take in to account these other secondary effects and their magnitude and consequences when making an overall assessment of the severity of a thermal challenge during transportation.

Behavioural responses indicative of rest/fatigue
Lying behaviour as an indicator of rest is relatively easy to quantify and can be categorized further by identification of ventral/lateral lying and whether lying is associated with the head on the ground and the eyes closed (Merrick and Sharp, 1971; Ruckebusch, 1975a). Whether lying behaviour is interpreted as indicating that the animals are comfortable with their environment and are resting, or are exhausted by the experience, would depend on the circumstances and the presence or absence of other signs. For example, in ruminants, lying associated with rumination is often interpreted as indicating either rest or lack of aversive response to the environment as the electroencephalogram of sheep and cattle performing this behaviour is indicative of a 'sleep-like' pattern which is disturbed in response to a stimulus such as a sudden noise (Ruckebusch, 1975b). The presence of movement and frequent interactions between animals are obvious signs that the animals are not resting.

Factors influencing the welfare of animals during transport
Transport/motion/vibration/driving skills
In cattle, Kenny and Tarrant (1987) found that it was the actual vehicular motion and the stimuli associated with transport that initiated a cortisol response, whereas there was no cortisol response to loading onto a stationary vehicle for a similar length of time. Rumination was inhibited during transport and there was more defaecation and a lower frequency of interactions between animals than before transport. In sheep, transport simulation produces a similar cortisol and adrenaline response

to that of isolation, which is considered to be a major psychological stressor in sheep (Parrott et al., 1994).

The quality of driving will affect the stability of the animals carried within the vehicle. Tarrant et al. (1988) related driving events such as cornering, braking and gear changes, to losses of balance in cattle and found that, when two driving events occurred simultaneously, this was responsible for the cattle making the greatest number of limb changes to maintain balance. Vehicle motion also causes postural instability in poultry resulting in aberrant behaviours and an increased risk of injury (Behrends et al., 1997).

It is well recognized that vibration and random motion induce nausea discomfort, fatigue and distress in human beings and that these effects may extend to transported livestock (Randall, 1992). WATO 1997 contains a provision that animals should not be caused unnecessary suffering from undue noise or vibration during transport. Vibration and noise can induce marked physiological responses in pigs (Stephens and Rader, 1983). The physiological responses depend upon the frequency and magnitude of the vibration arising from the structural components of the vehicle and the type of response may be related to the resonant frequency of the animal (Scott, 1994; Randall et al., 1996). The vibrations in commercial broiler transport containers during a journey are close to the resonant frequency of a 2-kg bird and as such may be regarded as a potential threat to the welfare of the animals (Randall et al., 1996). Vibration may cause changes in regional blood flow, cardiac output, blood pressure, respiratory patterns, gut motility and induce visceral blood pooling, pulmonary damage, impaired thermoregulation and skeletal muscle dysfunction (Stephens and Rader, 1983; Scott, 1994). Extensive studies in poultry have revealed that the predominant vibration frequencies occurring on commercial transporters (Randall et al., 1993) cause aversion (Rutter and Randall, 1993) and significant physiological and metabolic derangements including activation of the adrenal cortex, depletion of energy substrates, stress myopathy or muscle damage and muscle glycogen depletion (Warriss et al., 1997; Carlisle et al., 1998). In pigs, the cortisol response to transportation is greater when the vehicle is driven on 'rough' roads than when driven on 'smooth' roads (Bradshaw et al., 1996b). Pigs find vibration associated with transport more aversive than the noise associated with transport. When pigs had learnt to stop a transport simulator for 30-s periods by pressing a panel, they switched it off for three-quarters of the time. In a subsequent study, other pigs never learnt to switch the transporter on and did not learn to switch off noise without transport simulation (Stephens *et al.*, 1985). Some pigs experiencing low frequency oscillatory motion during transport will vomit or retch, probably indicating that they can experience motion sickness in a similar way to that of humans (Randall and Bradshaw, 1998). Nicol *et al.* (1991) found that broilers responded in a similar way to pigs, in that they found motion and noise aversive but there was no effect of noise alone. In the future it may be possible to protect animals from the effects of vibration by changing the type of vehicle suspension (air *v.* leaf) and the provision of vibration absorbing mats on the bed of the lorry. An understanding of the frequency and magnitudes of vibration which cause the greatest aversion and discomfort to different types of livestock should provide a sound scientific basis for strategies to improve welfare in transit.

Thermal environment
The thermal environment prevailing in commercial livestock transporters is potentially one of the major sources of stress and reduced welfare to which the animals are exposed. The mortality rate of pigs during transport increases markedly when the ambient temperature is greater than 17°C (Warriss and Brown, 1994) and 'dead on arrivals' increase in poultry in both cold and hot periods (Bayliss and Hinton, 1990; Hunter *et al.*, 1997; Mitchell *et al.*, 1997). Most animal transport vehicles rely upon a passive ventilation regime and thus the on-board micro-environment is partially dependent upon the external climatic conditions. The internal environment is, however, complex in that it is not only related to the incoming air but also to the heat, moisture and contaminant production of the animals in the transport compartment. Indeed the micro-environment may not be homogeneous due to uneven distributions of internal air flow. It is important to understand that the thermal environment is composed not only of air temperature but of water vapour density and air

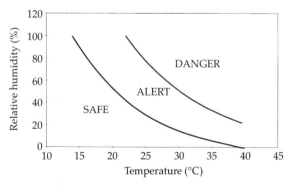

Figure 1 Thermal comfort zones — in crate conditions.

movement as well. The dry bulb temperature gradient determines the sensible heat exchange between animal and environment (convection, radiation and conduction) but the evaporative heat loss is clearly dependent upon the water vapour density gradient (Mitchell and Kettlewell, 1998). Air movement will enhance both sensible and insensible (evaporative) heat loss from an exposed surface. In animals relying heavily on evaporative cooling by panting or sweating in warm conditions, elevated humidity can prove extremely detrimental by inhibiting evaporation. A very high humidity may cause a profound heat stress at a relatively low dry bulb temperature under transport conditions. This problem is exacerbated by low ventilation rates which fail to remove heat and water vapour and do not offer direct convective cooling by an airstream. The situation is made worse still by constraints upon behavioural thermoregulation imposed by the design of the vehicle, stocking densities and floor conditions. Quantifying thermal stress in transit is vital (Nicol and Saville-Weeks, 1993). It is therefore necessary to characterize the physiological and behavioural responses of livestock, perhaps using transport simulation techniques, over a wide range of temperature-humidity combinations occurring in commercial practice, in order to define acceptable ranges and limits for each environmental parameter which may be applied to commercial production. Such values can then form the basis of environmental control systems and sound legislation and codes of practice to maximize the welfare of animals during transportation. Studies in broiler transportation have fully characterized the 'on-board' thermal environments during journeys in different seasons in the UK (Kettlewell and Mitchell, 1993; Kettlewell *et al.*, 1993). The findings indicated heterogeneous ventilation patterns leading to cold spots and a hot spot, the 'thermal core' in which the risk of heat stress was greatest. Using physiological indices of stress established in earlier studies (Mitchell *et al.*, 1992) physiological modelling has recently been employed to define the thermal comfort zones for broilers in transit (Mitchell and Kettlewell, 1998). This work exploited the concept of apparent equivalent temperature (AET), an integrated index of the total thermal load imposed on the birds in transit. By these means it was possible to define temperature-humidity combinations which induced minimal or no physiological stress (safe), moderate physiological stress (alert) in which hyperthermia, some tissue damage and elevated adreno-cortical activity will occur, and severe physiological stress (danger) in which conditions are unacceptable and mortalities will increase (see Figure 1). Under practical conditions, where relative humidities in the transport containers rarely fall below 70% because of obligatory water loss from the birds, it can be recommended that the maximum 'in-crate' allowable temperature, compatible with good welfare and productivity, should be 24 to 25°C. Thus research has provided the target temperature range for commercial broiler transport. It is, however, difficult to incorporate this into legislation and a more productive approach is to determine the cause of the thermal problems and provide strategies for their prevention. Further research has therefore examined the aerodynamics of commercial broiler transporters and characterized the external pressure fields which ultimately determine internal ventilation flows (Baker *et al.*, 1996; Dalley *et al.*, 1996; Hoxey *et al.*, 1996). This information can be employed to modify passive ventilation systems to improve ventilation of the thermal core of the vehicles and to reduce heat stress and mortality, and to substantially improve the welfare of the birds. In the context of 'writing the rules' it may be suggested that legislating for the provision of a ventilation system which will match the on-board thermal environment to an animal's biological requirements is more effective in improving welfare than prescribing the actual thermal limits with the inherent difficulties of monitoring and policing the commercial practice. Practical improvements in reducing the risk of cold stress in transported broilers have also been provided from concurrent thermal and dead-on-arrival mapping and physiological modelling techniques (Hunter *et al.*, 1997; Mitchell *et al.*, 1997). These studies demonstrated that ingress of water in specific locations (air inlets) led to wetted birds whose feather insulation was so compromised that hypothermia was rapidly induced even when ambient temperatures where 4 to 8°C. The construction of baffles removed this risk without reducing efficiency of ventilation of the rest of the load. Again it may be possible to legislate for a structure or ventilation system to avoid or prevent wetting, rather than to prescribe thermal conditions.

Ventilation requirements and future forced ventilation systems

A natural progression from the work relating the thermal environment, ventilation regimes and physiological stress in poultry is the application of the approach to other animals, in particular red-meat species. An attempt to provide a practical guide to the transportation of livestock in hot weather based on a temperature-humidity index (THI), similar in principle to the use of AET described above, has been made by the University of Nebraska (Wellman, 1996) and emphasizes the dangers of transportation of animals under hostile thermal conditions (see Figure 2). The importance of controlled ventilation to regulate the thermal micro-environment in pig transportation has been emphasized (Lambooy and Engel, 1991). If the thermal environment is considered to represent a major threat to the welfare of transported animals then control of this internal environment must be developed. Whilst it is possible to modify vehicle structure to improve passive ventilation flows this approach has severe limitations and is difficult to automate. Forced ventilation offers a viable alternative which can incorporate control strategies based on a knowledge of the animals' biological requirements and the heat loads to be managed. A powered or forced ventilation system requires the installation of fans of the appropriate capacity on the vehicle and the provision of the necessary power supply. The information required for the successful development of such a system consists of a knowledge of the thermal comfort zone of the species and age or size of the animal under transport conditions, i.e. at the appropriate stocking density, the heat and water production of the animals and the aerodynamic characteristics of the vehicle to ensure efficient location of fans and inlet/outlets. The acceptable ranges and limits for temperature and humidity have to be obtained from laboratory based physiological modelling and work is in progress relating to calves and pigs in the authors' groups. Metabolic heat and water productions can be obtained from the literature or calculated from a knowledge of body weight (Randall, 1993). If the 'thermostat setting' is known, i.e. the 'safe zone' of temperature and humidity to yield minimum physiological stress, then the ventilation requirement can be easily calculated from:

flow rate = total heat output / (specific heat capacity of air $\times$ acceptable air temperature rise)

where flow = m^3/s, specific heat capacity = 1226 J/m^3 per °C and the temperature rise = °C.

As a rule of thumb, if animals are loaded at the stocking densities laid down in WATO 1997, then on multi-deck transporters the total heat production will be about 12 kW per deck. More precise figures are given in Table 1.

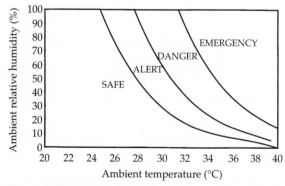

Figure 2 Temperature-humidity index — derived from NebGuide (Wellman, 1996).

Table 1 *Heat output per deck from typical laden transporter*

Species	Animals per deck	Heat output (kW)
Small calves (55 kg)	102	12·3
Heavy cattle (550 kg)	23	12·8
Shorn sheep (60 kg)	102	11·9
Unshorn sheep (60 kg)	76	8·9
Pigs (100 kg)	71	11·4

Thus, for a hypothetical deck of animals producing 12 kW of heat and where the maximum allowable temperature rise is 10°C, then a minimum vehicle ventilation rate of 0·97 m^3/s would be required. Fans are available which will achieve this and in practice much higher rates may be required in hot weather. Several fans should be installed giving a maximum ventilation rate of >5 m^3/s. To achieve maximum fan efficiency they should be used to extract air at sites of low pressure where air will naturally tend to leave the vehicle (Baker *et al.*, 1996; Dalley *et al.*, 1996; Hoxey *et al.*, 1996). The external pressure fields of moving transporters cause air to enter at the rear and exit at the front and thus the air moves in the same direction as the vehicle! This can be exploited by siting fans in the front of the vehicle to extract and having precisely defined inlets towards the rear. The advantages of mechanical ventilation for livestock vehicles are numerous. They provide precise environmental control, they are relatively closed and protect the animals from noise and threatening visual images, light levels can be controlled to calm the animals and they do not rely upon vehicle movement for their operation. This last feature means that thermal loads can be regulated even if the vehicle is stationary by design or is accidentally delayed. Vehicles of this type will probably be adopted for the transportation of all livestock in the future but currently are recommended for long journeys of over 8 h duration, as laid down in WATO 1997. Indeed the Council Regulation EC 411/98 (European Council, 1998) relating to 'the additional standards for vehicles used for the carriage of livestock in journeys exceeding 8 hours' states that such vehicles must have 'a forced ventilation system' or a ventilation system which ensures that a range of temperatures from 5 to 30°C can be maintained in the vehicle for all animals with a tolerance of +5°C depending on the outside temperature. It is clear that in this case the scientific research is helping to inform the writing of the rules.

Another environmental modification which might improve the welfare of animals in transit is the showering of pigs. Water spraying has been shown to be beneficial in lairage as assessed by meat quality (Weeding *et al.*, 1993). The strategy has not been fully evaluated in transportation but constraints such as floor surface condition and hygiene make implementation difficult. It might be proposed, however, that spraying would be practical in a fan ventilated vehicle where air flow could be increased to gain maximum benefit from evaporative cooling with minimal delivery of water. The relationships between the advantages of evaporative cooling of the animals, the potential rise in internal humidity and the ventilation rates required to efficiently dissipate both heat and water loads, requires more detailed investigation.

It is imperative that future vehicle designs and relevant legislation ensure that welfare is optimized by avoiding the imposition of both cold stress and heat stress in transported animals by prescribing the appropriate optimum conditions, ranges which can be tolerated and methods for environmental control that can be implemented in commercial practice.

Space allowance
Specification of optimal space allowance during transport has proved to be a difficult area when formulating legislation. Although specific ranges of space allowance are included within the European Union (EU) Directive, in the UK they are only contained within codes of practice and the legislation is not specific. Animals are not permitted to be transported in a way that is likely to cause injury or unnecessary suffering because of the amount of space provided. However, cattle, sheep and pigs must have sufficient space to be able to stand in their natural position and animals must have (unless it is unnecessary due to the species of animal or the nature of the journey) adequate space to lie down. The traditional view has been that animals require mutual support and therefore low space allowances during transport to minimize the risk of injury from vehicle movements. However, increasing the space allowance can provide a greater opportunity for the animals to lie down and adjust their posture during long journeys. Therefore during long journeys, the space provided should ideally allow: stability, normal posture and postural adjustments, without causing an increased risk of injury and psychological 'stress'. It is possible to calculate by using the body weight of the animals, the amount of space that different animals are likely to require during transportation (Randall, 1993). However, this does not take into account the behavioural responses of the animals during long distance transport. Tarrant *et al.* (1988) clearly showed that transporting steers at a low space allowance where they were tightly packed, resulted in greater injury and a greater plasma cortisol response than that found in steers transported at a higher space allowance. Contrary to providing greater stability from mutual support,

steers transported at the low space allowance had a greater frequency of losses of balance and falls than those at the higher space allowance. At the low space allowance some of the steers fell over and had difficulty getting up again. The steers that were unable to get up were trampled on by the other animals and this destabilized the animals that were standing. Even at the highest space allowance the cattle did not voluntarily lie down during the 4-h journey. In a subsequent experiment where steers were transported for 24 h and fewer steers fell over at the lowest space allowance, the frequency of losses of balance was reduced by mutual support. However, steers transported at the lowest space allowance had a greater cortisol response and more signs of injury than those transported at the higher space allowance (Tarrant et al., 1992). In sheep transported for 12 h, the provision of mutual support at a low space allowance reduced the frequency of losses of balance; however, at higher space allowances there was no greater risk of injury from either falls and collisions with the vehicle (Cockram et al., 1996). There was no effect of space allowance on the frequency of either trampling or riding and no effect on either the plasma cortisol concentration or the plasma creatine kinase activity. However, after 3 h of the journey, sheep (with a live weight of between 30 and 40 kg) transported at a space allowance of at least 0.27 m^2 per sheep lay down noticeably more than those transported tightly at a space allowance of 0.22 m^2 per sheep. The benefits of providing greater space are likely to be affected by factors that make it difficult for sheep to maintain their balance, e.g. poor driving and bad roads. In a survey of some of the factors affecting the risk of bruising in sheep transported from farms to a slaughterhouse, sheep transported by commercial hauliers at high space allowances (range 0.16 to 0.77 m^2 per sheep) were found to be at the greatest risk from bruising (Jarvis and Cockram, 1994). The literature on which to base optimal space allowances for pigs during transport has recently been reviewed by Warriss (1998). Lambooy and Engel (1991) found that pigs (110 kg live weight) spent more time lying down when they were transported at a space allowance of 0.59 m^2 per pig than at 0.47 m^2 per pig; all pigs were able to lie down at 0.47 m^2 per pig, but not at 0.39 m^2 per pig.

Social composition
WATO 1997 contains provisions for the segregation of certain types of animals to prevent injury. Although the Order contains phrases such as 'raised in compatible groups or are accustomed to one another', which would allow animals from a stable social group to be transported together, and phrases such as 'animals which are hostile to each other or are fractious', which would require segregation of

these animals, it is not effective in preventing all injury between animals. Mixing social groups of pigs at any stage of transportation will result in fighting and skin wounds (Guise and Penny, 1989).

Journey duration
Although most journey times for transporting sheep, pigs and broilers to slaughter in southern England are only 3 to 4 h (Warriss, 1996) some journeys can be considerably longer. Where there is the potential for animals to suffer during transportation if conditions are not optimal, it makes sense for farm animals to be slaughtered as near to the point of production as possible. However, if a statutory limit is imposed on journey length, it will have increased credibility if the limit is based on evidence that shows an adverse effect of continuing the journey much beyond this limit. If live animals must be transported over long distances and maximum journey times are imposed, resulting in the journey been broken up into a series of shorter journeys with a lairage stop after each section, there is a risk that the welfare of the animals might be worse than if the journey was completed without a mid-journey lairage period. This is because the total disruption time for the animals from farm to eventual destination will be longer; there is a potential for greater injury during unloading, handling and reloading; increased risk of infection from coming into contact with other animals and inadequately cleaned and disinfected premises; possibly greater psychological 'stress' from a novel environment and handlers; and no certainty that the animals will eat, drink and rest in their novel environment. In deciding whether to impose a maximum journey time and, if so, what the limit should be, not only must the type of animal and the quality of the journey be considered, but also the criteria on which to base the judgement. For broiler transport under current conditions, the criteria to use are relatively clear, in that Warriss et al. (1992) found that transporting broilers for longer than 4 h increased the risk of the broilers dying (for journeys of < 4 h mortality was 0.16% and for longer journeys it was found to be 0.28%). In addition, Cashman et al. (1989) found a positive linear relationship between journey time (up to 2 h) and tonic immobility (as a measure of fear) in broilers. From studies in cattle (Warriss et al., 1995), sheep (Cockram et al., 1996) and pigs (Bradshaw et al., 1996b) there is no evidence that the cortisol response to transportation increases with journey time. Maximal cortisol responses occurred after 3 h of a 12-h journey in sheep (Cockram et al., 1996) and after 1.5 h of a 8 h journey in pigs (Bradshaw et al., 1996b). If pigs (Lambooy, 1988) and sheep (Cockram et al., 1996) are provided with adequate space, increasing numbers of animals will gradually lie down after about 3 h of a long journey over good roads. Although the amount of lying

behaviour will be less during transport than during stationary confinement in similar circumstances, pigs and sheep may be able to obtain physical rest during a long journey and, if sufficient space is provided, there may not be a requirement to limit the maximum journey time to provide a period of physical rest. In WATO 1997, journey or travelling times, feeding and watering frequencies and rest periods are defined for each species and age of animal. Similar legislation has been implemented throughout the EU. For all animals travelling on 'basic' vehicles the maximum journey time is 8 h, calculated from the loading of the first animal to the unloading of the last animal. After such a journey the animals must be rested for at least 24 h in appropriate lairage facilities before another similarly limited journey can commence. For journeys of more than 8 h, vehicles must meet higher standards, as specified in the Council Regulation EC 411/98, and journeys conducted according to criteria defined in WATO 97. The journey 'breaks' on 'higher standard' vehicles are to allow rest, feeding and watering of the animals which do not have to be unloaded from the vehicle. It is thus necessary to have food and water available on the vehicle or the rest period to take place at a predesignated site where food and water might be provided. These journey durations on 'higher standard vehicles' are summarized in Table 2.

In the case of poultry, food and water must be provided for journeys of more than 12 h duration. In commercial practice this is generally not possible and so 12 h is the effective maximum journey time permitted. For day-old chicks, food and water must be provided at 'suitable intervals' on journeys lasting more than 24 h. They should not be transported for more than 36 h before food and water are provided. All these limitations and recommendations have been derived from the research available for each species and are constantly to be re-evaluated and debated. Continuing research efforts have an important rôle to play in improving this legislation and maximizing the protection of animals in a commercial transport environment.

Lairage periods: mid and post journey
Animals may be held in lairage either prior to slaughter or during long journeys (see above). The objectives of the procedure are to allow the animals to rest and recover from the rigours of the journey and to eat and drink if required. The efficacy of the strategy can only be judged by measurement of specific behavioural, physiological, biochemical and production parameters which reflect the response of the animals to the journey and the rate and extent of recovery towards a more normal or control biological state. Several studies have attempted the investigation of commercial lairage practice in this manner.

If sheep are provided with sufficient space and a smooth journey they can lie down during transport and they may not require a mid-journey lairage period to rest. If sheep become tired during a long journey, they would be expected to lie down more than normal after the journey. However, this was not found to be the case after sheep were transported for either 12 or 24 h. Their immediate priority after unloading was to eat and only after a period of 4 h to lie down for most of the time (Cockram *et al.*, 1997). Also, if sheep become progressively tired during a long journey, the provision of a mid-journey lairage to provide a period of rest would be expected to decrease the amount of lying behaviour seen during the remainder of the journey. However, the provision of a mid-journey rest period of 12 h during a 24 h journey did not affect the amount of lying behaviour observed during the remaining half of the journey, compared with that seen in sheep transported without a mid-journey lairage period. In sheep transported for 24 h without a mid-journey lairage period, there was some evidence of greater post-transport lying for about 1 h, 4 h after

Table 2 *Journey durations in 'higher standard vehicles', for different classes of livestock*

Class of livestock	Journey duration
Unweaned calves, lambs, kids and foals which are still on a milk diet and unweaned piglets	A maximum of 9 h, a rest period of at least one hour followed by a further maximum of 9 h
Other cattle , sheep and goats	A maximum of 14 h, a rest period of at least one hour followed by a further maximum of 14 h
Pigs	A maximum of 24 h with continuous access to liquid
Horses (except registered horses)	A maximum of 24 h with continuous access to liquid and if necessary food every 8 h

unloading than in those provided with a lairage of 12 h during a 24-h journey (Cockram *et al.*, 1997).

In pigs, commercial lairage may range from 1 to 20 h duration (Warriss and Bevis, 1986). Warriss *et al.* (1998) found that when pigs were provided with a 3-h lairage after journeys of > 120 km, their plasma cortisol concentration was not significantly different from those lairaged for 1 h or less. Pigs kept in overnight lairage had lower plasma cortisol concentrations than those lairaged for 3 h or less but they had significantly more bite wounds, indicating that a long lairage period for pigs can be detrimental. Whilst such studies have examined lairage periods, other studies have investigated factors such as space allowance, social environment and floor surfaces in lairages (Cockram, 1990 and 1991; Kim *et al.*, 1994; Jarvis and Cockram, 1995a; Abeyesinghe *et al.*, 1997) and the thermal environment in lairages. Weeding *et al.* (1993) demonstrated a significant improvement in meat quality in pigs sprayed with water during holding under warm to hot conditions, which was probably a consequence of evaporative cooling maintaining better thermoregulation. It may be proposed that this procedure would therefore support better welfare although the study also indicated that water spraying caused more pigs to stand, root around, chew the pen walls and fight and so may have some deleterious effects. Environmental control in lairage is an important issue but has perhaps received even less attention than transport thermal regimes. One study has characterized the conditions in commercial broiler lairages and examined the associated physiological and production responses (Mitchell *et al.*, 1998; Quinn *et al.*, 1998; Warriss *et al.*, 1999). Characterization and analysis of the thermal micro-environments existing in transport containers during commercial practice indicated that low air velocities (< 0·1 m/s) at bird level, i.e. poor ventilation, resulted in a potentially detrimental rise in temperature and water vapour content. These effects can occur in both winter and summer and the potentially stressful thermal environments may be achieved rapidly (within 1 h of arrival). Parallel measurements of physiological and biochemical responses of broilers suggested that lairage for up to 4 h (or beyond) results in disturbances in carbohydrate and lipid metabolism, including depletion of tissue glycogen reserves and decreased plasma tri-glyceride concentrations. These effects are progressive and will tend to result in ante-mortem fatigue and post-mortem changes in meat quality. It was proposed that practical 'target' conditions should be a temperature of no more than 20°C and an accompanying relative humidity of < 0·65. Further research to provide recommendations for optimum lairage durations and conditions should be undertaken.

Food and water intervals

In considering the length of time that animals are without food and water when they are transported to slaughter, it is very important to consider the total time involved, especially if this includes a visit to a livestock market. Warriss and Bevis (1986) surveyed journey times to slaughter for pigs in southern England and found that the combined transport and lairage times could be as long as 32 h. Before the introduction of the current order (WATO 1997) the journey time, any time at a market and the time spent in the lairage before slaughter were considered separately when determining the length of time before the animals had to be offered food and water. This had at least the theoretical possibility that animals might not have been offered food for extended periods of time. Jarvis *et al.* (1996 a, b and c) showed that blood taken at the time of slaughter from cattle and sheep that arrived at the slaughterhouse via a market rather than direct from a farm tended to show evidence of a greater mobilization of body energy reserves and more evidence of dehydration. This indicated that cattle and sheep from markets may have experienced a longer period of food and water restriction than animals sent to slaughter direct from farms.

Decisions on the length of time that animals should be transported without food and water should depend upon the environmental conditions (for example, at high temperatures insensible water losses will be greater than at cool temperatures) but they will also be affected by the criteria used to make the judgement. Several different criteria could be used to determine the intervals at which an animal should be provided with food and/or water during a journey. One extreme criterion could be to set the limit according to how long animals could survive without food and water and then subsequently make a full recovery when food and water were available. Another possibility would be to try and determine after what time animals show signs of suffering as a result of the absence of food and water. A third possibility would be to determine under a variety of conditions the time before animals showed either clinical or physiological evidence of dehydration or starvation. Another possibility would be to determine after what period of time the animals made significant physiological changes in order to (a) either conserve body water or redistribute body water in response to water restriction and (b) mobilize body energy reserves in response to an energy deficiency. The behaviour of the animal when presented with food and or water could also be used to determine the degree of thirst or hunger that the animal might show after various periods of food and/or water restriction. These five approaches to the same question would be likely to produce answers which would recommend successively shorter periods of time before animals should be provided with food/water.

Sheep. To take sheep as an example, we could decide that sheep should be offered water as often as is necessary to prevent thirst (as in The Welfare of Animals at Markets Order (Great Britain Parliament, 1990)). This seems reasonable as freedom from thirst is part of the Farm Animal Welfare Council's five freedoms (Farm Animal Welfare Council, 1993). However, we have no direct way of assessing thirst in farm animals. Thirst in humans is associated with dryness of the mouth and throat (Fitzsimons, 1972) but we cannot automatically assume that sheep perceive thirst in the same way as humans. Although the passage of water over oropharyngeal receptors can temporarily inhibit drinking in water deprived sheep, drinking is mainly controlled by other factors, such as the presence of water in the rumen (Bott *et al.*, 1965) and receptors in the interstitial fluid (Park *et al.*, 1986). It is a reasonable working assumption that a dehydrated animal that eagerly seeks out and consumes water is thirsty (Fitzsimons, 1972), however, the onset of drinking may not always be a reliable indicator of the development of a negative water balance. This is because most drinking occurs when there is no current water deficit but allows the animal to anticipate its future water requirements. This secondary drinking is affected by environmental conditions, circadian rhythm, pattern of feeding and diet (Fitzsimons, 1972). However, primary drinking is an emergency response to a deficit of body fluid and occurs at any time of the day or night. Sheep can replace a water deficit equivalent to proportionately 0·07 to 0·10 of body weight within 10 min of access to drinking water (Bott *et al.*, 1965). Most of the increased post-transport water intake seen in sheep after a 12-h journey (Cockram *et al.*, 1997) is secondary to an increased food intake. However, when sheep are offered water but no food after a 15 h journey, they drink more water and drink sooner than those that had not been transported. However, drinking is often not an immediate priority after transport (the median time after unloading taken by sheep without access to hay to obtain their first drink was over 5 h) (M. S. Cockram, unpublished observations). *This would suggest that sheep should be offered water at intervals of less than 15 h.* However, ruminants can withstand greater dehydration than most simple stomached mammals (Cole, 1995). This capacity is related to their ability during dehydration to use the water present in the rumen (Silanikove, 1994). During the first 24 h that sheep are without food and water, most of the body-weight loss can be attributed to water loss from the rumen and the water absorbed from the alimentary tract is likely to be sufficient to

prevent dehydration (Hecker *et al.*, 1964). In sheep, the homeostatic responses to dehydration that act to conserve body fluids, include stimulation of thirst and increased secretion of vasopressin with subsequent reduction in urinary water excretion (McKinley *et al.*, 1983). Even at environmental temperatures of up to 32°C, the plasma volume can be maintained in Merino sheep without access to drinking water for at least 3 days (MacFarlane *et al.*, 1961). *This would suggest that sheep could be offered water at intervals of up to 72 h and they would not experience any major undue consequences.* If dehydration continues, the extracellular fluid volume decreases, sodium is retained and plasma osmolality increases. In sheep transported at environmental temperatures of less than 25°C, no biochemical signs of dehydration (as assessed by the packed cell volume, plasma osmolality, and the plasma concentrations of total protein, sodium and vasopressin) were seen during 24 h of transport (Cockram *et al.*, 1997). *This would suggest that sheep could be transported without access to water for periods of up to 24 h and not experience any major undue consequences.* However, at higher air temperatures than that normally found for most of the time in the UK (e.g. greater than 25°C), evaporative water losses are likely be appreciably greater and the rate of dehydration of the sheep would be faster (Degen and Shkolnik, 1978). For example, Knowles *et al.* (1994b) found that when sheep were transported from the UK to southern France on journeys lasting for 18 and 24 h there was some evidence of dehydration post transport. However, the remarkable tolerance of sheep to water deprivation was illustrated by Parrott *et al.* (1996) who found no evidence of either increased plasma osmolality or increased plasma cortisol concentration when sheep were kept in an environmental temperature of 35°C for 48 h without either food or water. *This would suggest that sheep could be offered water at intervals of up to 48 h and not experience any major undue consequences.*

After a 12 h journey, sheep appear to be hungry. This is shown by their immediate eating behaviour when presented with hay, by their increased hay intake and by spending most of the 3 h after unloading standing and eating (Cockram *et al.*, 1997). Warriss *et al.* (1989) found that after 24 h of fasting the liver glycogen concentration in sheep had been reduced to almost zero and there were increases in both the plasma concentrations of free fatty acids and β-hydroxybutyrate. After 15 h of transport without access to food, sheep show evidence of mobilization of body reserves, however there is no evidence that this 'hunger' is associated with a stress response (Cockram *et al.*, 1997). Freedom from hunger is also part of the Farm Animal Welfare Council's five freedoms (Farm Animal Welfare Council, 1993) and there is some evidence, reviewed by Forbes (1995), to suggest that there is a hunger mechanism in ruminants that can initiate feeding. However, it is unclear whether sheep 'suffer' and experience any emotional effects due to a 12-h period without food.

If a decision is made to break a journey to provide a period of time for access to water and if necessary food (as in WATO 1997) it is important to ensure that the welfare of the sheep is not made worse by this mid-journey lairage period. Given the possibility that some sheep in some circumstances might develop a thirst during a long journey, the provision of drinking water in a way that was familiar to the sheep could be beneficial. As sheep appear to become hungry after a relatively short period without access to food, the provision of food during a mid-journey lairage period might also be beneficial. Cockram *et al.* (1997) found that providing sheep with a 3-h lairage period (where there was access to hay) during a 24-h journey resulted in lower plasma concentrations of β-hydroxybutyrate and free fatty acids during the remaining 12 h of the journey than during the last 12 h of a 24-h journey (where the sheep were transported continuously without a lairage period). However, even when sheep were in lairage for 12 h in the middle of a 24-h journey, they also mobilized body energy reserves during the remainder of the journey, suggesting that the lairage period did not avoid all the potential problems related to food restriction during the journey. Sheep transported for 24 h without a lairage stop (24 h without food) ate more post transport than those that had been lairaged during the journey (12 h without food) suggesting the possibility that a lairage stop could reduce the severity of the 'hunger' experienced by the sheep. If sheep are provided with food during a lairage stop it is very important that they are given sufficient time and access to drinking water during the lairage period before they are reloaded to continue their journey. There is a potential problem with the EU directive and WATO 1997 in this respect, in that at least theoretically sheep could be offered water and food within a period as short as 1 h. For sheep, a 1 h lairage period is not sufficient time for mid-journey lairage. A significant part of this time would be spent unloading/loading and penning the sheep. If offered hay, the sheep would spend most of this time eating and may not have sufficient time to drink. Cockram *et al.* (1997) found that even when sheep were provided with a 3-h lairage period after 12 h of transport, they spent most of this time eating hay. After the intake of a large amount of dry food such as hay, a large volume of saliva is produced and there is an increase in rumen osmolality, resulting in a movement of fluid into the rumen. This can induce a period where plasma osmolality is increased (Ternouth, 1968). If during a

short lairage period, sheep do not have access to drinking water after feeding they can become dehydrated during the remainder of the journey. Cockram *et al.* (1997) found that this did not occur when sheep were unloaded after a 12-h journey and provided with food and water for a 3-h lairage period before they were transported for a further 12 h. However, dehydration during the remaining 12 h of a 24-h journey did occur when sheep were offered hay and water for 3 h whilst they remained on the vehicle. Although sheep readily ate hay during the 3-h stationary period on the vehicle, they did not drink sufficient water. This resulted in some evidence of dehydration during the remainder of the journey and a greater water intake post transport than in those transported continuously for 24 h without a lairage stop. Therefore, sheep should always be unloaded from the vehicle and offered food and water in a lairage, unless there is clear evidence that the sheep have sufficient time and access to drink and the means of providing water on the vehicle allows the sheep to obtain sufficient drinking water before the journey restarts.

The provision for sheep within WATO 1997 for a 24-h post-transport lairage period after a maximum of two 14 h journeys (with a mid-journey lairage period) before transport can be resumed appears to be adequate. Cockram *et al.* (1997) found that sheep spent most of a 3-h lairage period after a 12-h journey eating and there might not have been sufficient time during this short period to completely replace any nutrient deficit. Although no effect of lairage duration on post-transport hay intake was found, sheep in lairage for 12 h during a 24-h journey spent less time eating during the 3rd h post transport, than those in lairage for 3 h during the 24-h journey, suggesting that a mid-journey lairage period of 12 h was more beneficial than a 3-h lairage period. If the time during which sheep after transport show greater than normal eating behaviour is taken as the criterion, after a 24-h journey without food, sheep require at least 5 h access to hay and after a 24-h journey with a lairage of 3 h they require at least 4 h access to hay. After 24 h of transport without access to food, raised plasma concentrations of free fatty acids and β-hydroxybutyrate returned to normal by about 6 h. However, after a journey of 24 h, the behaviour of sheep did not return to normal until 11 to 15 h after unloading. This suggests that a lairage period of at least this duration is required to fully recover from the effects of food restriction and transport. Based on the time taken for plasma creatine kinase activity to fall to low values, Knowles *et al.* (1993) concluded that up to 144 h are required for sheep to recover from a 14-h journey. However, this conclusion is difficult to interpret as the half-life of plasma creatine kinase activity in sheep has been estimated to be 2 h (Houpert *et al.*, 1995) and if the plasma creatine kinase activity was a response to either the journey or unloading, the activity should have fallen to low levels within 24 h of unloading.

Cattle. Adult cattle can also withstand prolonged periods without access to water. Warriss *et al.* (1995) found no evidence of dehydration after journeys of up to 15 h. Schaefer *et al.* (1992) transported steers for 4 h and then left them in a lairage for 36 h without access to either water or food and there were no changes in serum osmolality that would have indicated dehydration. Frohli and Blum (1988) found an increased plasma free fatty acid concentration in cattle after 24 h of fasting but the plasma glucose concentration was not significantly decreased until 48 h of fasting and the plasma β-hydroxybutyrate concentration was not significantly increased until 72 h after fasting. In unweaned calves, Knowles *et al.* (1997) only found a slight increase in plasma total protein concentration after 24 h of transport without access to food or water, with no significant changes in either plasma osmolality or the plasma concentrations of free fatty acids and β-hydroxybutyrate.

Pigs. Pigs are more susceptible to water restriction than either sheep or cattle and show increased plasma osmolality after 24 h without food and water (Parrott *et al.*, 1988). Pigs also show greater responses than ruminants to fasting. Pigs use almost all of their liver glycogen within the first 24 h of fasting (Warriss and Bevis, 1987) and show increased plasma concentrations of free fatty acids and decreased plasma glucose concentration after 16 h of fasting (Barb *et al.*, 1997). It is often recommended that pigs should be starved before transport to (a) reduce the risk of vomiting during transport, (b) reduce the risk of death during transport or lairage and (c) in slaughtered pigs to minimize the risk of carcass contamination during dressing. However, Guise *et al.* (1995) found no significant relationship between the interval since the last food and the weight of the stomach contents at slaughter. The interval between the last food and slaughter was between 3·5 and 46 h, and Warriss and Bevis (1987) estimated that a quarter of pigs surveyed at slaughterhouses in southern England had been starved for longer than 30 h by the time of slaughter. This suggests that although fasting pigs before slaughter could reduce the risk of vomiting and death during transport, pigs could experience hunger for a long period before slaughter.

Poultry. Knowles *et al.* (1996) found no evidence of dehydration in broilers transported to slaughter (time between transport from the farm to slaughter was up to 4 h). However, Warriss *et al.* (1993) found a significant decrease in liver glycogen concentration after up to 10 h of pre-transport starvation followed by 6 h of transport.

Handling
If animals are handled correctly, the operation is achieved more efficiently, the animals and the handlers are calmer and there is less risk of injury. Correct handling requires, preparation, co-ordination of effort by trained handlers, correct design of handling facilities and utilization of the natural behaviour of animals. Principles involved in the handling of animals before and after transport were reviewed by Grandin (1993). Current legislation (WATO 1997) includes many of these principles: lighting to encourage animals to move into areas that would otherwise be too dark, ramps with side protection that are not too steep and use of permanent unloading ramps or bridges. There is detailed information in the scientific literature on appropriate facilities for handling of some animals before and after transport. Loading has a greater effect on pigs than on cattle and sheep. Loading of either steers (Kenny and Tarrant, 1987) or sheep (Cockram *et al.*, 1996) on to a single deck transporter that remains stationary does not result in a cortisol response, however loading pigs on to a stationary vehicle can result in a cortisol response (Bradshaw *et al.*, 1996b). The design of loading and unloading facilities are important. Groups of sheep move up and down wide ramps quicker than they do on narrow (one sheep width) ramps (Hitchcock and Hutson, 1979). The time taken by groups of sheep either to go up or down a wide ramp or up a narrow ramp increases markedly at angles of 30° or greater, and increases markedly at angles of 20° or greater for sheep going down a narrow ramp (Hitchcock and Hutson, 1979). The optimal angle (20°), width (710 mm for pigs going down a 22° slope), cleat spacing (50 mm) and cleat height (10 mm) for loading ramps has been determined for 8-week-old pigs by Phillips *et al.* (1988 and 1989) and the optimal angle (20°) and cleat spacing (150 mm) for loading ramps has been determined for 55 kg live weight pigs by Warriss *et al.* (1991).

WATO 1997 prohibits the use of certain handling methods, such as lifting or dragging sheep by the fleece, which are likely to cause injury and suffering. The use of sticks, electrical goads and other driving instruments is either prohibited or their use is restricted. The amount and type of handling that animals experience affects the degree of injury observed at slaughter. McNally and Warriss (1996) found more bruising and more stick marks in cattle sent to slaughter via an auction market rather than sent to slaughter direct from farms. Jarvis and Cockram (1995b) observed wool-pulls by handlers, and falls and hits into structures when sheep were at an auction market, however, the greatest number of potentially traumatic events observed were riding interactions between sheep (these interactions were greatest when the sheep were either confined in a small area or moved too quickly along a passageway by a handler). The risk of inappropriate handling of animals is reduced where the handling facilities are correctly designed and maintained and the handlers have received training.

Although poultry are protected by the general section within WATO 1997 which prohibits the transport (including loading and unloading) of any animal in a way which causes or is likely to cause injury or unnecessary suffering, they are at risk during handling before transport. Carrying broilers upside down when transferring them from the house to a crate produces a greater plasma corticosterone response than carrying them in an upright position (Kannan and Mench, 1996). The use of a fixed crate system compared with either loose crates or metal/plastic modules to load broilers produces a longer duration of tonic immobility (an indicator of fear) (Cashman et al., 1989). Injury in broilers transported to slaughter is a particular problem. In a survey by Gregory and Austin (1992), 0·19% of the birds were found dead-on-arrival at the slaughterhouse. Thirty-five per cent of these birds had a traumatic injury, such as hip dislocation/fracture probably caused by the method of carrying the hindlegs of the birds by hand; ruptured liver and intraperitoneal haemorrhage, possibly caused by compression; and head trauma possibly caused during the closure of either lids or drawers on a module system. In addition, bone fractures were found throughout the skeleton. The legislation contains a provision that animals should not be loaded and unloaded in such a way that they are caused injury or unnecessary suffering by contact with any part of the means of transport or receptacle or with any obstruction. Spent laying hens, particularly those from battery cages, are at even greater risk of skeletal fractures during handling and transport (Reed et al., 1993). This is because their bones are weakened by osteoporosis and they can come into contact with the cage and food trough during removal from the cage. Rough handling, carrying too many birds, and carrying birds by only one leg can affect the risk of fractures (Gregory and Wilkins, 1989). Keeping laying hens in barren battery cages will increase the risk of potentially damaging behaviour exhibited by the birds during their removal from the cage (Reed et al., 1993).

Fitness of animals for transport
There is potentially a large financial incentive to send cull animals or animals with an existing pathology to a slaughterhouse for human consumption. Parker and Hinton (1990) surveyed disease conditions in culled adult cattle sent to a slaughterhouse. Seventeen per cent of the culls were slaughtered on the farm and 30% of the culls were rejected at the slaughterhouse for human consumption. The disease conditions found in the cull cattle were lameness (42%), mastitis (17%), chronic infections (15%), complications of parturition (10%), fractures and dislocations (7%), central nervous system disorders (4%) and miscellaneous (5%). Decisions on the fitness of animals for transport present many difficulties. Pre-existing health problems are important risk factors affecting mortality of animals during transport (Bayliss and Hinton, 1990; Knowles et al., 1994a). Under WATO 1997, an animal is not considered fit for its intended journey if it is ill, injured, infirm or fatigued, unless it is only slightly injured, ill, infirm or fatigued and the intended journey is not likely to cause it unnecessary suffering. The wording of this Order is an improvement on the previous Order, in that if an animal shows any form of pathological change or a specific disease it is not automatically classified as an unfit animal. However, a pathological lesion, such as a lump or swelling, no matter how small, will have a degree of inflammation and, therefore, an animal is likely to experience some degree of pain. If pressure or movement associated with transport is applied to a visible lesion, or diseased tissue (for example, in lameness), it is likely that this will cause pain (Muirhead, 1993). The legislation allows cattle, sheep, goats and pigs to be transported to the nearest available place for veterinary treatment or diagnosis or to nearest available place for slaughter if the animal is not likely to be subject to unnecessary suffering by reason of its unfitness. However, it is likely that if the animal can be classified as unfit for transport it will be subjected to some degree of suffering during transport. This suffering would not be necessary as the animal could have been slaughtered on the farm rather than transported to either a slaughterhouse or a place for veterinary treatment.

Welfare research and transport legislation — 'the scientific basis for the rules'
The framing of legislation to protect the welfare of animals in transit must be based upon sound scientific analysis of the problems and appropriate scientific strategies for reductions in physiological stress and behavioural disturbances. Transport legislation has to be applicable to a wide range of farmed animals including the main farm animals : cattle, sheep, pigs, and chickens, but also the less numerous farmed animals: including turkeys, geese, ducks, goats, deer, rabbits, ostriches and other

ratites, and fish. These animals differ in anatomy (e.g. weight and shape), physiology and diet. In addition their response to transport is likely to vary with age, genotype, sex, previous experience, health and physiological state.

In the face of the complexity of this topic and the apparent conflicts between philosophical, ethical, moral and objective scientific thought and with the emphasis of much previous research tending to favour the identification of problems, not the provision of solutions, it is unsurprising that an instinctive suspicion exists on the part of animal producers and hauliers towards transport welfare research and its applications. Hopefully such fears may be allayed by undertaking research which is relevant to the welfare of the animals concerned and the objectives and constraints of commercial animal production. It is proposed that it is reasonable and valid to employ scientific method to identify potential sources of stress and reduced welfare during transportation and deficiencies in current practices. The remit of the researcher, however, should not be limited to merely confirming the presence of stress. A more constructive and profitable course is to exploit the knowledge thus gained to alleviate or prevent the stresses by basing improved designs and procedures on a sound scientific foundation. Thus, only through thorough characterization of animals' requirements in-transit and the scientific definition of acceptable ranges for environmental variables can genuine progress and improvements in transport methods and practices be achieved.

It is therefore proposed that co-operation and complementary collaboration between multi-disciplinary scientific groups and the animal production and transport industries represent the way forward. The notion of such interactions and their benefits has existed for some time, but the culture change required to promote integration of the activities of the academic scientific and commercial communities has been absent until recently. The present economic and political climate has encouraged the development of a more holistic approach to research on animal transportation. This is in marked contrast to previous fragmentary or piecemeal studies involving single discipline projects. Current programmes are attempting to optimize welfare and productivity where compatible and to provide long-term strategies for vehicle design and development of meaningful codes of transport practice and legislation

References

Abeyesinghe, S. M., Goddard, P. J. and Cockram, M. S. 1997. The behavioural and physiological responses of farmed red deer (*Cervus elaphus*) penned adjacent to other species. *Applied Animal Behaviour Science* 55: 163-175.

Artursson, K., Wallgren, P. and Alm, G. V. 1989. Appearance of interferon-alpha in serum and signs of reduced immune function in pigs after transport and installation in a fattening farm. *Veterinary Immunology and Immunopathology* 23: 345-353.

Atkinson, P. J. 1992. Investigation of the effects of transport and lairage on hydration state and resting behaviour of calves for export. *Veterinary Record* 130: 413-416.

Baker, C. J., Dalley, S., Yang, X., Kettlewell, P. and Hoxey, R. 1996. An investigation of the aerodynamic and ventilation characteristics of poultry transport vehicles. 2. Wind-tunnel experiments. *Journal of Agricultural Engineering Research* 65: 97-113.

Baldock, N. M. and Sibly, R. M. 1990. Effects of handling and transportation on the heart rate and behaviour of sheep. *Applied Animal Behaviour Science* 28: 15-39.

Barb, C. R., Kraeling, R. R., Rampacek, G. B. and Dove, C. R. 1997. Metabolic changes during the transition from the fed to the acute feed-deprived state in prepuberal and mature gilts. *Journal of Animal Science* 75: 781-789.

Barnett, J. L. and Hemsworth, P. H. 1990. The validity of physiological and behavioural measures of animal welfare. *Applied Animal Behaviour Science* 25: 177-187.

Bayliss, P. A. and Hinton, M. H. 1990. Transportation of broilers with special reference to mortality rates. *Applied Animal Behaviour Science* 28: 93-118.

Behrends, J. I., Randall, J. M., Stiles, M. A. and Kettlewell, P. J. 1997. Vibration of a poultry transporter and bird postural stability. In *Livestock environment V, volume I.* (eds R. W. Bottcher and S. J. Hoff), *proceedings of the fifth international symposium*, Bloomington, Minnesota, USA, 29-31 May 1997, pp. 109-114. American Society of Agricultural Engineers, St Joseph, Michigan, USA.

Bekoff, M. 1994. Cognitive ethology and the treatment of non-human animals: how matters of mind inform matters of welfare. *Animal Welfare* 3: 75-96.

Birchall, A. 1990. The rough road to slaughter. *New Scientist* 128: 33-36.

Bligh, J. 1985. Temperature regulation. In *Stress physiology of livestock I: basic principles* (ed. M. K. Yousef), pp. 75-96. CRC Press, Boca Raton, Florida, USA.

Bonner, J. 1995. Roads to the abattoir. New Scientist 1968: 30-31.

Bott, E., Denton, D. A. and Weller, S. 1965. Water drinking in sheep with oesophageal fistulae. *Journal of Physiology* 176: 323-336.

Bradshaw, R. H., Parrott, R. F., Forsling, M. L., Goode, J. A., Lloyd, D. M., Rodway, R. G. and Broom, D. M. 1996a. Stress and travel sickness in pigs: effects of road transport on plasma concentrations of cortisol, beta-endorphin and lysine vasopressin. *Animal Science* 63: 507-516.

Bradshaw, R. H., Parrott, R. F., Goode, J. A., Lloyd, D. M., Rodway, R. G. and Broom, D. M. 1996b. Behavioural and hormonal responses of pigs during transport: effect of mixing and duration of journey. *Animal Science* 62: 547-554.

Carlisle, A. J., Mitchell, M. A., Hunter, R. R., Duggan, J. A. and Kettlewell, P. J. 1998. Physiological responses of broiler chickens to the vibrations experienced during road transportation. *British Poultry Science Supplement* **39**: S48-S49.

Cashman, P. J., Nicol, C. J. and Jones, R. B. 1989. Effects of transportation on the tonic immobility fear reactions of broilers. *British Poultry Science* **30**: 211-221.

Cockram, M. S. 1990. Some factors influencing behaviour of cattle in a slaughterhouse lairage. *Animal Production* **50**: 475-481.

Cockram, M. S. 1991. Resting behaviour of cattle in a slaughterhouse lairage. *British Veterinary Journal* **147**: 109-119.

Cockram, M. S., Kent, J. E., Goddard, P. J., Waran, N. K., McGilp, I. M., Jackson, R. E., Muwanga, G. M. and Prytherch, S. 1996. Effect of space allowance during transport on the behavioural and physiological responses of lambs during and after transport. *Animal Science* **62**: 461-477.

Cockram, M. S., Kent, J. E., Jackson, R. E., Goddard, P. J., Doherty, O. M., McGilp, I. M., Fox, A., Studdert-Kennedy, T. C., McConnell, T. I. and O'Riordan, T. 1997. Effect of lairage during 24 h of transport on the behavioural and physiological responses of sheep. *Animal Science* **65**: 391-402.

Cole, N. A. 1995. Influence of a 3-day feed and water-deprivation period on gut fill, tissue weights, and tissue composition in mature wethers. *Journal of Animal Science* **73**: 2548-2557.

Council of the European Community. 1991. Directive 91/628/EEC of 19 November 1991 on the protection of animals during transport and amending Directives 90/425/EEC and 91/496/EEC. *Official Journal of the European Communities* **L340**: 17-38.

Council of the European Community. 1995. Directive 95/29/EC of June 1995 amending Directive 91/628/EEC concerning the protection of animals during transport. *Official Journal of the European Communities* **L148**: 52-63.

Council of the European Community. 1998. Directive 411/98/EC of February 1988 amending Directive 91/628/EEC concerning the protection of animal during transport. Additional standards for road vehicles used for the carriage of livestock on journeys exceeding 8 hours. *Official Journal of the European Communities* **L52**: 8-11.

Dalin, A. M., Magnusson, U., Haggendal, J. and Nyberg, L. 1993. The effect of transport stress on plasma-levels of catecholamines, cortisol, corticosteroid-binding globulin, blood-cell count, and lymphocyte-proliferation in pigs. *Acta Veterinaria Scandinavica* **34**: 59-68.

Dalley, S., Baker, C. J., Yang, X., Kettlewell, P. and Hoxey, R. 1996. An investigation of the aerodynamic and ventilation characteristics of poultry transport vehicles. 3. Internal flow-field calculations. *Journal of Agricultural Engineering Research* **65**: 115-127.

Degen, A. A. and Shkolnik, A. 1978. Thermoregulation in fat-tailed Awassi, a desert sheep, and in German mutton Merino, a mesic sheep. *Physiological Zoology* **51**: 333-339.

Doherty, O., Booth, M., Waran, N., Salthouse, C. and Cuddeford, D. 1997. Study of the heart rate and energy expenditure of ponies during transport. *Veterinary Record* **141**: 589-592.

Duncan, I. J. H. and Fraser, D. 1997. Understanding animal welfare. In *Animal welfare* (ed. M. C. Appleby and B. O. Hughes), pp. 19-31. CAB International, Wallingford, Oxon.

Farm Animal Welfare Council. 1993. *Report on priorities for animal welfare research and development.* Ministry of Agriculture, Fisheries and Food, Surbiton.

Fitzsimons, J. T. 1972. Thirst. *Physiological Reviews* **52**: 468-561.

Forbes, J. M. 1995. *Voluntary food intake and diet selection in farm animals.* CAB International, Wallingford, Oxon.

Franc, C., Bartos, L., Hanys, Z. and Tomes, Z. 1988. Pre-slaughter social activity of young bulls relating to the occurrence of dark-cutting beef. *Animal Production* **46**: 153-161.

Frohli, D. and Blum, J. W. 1988. Effects of fasting on blood plasma levels, metabolism and metabolic effects of epinephrine and norepinephrine in steers. *Acta Endocrinologica (Copenhagen)* **118**: 254-259.

George, J. C. 1984. Thermogenesis in birds. In *Thermal physiology* (ed. J. R. Hales), pp. 467-473. Raven Press, New York.

Grandin, T. 1993. *Livestock handling and transport.* CAB International, Wallingford.

Great Britain Parliament. 1990. *The welfare of animals at markets order. Statutory instrument 1990/2628.* Her Majesty's Stationery Office, London.

Great Britain Parliament. 1997. *The welfare of Animals (Transport) Order. Statutory instrument 1997/1480.* Her Majesty's Stationery Office, London.

Gregory, N. G. and Austin, S. D. 1992. Causes of trauma in broilers arriving dead at poultry-processing plants. *Veterinary Record* **131**: 501-503.

Gregory, N. G. and Wilkins, L. J. 1989. Broken bones in domestic fowl: handling and processing damage in end-of-lay battery hens. *British Poultry Science* **30**: 555-582.

Grigor, P. N., Goddard, P. J. and Littlewood, C. A. 1998. The relative aversiveness to farmed red deer of transport, physical restraint, human proximity and social isolation. *Applied Animal Behaviour Science* **56**: 255-262.

Guise, H. J. and Penny, R. H. C. 1989. Factors influencing the welfare and carcass and meat quality of pigs. 2. Mixing unfamiliar pigs. *Animal Production* **49**: 517-521.

Guise, H. J., Penny, R. H. C., Baynes, P. J., Abbott, T. A., Hunter, E. J. and Johnston, A. M. 1995. Abattoir observations of the weights of stomachs and their contents in pigs slaughtered at known times after their last feed. *British Veterinary Journal* **151**: 659-670.

Hecker, J. F., Budtz-Olsen, O. E. and Ostwald, M. 1964. The rumen as a water store in sheep. *Australian Journal of Agricultural Research* **15**: 961-968.

Hitchcock, D. K. and Hutson, G. D. 1979. The movement of sheep on inclines. *Australian Journal of Experimental Agriculture and Animal Husbandry* **19**: 176-182.

Houpert, P., Serthelon, J. P., Lefebvre, H. P., Tountain, P. L. and Braun, J. P. 1995. *In vivo* non-invasive quantification of muscle damage following a single intramuscular injection of phenylbutazone in sheep. *Veterinary and Human Toxicology* **37**: 105-110.

Hoxey, R. P., Kettlewell, P. J., Meehan, A. M., Baker, C. J. and Yang, X. 1996. An investigation of the aerodynamic and ventilation characteristics of poultry transport vehicles. 1. Full-scale measurements. *Journal of Agricultural Engineering Research* 65: 77-83.

Hunter, R. R., Mitchell, M. A. and Matheu, C. 1997. Distribution of 'dead on arrivals' within the bio-load on commercial broiler transporters: correlation with climate conditions and ventilation regimen. *British Poultry Science* 38: (supplement) S7-S9.

Ingram, D. L. and Dauncey, M. J. 1985. Thermoregulatory behaviour. In *Stress physiology of livestock I: basic principles* (ed. M. K. Yousef), pp. 97-108. CRC Press, Boca Raton, Florida USA.

Jarvis, A. M. and Cockram, M. S. 1994. Effect of handling and transport on bruising of sheep sent directly from farms to slaughter. *Veterinary Record* 135: 523-527.

Jarvis, A. M. and Cockram, M. S. 1995a. Some factors affecting resting behaviour of sheep in slaughterhouse lairages after transport from farms. *Animal Welfare* 4: 53-60.

Jarvis, A. M. and Cockram, M. S. 1995b. Handling of sheep at markets and the incidence of bruising. *Veterinary Record* 136: 582-585.

Jarvis, A. M., Cockram, M. S. and McGilp, I. M. 1996a. Bruising and biochemical measures of stress, dehydration and injury determined at slaughter in sheep transported from farms or markets. *British Veterinary Journal* 152: 719-722.

Jarvis, A. M., Harrington, D. W. J. and Cockram, M. S. 1996b. Effect of source and lairage on some behavioural and biochemical measurements of feed restriction and dehydration in cattle at a slaughterhouse. *Applied Animal Behaviour Science* 50: 83-94.

Jarvis, A. M., Messer, C. D. A. and Cockram, M. S. 1996c. Handling, bruising and dehydration of cattle at the time of slaughter. *Animal Welfare* 5: 259-270.

Jarvis, A. M., Selkirk, L. and Cockram, M. S. 1995. The influence of source, sex class and pre-slaughter handling on the bruising of cattle at two slaughterhouses. *Livestock Production Science* 43: 215-224.

Kannan, G. and Mench, J. A. 1996. Influence of different handling methods and crating periods on plasma-corticosterone concentrations in broilers. *British Poultry Science* 37: 21-31.

Kenny, F. J. and Tarrant, P. V. 1987. The physiological and behavioral-responses of crossbred Friesian steers to short-haul transport by road. *Livestock Production Science* 17: 63-75.

Kettlewell, P. J. and Mitchell, M. A. 1993. The thermal environment on poultry transport vehicles. In *Livestock environment IV* (ed. E. Collins and C. Boon), *proceedings of the fourth international symposium of the American Society of Agricultural Engineers*, pp. 552-559.

Kettlewell, P. J., Mitchell, M. A. and Meehan, A. 1993. The distribution of thermal loads within poultry transport vehicles. *Agricultural Engineer* 48: 26-30.

Kettlewell, P. J., Mitchell, M. A. and Meeks, I. R. 1997. An implantable radio-telemetry system for the remote monitoring of heart rate and deep body temperature in poultry. *Computers and Electronics in Agriculture* 17: 161-175.

Kim, F. B., Jackson, R. E., Gordon, G. D. H. and Cockram, M. S. 1994. Resting behaviour of sheep in a slaughterhouse lairage. *Applied Animal Behaviour Science* 40: 45-54.

Knowles, T. G., Ball, R. C., Warriss, P. D. and Edwards, J. E. 1996. A survey to investigate potential dehydration in slaughtered broiler- chickens. *British Veterinary Journal* 152: 307-314.

Knowles, T. G., Maunder, D. H. L., Warriss, P. D. and Jones, T. W. H. 1994a. Factors affecting the mortality of lambs in transit to or in lairage at a slaughterhouse, and reasons for carcase condemnations. *Veterinary Record* 135: 109-111.

Knowles, T. G., Warriss, P. D., Brown, S. N., Edwards, J. E., Watkins, P. E. and Phillips, A. J. 1997. Effects on calves less than one month old of feeding or not feeding them during road transport of up to 24 hours. *Veterinary Record* 140: 116-124.

Knowles, T. G., Warriss, P. D., Brown, S. N. and Kestin, S. C. 1994b. Long distance transport of export lambs. *Veterinary Record* 134: 107-110.

Knowles, T. G., Warriss, P. D., Brown, S. N., Kestin, S. C., Rhind, S. M., Edwards, J. E., Anil, M. H. and Dolan, S. K. 1993. Long distance transport of lambs and the time needed for subsequent recovery. *Veterinary Record* 133: 286-293.

Lambooy, E. 1988. Road transport of pigs over a long-distance: some aspects of behaviour, temperature and humidity during transport and some effects of the last two factors. *Animal Production* 46: 257-263.

Lambooy, E. and Engel, B. 1991. Transport of slaughter pigs by truck over a long-distance — some aspects of loading density and ventilation. *Livestock Production Science* 28: 163-174.

Lambooy, E., Garssen, G. J., Walstra, P., Mateman, G. and Merkus, G. S. M. 1985. Transport of pigs by car for two days — some aspects of watering and loading density. *Livestock Production Science* 13: 289-299.

Lefebvre, H. P., Braun, J. P., Laroute, V., Tripodi, A., Bret, L. and Toutain, P. L. 1995. Non-invasive quantification of organ damage. *Comparative Haematology International* 5: 120-124.

MacFarlane, W. V., Morris, R. J. H., Howard, B., McDonald, J. and Budtz-Olsen, O. E. 1961. Water and electrolyte changes in tropical Merino sheep exposed to dehydration during summer. *Australian Journal of Agricultural Research* 12: 889-912.

McKinley, M. J., Denton, D. A., Nelson, J. F. and Weisinger, R. S. 1983. Dehydration induces sodium depletion in rats, rabbits, and sheep. *American Journal of Physiology* 245: R287-R292.

McNally, P. W. and Warriss, P. D. 1996. Recent bruising in cattle at abattoirs. *Veterinary Record* 138: 126-128.

Mason, G. and Mendl, M. 1993. Why is there no simple way of measuring animal welfare? *Animal Welfare* 2: 301-319.

Mendl, M. 1991. Some problems with the concept of a cut-off point for determining when an animal's welfare is at risk. *Applied Animal Behaviour Science* 31: 139-146.

Merrick, A. W. and Sharp, D. W. 1971. Electroencephalography of resting behaviour in cattle, with observations on the question of sleep. *American Journal of Veterinary Research* **32**: 1893-1897.

Mitchell, M. A. 1986. The effects of air movement upon respiratory evaporative heat loss from the domestic fowl at high ambient-temperatures. *Journal of Physiology, London* **378**: P 72.

Mitchell, M. A., Carlisle, A. J., Hunter, R. R. and Kettlewell, P. J. 1997. Welfare of broilers during transportation: cold stress in winter — causes and solutions. *Proceedings of the fifth European symposium on poultry welfare* (ed. P. Koene and H. J. Blokhuis), WPSA, University of Wageningen and Institute of Animal Science and Health, The Netherlands.

Mitchell, M. A. and Kettlewell, P. J. 1998. Physiological stress and welfare of broiler chickens in transit: Solutions not problems! *Poultry Science* **77**: 1803-1814.

Mitchell, M. A., Kettlewell, P. J., Quinn, A. D., Warriss, P. and Baxter, C. 1998. Alleviation of thermal stress experienced by pountry whilst held on stationary transport vehicles and in lairage. *MAFF Open Contract Report CSA 2826*.

Mitchell, M. A., Kettlewell, P. J. and Maxwell, M. H. 1992. Indicators of physiological stress in broiler chickens during road transportation. *Animal Welfare* **1**: 91-103.

Mitchell, M. A. and Sandercock, D. A. 1995. Creatine kinase isoenzyme profiles in the plasma of the domestic fowl (*Gallus domesticus*) — effects of acute heat stress. *Research in Veterinary Science* **59**: 30-34.

Moberg, G. P. 1985. Biological response to stress: key to assessment of animal well-being? In *Animal stress* (ed. G. P. Moberg), pp. 27-49. American Physiological Society, Bethesda.

Muirhead, M. R. 1993. Casualty slaughter prosecution. *Veterinary Record* **132**: 23.

Murata, H. and Hirose, H. 1991. Suppression of bovine lymphocyte and macrophage functions by sera from road-transported calves. *British Veterinary Journal* **147**: 455-462.

Nanda, A. S., Dobson, H. and Ward, W. R. 1990. Relationship between an increase in plasma-cortisol during transport induced stress and failure of estradiol to induce a luteinizing-hormone surge in dairy-cows. *Research in Veterinary Science* **49**: 25-28.

Nicol, C. J., Blakeborough, A. and Scott, G. B. 1991. Aversiveness of motion and noise to broiler-chickens. *British Poultry Science* **32**: 249-260.

Nicol, C. and Saville-Weeks, C. 1993. Poultry handling and transport. In *Livestock handling and transport* (ed. T. Grandin), pp. 273-288. CAB International, Oxon, UK.

Park, R. G., Congiu, M., Denton, D. A. and McKinley, M. J. 1986. Volume influences on thirst and vasopressin secretion in dehydrated sheep. *American Journal of Physiology* **251**: R621-R626.

Parker, D. W. H. and Hinton, M. 1990. Disease conditions diagnosed in culled adult cattle sent to an abattoir either with or without a veterinary certificate. *Veterinary Record* **126**: 189-190.

Parrott, R. F., Bradshaw, R. H., Lloyd, D. M. and Goode, J. A. 1998. Effects of transport and indomethacin on telemetered body temperature and release of cortisol and prolactin in pre-pubertal pigs. *Research in Veterinary Science* **64**: 51-55.

Parrott, R. F., Lloyd, D. M. and Goode, J. A. 1996. Stress hormone responses of sheep to food and water deprivation at high and low ambient temperatures. *Animal Welfare* **5**: 45-56.

Parrott, R. F., Misson, B. H. and Riva, C. F. de La 1994. Differential stressor effects on the concentrations of cortisol, prolactin and catecholamines in the blood of sheep. *Research in Veterinary Science* **56**: 234-239.

Parrott, R. F., Thornton, S. N., Baldwin, B. A. and Forsling, M. L. 1988. Changes in vasopressin and cortisol secretion during operant drinking in dehydrated pigs. *American Journal of Physiology* **255**: R 248-R 251.

Phillips, P. A., Thompson, B. K. and Fraser, D. 1988. Preference tests of ramp designs for young pigs. *Canadian Journal of Animal Science* **68**: 41-48.

Phillips, P. A., Thompson, B. K. and Fraser, D. 1989. The importance of cleat spacing in ramp design for young pigs. *Canadian Journal of Animal Science* **69**: 483-486.

Quinn, A. D., Kettlewell, P. J., Mitchell, M. A. and Knowles, T. 1998. Air movement and the thermal microclimates observed in poultry lairages. *British Poultry Science* **39**: 469-476.

Randall, J. M. 1992. Human subjective response to lorry vibration — implications for farm animal transport. *Journal of Agricultural Engineering Research* **52**: 295-307.

Randall, J. M. 1993. Environmental parameters necessary to define comfort for pigs, cattle and sheep in livestock transporters. *Animal Production* **57**: 299-307.

Randall, J. M. and Bradshaw, R. H. 1998. Vehicle motion and motion sickness in pigs. *Animal Science* **66**: 239-245.

Randall, J. M., Cove, M. T. and White, R. P. 1996. Resonant frequencies of broiler chickens. *Animal Science* **62**: 369-374.

Randall, J. M., Streader, W. V. and Meehan, A. M. 1993. Vibration on poultry transporters. *British Poultry Science* **34**: 635-642.

Reed, H. J., Wilkins, L. J., Austin, S. D. and Gregory, N. G. 1993. The effect of environmental enrichment during rearing on fear reactions and depopulation trauma in adult caged hens. *Applied Animal Behaviour Science* **36**: 39-46.

Ribble, C. S., Meek, A. H., Shewen, P. E., Guichon, P. T. and Jim, G. K. 1995. Effect of pretransit mixing on fatal fibrinous pneumonia in calves. *Journal of the American Veterinary Medical Association* **207**: 616-619.

Ruckebusch, Y. 1975a. The hypnogram as an index of adaptation of farm animals to changes in their environment. *Applied Animal Ethology* **2**: 3-18.

Ruckebusch, Y. 1975b. Motility of the ruminant stomach associated with states of sleep. In *Digestion and metabolism in the ruminant* (ed. I. W. McDonald and A. C. I. Warner), pp. 77-90. University of New Zealand Publishing Unit, Armidale, Australia.

Rutter, S. M. and Randall, J. M. 1993. Aversion of domestic-fowl to whole-body vibratory motion. *Applied Animal Behaviour Science* **37**: 69-73.

Sather, A. P., Jones, S. D. M., Squires, E. J., Schaefer, A. L., Robertson, W. M., Tong, A. K. W. and Zawadski, S. 1995. Antemortem handling effects on the behaviour, carcass yield and meat quality of market weight entire male pigs. *Canadian Journal of Animal Science* 75: 45-56.

Schaefer, A. L., Jones, S. D. M., Tong, A. K. W., Young, B. A., Murray, N. L. and Lepage, P. 1992. Effects of post-transport electrolyte supplementation on tissue electrolytes, haematology, urine osmolality and weight loss in beef bulls. *Livestock Production Science* 30: 333-346.

Scott, G. B. 1994. Effects of short-term whole-body vibration on animals with particular reference to poultry. *World's Poultry Science Journal* 50: 25-38.

Sherwin, C. M., Kestin, S. C., Nicol, C. J., Knowles, T. G., Brown, S. N., Reed, H. J. and Warriss, P. D. 1993. Variation in behavioral indexes of fearfulness and fatigue in transported broilers. *British Veterinary Journal* 149: 571-578.

Silanikove, N. 1994. The struggle to maintain hydration and osmoregulation in animals experiencing severe dehydration and rapid rehydration — the story of ruminants. *Experimental Physiology* 79: 281-300.

Stephens, D. B., Bailey, K. J., Sharman, D. F. and Ingram, D. L. 1985. An analysis of some behavioural effects of the vibration and noise components of transport in pigs. *Quarterly Journal of Experimental Physiology* 70: 211-217.

Stephens, D. B. and Rader, R. D. 1983. Effects of vibration, noise and restraint on heart-rate, blood-pressure and renal blood-flow in the pig. *Journal of the Royal Society of Medicine* 76: 841-847.

Tarrant, P. V. 1989. The effects of handling, transport, slaughter and chilling on meat quality and yield in pigs — a review. *Irish Journal of Food Science and Technology* 13: 79-107.

Tarrant, P. V., Kenny, F. J. and Harrington, D. 1988. The effect of stocking density during four hour transport to slaughter on behaviour, blood constituents and carcass bruising in Friesian steers. *Meat Science* 24: 209-222.

Tarrant, P. V., Kenny, F. J., Harrington, D. and Murphy, M. 1992. Long-distance transportation of steers to slaughter — effect of stocking density on physiology, behaviour and carcass quality. *Livestock Production Science* 30: 223-238.

Ternouth, J. H. 1968. Changes in the thiosulphate space and some constituents of the blood of sheep after feeding. *Research in Veterinary Science* 9: 345-349.

Thompson, G. E. 1977. Physiological effects of cold exposure. *International Review of Physiology, Environmental Physiology II* 15: 30-69.

Thoren-Tolling, K. 1991. Serum creatine-kinase activity as a selection criterion for stress susceptibility after standardized stress in pigs. *Annales de Recherches Vétérinaires* 22: 395-403.

Villé, H., Bertels, S., Geers, R., Janssens, S., Goedseels, V., Parduyns, G., Bael, J. van, Goossens, K., Bosschaerts, L., Ley, J. de and Heylen, L. 1993. Electrocardiogram parameters of piglets during housing, handling and transport. *Animal Production* 56: 211-216.

Warriss, P. D. 1996. The welfare of animals during transport. *The Veterinary Annual* 36: 73-85.

Warriss, P. D. 1998. Choosing appropriate space allowances for slaughter pigs transported by road: a review. *Veterinary Record* 142: 449-454.

Warriss, P. D. and Bevis, E. A. 1986. Transport and lairage times in British slaughter pigs. *British Veterinary Journal* 142: 124-130.

Warriss, P. D. and Bevis, E. A. 1987. Liver glycogen in slaughtered pigs and estimated time of fasting before slaughter. *British Veterinary Journal* 143: 354-360.

Warriss, P. D., Bevis, E. A., Brown, S. N. and Ashby, J. G. 1989. An examination of potential indexes of fasting time in commercially slaughtered sheep. *British Veterinary Journal* 145: 242-248.

Warriss, P. D., Bevis, E. A., Brown, S. N. and Edwards, J. E. 1992. Longer journeys to processing plants are associated with higher mortality in broiler-chickens. *British Poultry Science* 33: 201-206.

Warriss, P. D., Bevis, E. A., Edwards, J. E., Brown, S. N. and Knowles, T. G. 1991. Effect of the angle of slope on the ease with which pigs negotiate loading ramps. *Veterinary Record* 128: 419-421.

Warriss, P. D. and Brown, S. N. 1994. A survey of mortality in slaughter pigs during transport and lairage. *Veterinary Record* 134: 513-515.

Warriss, P. D., Brown, S. N., Edwards, J. E. and Knowles, T. G. 1998. Effect of lairage time on levels of stress and meat quality in pigs. *Animal Science* 66: 255-261.

Warriss, P. D., Brown, S. N., Knowles, T. G. and Edwards, J. E. 1999. Effects of commercial transportation and lairage upon tissue glycogen stores, body temperature and hydration state in broiler chickens. *Veterinary Record* In press.

Warriss, P. D., Brown, S. N., Knowles, T. G., Edwards, J. E. and Duggan, J. A. 1997. Potential effect of vibration during transport on glycogen reserves in broiler chickens. *Veterinary Journal* 153: 215-219.

Warriss, P. D., Brown, S. N., Knowles, T. G., Kestin, S. C., Edwards, J. E., Dolan, S. K. and Phillips, A. J. 1995. Effects on cattle of transport by road for up to 15 hours. *Veterinary Record* 136: 319-323.

Warriss, P. D., Kestin, S. C., Brown, S. N., Knowles, T. G., Wilkins, L. J., Edwards, J. E., Austin, S. D. and Nicol, C. J. 1993. The depletion of glycogen stores and indexes of dehydration in transported broilers. *British Veterinary Journal* 149: 391-398.

Weeding, C. M., Guise, H. J. and Penny, R. H. C. 1993. Factors influencing the welfare and carcass and meat quality of pigs: the use of water sprays in lairage. *Animal Production* 56: 393-397.

Wellman, A. C. 1996. Hot weather livestock stress. In *NebGuide*. University of Nebraska.

Wiepkema, P. R. and Koolhaas, J. M. 1993. Stress and animal welfare. *Animal Welfare* 2: 195-218.

Wray, C., Todd, N., McLaren, I. M. and Beedell, Y. E. 1991. The epidemiology of salmonella in calves: the role of markets and vehicles. *Epidemiology and Infection* 107: 521-525.

Farm animal welfare — who writes the rules?
Occasional Publication No. 23 — British Society of Animal Science 1999
edited by A. J. F. Russel, C. A. Morgan, C. J. Savory, M. C. Appleby and T. L. J. Lawrence

The influence of housing research on welfare legislation

S. A. Edwards[1]†, J. Robertson[1] and M. Kelly[2]

[1]Animal Biology Division, Scottish Agricultural College, Craibstone Estate, Bucksburn, Aberdeen, AB21 9YA
[2]Building Design Department, Environment Division, Scottish Agricultural College, Auchincruive, Ayr KA6 5HW

Abstract

The design and management of housing play a major rôle in the welfare of most farm animal species and are implicated in all of the 'five freedoms'. Housing has always been an aspect of livestock production systems which is readily amenable to legislation and the majority of current UK (and EU) welfare legislation relates generally or specifically to housing. An area of concern in current legislation is the tendency to legislate on housing systems rather than animal state, which leads to disagreements in interpretation and anomalies in implementation. Housing legislation is furthest advanced in the simple-stomached species, rather than in ruminant species which have traditionally been farmed more extensively. However, issues of housing and welfare certainly require to be addressed in other species. Whilst scientific research does underlie many of the existing housing regulations, it has not always been correctly interpreted or sensibly applied. Many dilemmas exist when overviewing the balance of scientific evidence relating to contentious housing systems in all species. In many areas, requirements of quality assurance schemes are now more rigorous and wide reaching than legislation but these are not always based on scientific evidence. However, many component-specific recommendations have been scientifically established and animal welfare could be significantly improved by their application. In the future, advances in fundamental science are needed to better establish legislative criteria. Applied scientists should continue to be used as independent advisers in consideration of future legislation and should be more proactive in information transfer outwith the normal scientific media.

† Present address: Department of Agriculture, University of Aberdeen, Aberdeen AB24 5UA.

The importance of housing for animal welfare

The design and management of housing plays a major rôle in the welfare of most farm animal species. As the livestock industry has sought to become more biologically and economically efficient, methods to allow greater control of all factors impinging on animal performance have been developed. This trend has resulted in widespread use of advanced breeding programmes and technologies, more complex diets and more sophisticated environmental control systems. Welfare is now commonly defined for legislative and political purposes in terms of the 'five freedoms' and housing can have a significant effect on the extent to which each of these freedoms can be met. 'Freedom from hunger and thirst' depends not only on the diet offered but also on the adequacy of feeding and watering facilities, both in terms of design suitability and accessibility (Metz, 1983; Barber et al., 1989). 'Freedom from thermal and physical discomfort' depends on the adequacy of environmental temperature control, linked to other related environmental factors such as airspeed, thermal conductivity of flooring and provision of radiant heat (Bruce and Clark, 1979). It also depends on the appropriateness of building materials and especially flooring, with or without provision of bedding (Webb and Nilsson, 1983). 'Freedom from injury and disease' depends on the ability to maintain appropriate hygiene, both at the floor surface (Blom et al., 1985) and in the aerial environment (Robertson, 1994 and 1998), whilst avoiding acutely or chronically injurious physical structures. 'Freedom from fear and stress', whilst depending on all of the above factors, also requires the facility to achieve and maintain appropriate social interactions with both conspecifics and human carers (Grandin, 1980; Zayan, 1985). Finally and often most contentiously, 'Freedom to exhibit normal behaviour' implies that housing must provide the necessary environmental conditions to elicit or facilitate the specific behavioural patterns which can be demonstrated to comprise 'behavioural needs' for the species (Stolba and Wood-Gush, 1984). The concept of behavioural needs is not a simple one (Edwards, 1995a) and does not imply that all behaviours seen in natural circumstances need to be reproduced in the housed environment but it is now widely accepted that animals do have psychological rather than just physical needs for which housing systems must be designed to cater. Whilst the scientific understanding of and agreement about, the physical needs of animals is approaching unanimity, the same cannot yet be said in relation to behavioural needs.

Housing and current legislation

Housing has always been an aspect of livestock production systems which is readily amenable to legislation. It is highly visible, with a degree of permanence, subject to modification and comprises many easily measurable components in comparison with other more dynamic activities such as feeding or handling. For this reason, it is not surprising that the majority of current UK welfare legislation clauses (and EU welfare directives) relate generally or specifically to housing. In the most recent farm animal legislation 'The Welfare of Livestock Regulations 1994' (Statutory Instrument No. 2126; Great Britain Parliament, 1994), the following breakdown can be found (Table 1).

The interpretation in Table 1 is conservative; for example the requirement to clean pens is taken as a stockman, rather than a building related, requirement. Even so, 65% of legislation in all schedules is specifically related to housing, whilst few clauses relate to livestock in extensively managed situations. It would be wrong to suggest that welfare problems do not exist in extensive systems (e.g. Farm Animal Welfare Council (FAWC), 1996) but they are perceived by the general public as being more 'natural' and therefore acceptable and possibly by legislators as being less easy to define, measure and enforce.

Housing systems and welfare objectives

An area of concern in current legislation is the tendency to legislate on housing systems (e.g. sow stalls, calf crates, chicken battery cages) rather than

Table 1 *Summary of the relative importance of housing in the Welfare of Livestock Regulations (GB Parliament, 1994)*

Schedule	Total clauses	Number relating to housing
1. Laying hens	16	11
2. Calves	20	11
3. Pigs	34	23
4. General	15	10
5. Overall	85	55

the welfare state of the animal. In reality, housing systems are complex entities made up of multiple interacting physical and social components and not the simple housing descriptors which they are often deemed to be (Edwards, 1995b). Making scientifically supportable legislation on housing systems is therefore fraught with difficulties. The first is the problem of unwarranted generalization. Because of the large scale and diverse nature of systems, experimental evaluation frequently involves replication of animals within the system to assess its effects on welfare, rather than true replication of the system itself. Since quite small changes in design or management can exert major influences on the success and acceptability of any given system (e.g. Edwards and Riley, 1986), only larger scale, multi-site evaluation will yield a true picture.

A second problem with system evaluation is the choice of criteria used for assessment. It is now widely accepted that welfare assessment must be multifactorial, encompassing physical, physiological and behavioural elements (English and Edwards, 1999) but less well agreed as to the correct course of action when such assessments appear to conflict (Mason and Mendl, 1993). Equally, the concept that animal welfare may be modified by a housing change in different directions for different individuals is difficult to deal with. Figure 1 illustrates some of these dilemmas. If welfare could be measured as a unitary parameter (an ability still beyond science), should one adopt a system where, with the same group average welfare, more individual animals have good welfare but also more have bad (population A), or one where more of the population falls into the average category (population B)? Such an example might arise when considering whether to impose a fixed or free-choice thermal environment on a group. The imposed environment may be adequate but not the optimal preference for all and the free choice situation may allow dominant animals to occupy preferred zones but exclude subdominant individuals through social competition. More problematic is whether one should raise the welfare of the majority at the expense of the few (population C) or protect the vulnerable individual by limiting welfare of the mass (population D). Such an example might arise when permitting uncontrolled social interaction or imposing behavioural restriction on the mother for the benefit of her offspring.

Further legislative conflicts are likely to arise when animal welfare considerations conflict with other political considerations. Some may be truly ethical conflicts, as with the need to balance animal welfare considerations against risks to human food safety; e.g. the provision of straw as a behavioural substrate

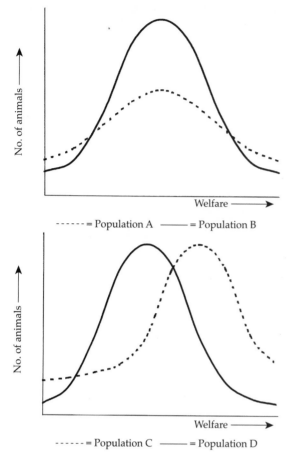

= Population A   = Population B

= Population C   = Population D

Figure 1 The possible consequences of system change for welfare within populations of animals.

With such complex considerations involved in legislative decisions, it is valid to ask whose views should influence the final decision. When looking specifically at the rôle played by scientists active in housing research in recently implemented and impending legislation, it is apparent that their voice has been influential but not exclusively so. Obtaining indisputable scientific fact is an expensive and slow process which often seems to the outsider to be artificial and of limited relevance to commercial practice. The view of practitioners within the industry under debate (farmers, veterinarians and staff in ancillary industries) is well informed but seen as being biased and economically slanted (although with the high level of sponsorship of research by various interest groups which currently pertains, it cannot always be said that scientists are economically uninfluenced). The view of the general public is relatively uninformed but highly relevant to the requirements of the market and of society in general. Legislation must therefore reflect ultimately the ethical views of the majority at any given point in time and science should seek to actively inform such decisions wherever possible.

The scientific base for recent and proposed legislation

The following discussion of current issues focuses on the major farm species which have legislative documentation, namely poultry, pigs and cattle. Whilst the housing of other, formerly more extensively kept, species is increasing, legislation has not yet specifically addressed these. Thus housing of sheep receives no specific mention in current legislation and other aspects of production predominate in welfare considerations in this species (Vipond and Hosie, 1997). The only other species mentioned in the Welfare of Livestock Regulations (Great Britain Parliament, 1994) is the rabbit but requirements here are very general. Housing of exotic farmed species (e.g. mink, camelids, ostriches) all raise welfare issues but these are not widespread industries within the UK context.

Poultry housing

To date, housing legislation has been most advanced within the intensive livestock industries involving pigs and poultry. Greatest concern in the poultry industry has related to the laying hen and resulted in the first of the modern UK series of species-specific housing legislation: the Welfare of Battery Hen Regulations (Great Britain Parliament, 1987). The greatest issue has been the use of the battery cage and the degree of confinement and behavioural restriction which this involves. Welfare concerns arise through the lack of space, absence of nestboxes and perches and flooring without manipulable substrate (FAWC, 1997a). Producers argue that

may increase risk of microbial proliferation in the environment (Allen and Hinton, 1993). Other conflicts may arise between animal welfare and socio-economic considerations; e.g. the cost of implementing changes in production systems which improve animal welfare might make the national industry less competitive in a global (free) market economy and hence prejudice survival of rural communities. Whilst animal welfare, like other moral issues, should not be influenced by economics, it is inevitable that it will be. Poorly designed, constructed or managed systems which, due to economic constraints, comply with the letter but not the spirit of welfare legalisation will threaten and not enhance welfare. The housing researcher and legislator therefore need to be aware of the robustness of a system to both construction and managment modification, since these will impinge on the real welfare experienced by the animals which occupy that housing.

colony based alternatives result in greater problems of aggression and cannibalism and poorer environmental control, hygiene and health.

Considering initially only the issue of space, there is still no international common standard for this. Within the EU, implementation of Directive 88/166/EEC has resulted in a figure of >450 cm^2 per bird in battery cages, although higher allowances are being sought (FAWC, 1997a). Scientists have yet to adequately resolve this issue, since attempts to determine the space requirement for acceptable welfare have failed to give consistent results. Whilst the space occupied by different behavioural activities has been measured (e.g. Dawkins and Hardie, 1989), the needs for exercise and social interaction and the way in which this is modified by group size and the possibilities for sharing of free space are still uncertain. Different behavioural and physiological approaches designed to measure the motivation to obtain increased space, or the point at which space becomes inadequate have failed to produce clear guidelines (Craig et al., 1986; Faure, 1994). Lack of exercise has been shown clearly as a causal factor in poor bone strength and increased prevalence of fractures (Fleming et al., 1994), although many studies have confounded space and housing system.

Scientific evidence indicates a number of behavioural needs which are not provided for by the commercial battery cage, including nesting, dust bathing, foraging and possibly perching. Of these, the inability to perform pre-laying behaviour has been suggested to constitute the most important welfare problem for the hen, resulting in stereotyped escape behaviour or pacing indicative of frustration (FAWC, 1997a). The need for litter is more contentious, since its elasticity of demand in operant tests seems to depend on the precise methodology of testing (Lagadic and Faure, 1987; Matthews et al., 1993). The development of enriched cages, designed to allow scope for expression of these behaviours, has been scientifically successful but, as yet has made no impact on the industry (Sherwin, 1994).

Most commonly, alternatives focus on large colony systems where most cost effective space utilization can be achieved. These include aviaries and percheries, utilizing three-dimensional space and also deep litter and strawyard systems (Commission of the European Community, 1989). Proponents of the battery cage point to the scientific evidence of equally great welfare problems in such systems, in particular the greater prevalence of cannibalism (Hughes, 1990) and poorer control of parasites in alternatives where there can be contact with droppings (Morgenstern and Lobsiger, 1993). Increases in group size are associated with increased feather pecking and cannibalism, fearfulness, hysteria and mortality but these are not simple, system-dependent problems. Feather pecking has been shown to be multifactorial in causation, being influenced by flock size, density, lighting, nutrition and flooring or substrate. It may be reduced in cage conditions by environmental enrichment with a straw basket (Norgaard-Nielsen et al., 1993) but is not necessarily absent in more enriched housing systems. Cannibalism, whilst more severe in larger flock sizes, also depends on genotype, since different strains of birds show different levels of injurious behaviour.

Reviewing the scientific contribution to this debate on housing for laying hens, FAWC (1997a) tellingly state that 'Scientific research is good at isolating specific effects stemming from particular causes but may be less effective in helping us understand the complex interrelationship between the various parameters affecting commercial production'.

Whilst currently less debated than the laying hen, welfare issues linked to housing are also significant in the broiler industry. Questions on group size, stocking density and associated environmental conditions require to be addressed and the scientific information regarding criteria for these environmental parameters which safeguard bird welfare needs to be implemented in practice (Al Homidan et al., 1998).

Pig housing
The pig industry has perhaps faced the greatest number of welfare issues in relation to housing, although it was not until the advent of the Welfare of Pigs Regulations (Great Britain Parliament, 1991) that species-specific UK legislation was first implemented. After many years of debate, the UK decided to take unilateral action within the EU and follow the lead of a number of small pig producing nations (Sweden, Norway, Switzerland, Austria) in banning the use of individual confinement systems (stalls and tethers) for pregnant sows. The scientific evidence supporting this decision included information on lameness and reduced bone strength but related primarily to the increased incidence of abnormal stereotypic behaviours seen in such systems. Subsequent research suggested a misinterpretation of such data and underestimation of the rôle of hunger, which has been shown to give rise to abnormal oral behaviour in both confined and loose-housed systems (Terlouw et al., 1991; Spoolder et al., 1995). Welfare problems associated with aggression and inequality of access to resources can be extreme in alternative group-housing systems, which require a high standard of design and management to operate beneficially for the animals (Edwards, 1992).

With the implementation of legislation on dry sows, attention shifted to the other situation in which sows are confined, the farrowing crate. Scientific evidence called upon in this debate has focused on two issues — the degree of welfare compromise for the sow and the degree of welfare benefit for the piglets. All behavioural research indicates that nestbuilding is a strongly motivated, inherent behaviour in pigs and that its prevention results in both behavioural abnormality and physiological stress (Lawrence et al., 1997). However, the extent of this stress is questionable, with only small and transient effects on blood cortisol (even less so with increased parity; Jarvis et al., 1998) and no demonstrably detrimental effects on the production of oxytocin or the process of parturition. This, together with the scientific confounding in all work to date of confinement in crates and provision of straw as a nesting substrate, does not provide strong scientific support for public concern. On the other hand, most applied scientific literature indicates beneficial effects of the farrowing crate system on piglet survival (Edwards and Fraser, 1997). Instances of successful alternatives have been reported but have generally failed to translate well into large scale practice. Scientific evidence has therefore made politicians reluctant to legislate despite high pressure from public opinion on this topic.

In the growing pig, the major legislative issues are those of space and environmental enrichment. Recommendations on lying space requirements have existed in Welfare Codes for some time but it is only recently that specific space requirements have become a legal requirement (Welfare of Livestock Regulations, 1994). Whilst there is a good scientific basis for lying space requirements based on pig allometry (Petherick, 1983), it would appear that science has contributed relatively little to the detailed formulation of the current legislation. The imposition of space allowances according to arbitrary weight bands has no scientific basis and causes great practical difficulties. Recently commissioned scientific research has demonstrated the acceptability of a more biologically based alternative (Spoolder et al., 1999) and such information has been utilized in the interpretation of current legislation (MAFF, 1997) and pressure for future amendment of such legislation. The question of suitable volumetric space and ventilation continues to be largely ignored, in spite of the direct correlation with air quality. This is addressed in the legislation as a need for 'adequate ventilation', even though science has produced clear guidance.

Perhaps the greatest debate for future legislation is the issue of environmental enrichment. Current legislation states that 'In addition to the measures normally taken to prevent tail biting and other vices and in order to enable them to satisfy their behavioural needs, all pigs, taking into account environment and stocking density, must have access to straw or other material or object suitable to satisfy those needs', but scientific definition of which are the behavioural needs in question and which other materials or objects are suitable substitutes for straw is still lacking. Whilst straw can be demonstrated to contribute in a number of ways to pig welfare (e.g. in respect of its properties of thermal insulation, physical cushioning, nutritional bulk) the importance of its rôle as a behavioural substrate providing environmental enrichment is uncertain, as is the extent to which the pig has a 'behavioural need' for exploration (Rushen, 1993). More recent cognitive models of exploration provide a better conceptual base for denoting exploration as a behavioural need (Wemelsfelder and Birke, 1997). Information gathering and processing are seen as critical to the behavioural development of the animal and its ability to subsequently deal appropriately with unexpected or novel events. However, better scientific definition of the acceptable ways to meet any such need is required before legislation can be considered.

Cattle housing

Welfare legislation for ruminants has not been as focussed or contentious as in the pig and poultry sectors. Calf housing bears the brunt of the legislation, with the Welfare of Calves Regulations (Great Britain Parliament, 1987) and the Welfare of Livestock Regulations (Great Britain Parliament, 1994) aimed primarily at issues relating to housed calves and stimulated by concerns about veal production methods. The legislation states that calves must not be kept in permanent darkness and gives minimum acceptable pen dimensions relative to calf size. These dimensions accord with results of studies of the preferred lying patterns of calves (Ketelaar-de-Lauwere and Smits, 1991) but the extent to which such lying patterns are welfare needs has not been scientifically demonstrated. Social contact may be important for the welfare of calves but comparisons of calves housed individually or in groups demonstrate conflicting benefits. Group-housed calves show a reduced frequency of abnormal behaviours and more appropriate behavioural development (Webster et al., 1985) but a greater frequency of intersucking and risk of disease (Perez et al., 1990).

The number of cattle tied by the neck in the UK continues to decline. Such animals must have tethers which allow them to lie down, rest and groom, without the risk of strangulation or injury. FAWC (1997b) recommends that tethered cattle be untied and exercised at least once a day. This creates additional labour costs, which hasten the trend towards loose housing systems. In Sweden, where smaller herd sizes make tethering more prevalent, the Swedish Animal Protection Law from January 1999 specifies a minimum requirement for tie-up standings (Gustafsson and Magnusson, 1994). This is likely to lead to higher capital investment costs, since existing units are too small to meet the requirements. Under such circumstances, a prolonged lead-in time to legislation allows the industry to adapt and spread the capital cost over an acceptable timescale.

Pollution control regulations in the 1990s led to a renewed interest in loose housing on straw, in areas where straw was affordable. However, surveys have indicated that the incidence of mastitis in straw yards for dairy cows is greater than for cubicles (Berry, 1998). Cows lie down for longer in straw yards than in cubicles and so it is possible that there are increased periods of contact with environmental pathogens. Lameness is more prevalent in cubicles but many factors are involved, including slippery passages, cubicle beds which are too small and badly designed cubicle divisions (Logue *et al.*, 1995). Much effort is now going into researching and developing comfortable cubicle beds and a wide range of products are now on the market, including rubber-filled mattresses and water beds. If there is a trend towards all year round housing of dairy cows, the facilities must be good, since there is no cow recovery period at turn-out. Housed cows can develop oral sterotypies, (Redbo, 1990) and the extent to which behavioural needs associated with grazing at pasture exist in the cow has yet to be investigated scientifically.

Slatted floors are common for beef cattle, especially in grassland areas short of straw. This form of housing can result in increased foot injury (Dumelow, 1993) and attempts have been made to make the system more animal-friendly, with rubber toppings, overlays and linked solid or bedded lying areas. Generally these have not been successful and have lead to dirty cattle. The cleanliness of cattle at slaughter is becoming a major issue and the recent State Veterinary Service Audit Report on the work of the Meat Hygiene Service (SVS, 1998) recommends tougher action to stop dirty animals going forward for slaughter. Clipping cattle at the abattoir will become more common, with the processor attempting to put the cost back to the mart or individual farmer. A conflict between animal welfare and food safety considerations will therefore become more pronounced.

Recommendations and quality assurance schemes
In aspects of housing other than the specific species issues discussed above, legislation is quite vague; for example, the need for adequate provision of food and water. However, quality assurance (QA) schemes have taken such sentiments and elaborated them into specific and measurable requirements which, because of the predominance of such schemes in certain commodity markets, are effectively as obligatory as any legislation. In all animal sectors, consumers' concerns, informed or otherwise, about the humane treatment of animals, coupled with a growing interest and awareness in food quality and safety, are major forces for change. QA schemes for livestock production systems are a powerful means of implementing housing design standards, without the rigour often necessary within the legislative process. Once again, such standards are not always based on rigorous science. One such example relates to provision of drinking facilities for pigs, where requirements based on recommendations in the UK Welfare Codes have been used, despite the complete lack of a scientifically determined basis. The only recent research on this subject suggests that such generous requirements are not necessary under typical and well managed modern circumstances (Turner and Edwards, 1999), although the degree of safety margin for commercial variation which should be built in to such specifications does require consideration. Similarly, the feeding space requirement figures used by some QA schemes would appear to rely mainly on commercial experience, since scientific information is still highly conflicting. It is vital that those producing QA documentation are fully aware of the commercial implications, as well as the scientific evidence supporting their QA requirements.

However, QA schemes and future legislation should not ignore the fact that scientifically based design criteria do exist for many components of livestock housing, including flooring surfaces and ventilation systems and air quality (e.g. British Standards Institute). Such information could give more precision to vague requirements and implementation within the industry would improve animal welfare measurably.

The current and future rôle of scientists
There is no doubt that scientists have an important rôle to play in the formulation of future welfare legislation relating to livestock housing. The contribution of scientists will be essential in a number of areas. At the fundamental level, clarification of what comprises the true behavioural needs of animals for acceptable welfare is key to all decisions, as is a reliable measure of the extent to which overall welfare is compromised in any given situation. Within the constraints imposed by such knowledge, it is then the rôle of applied scientists to

integrate such requirements within acceptable working systems which can be developed to the level of practical use. Such a process involves close interaction with all sectors of the industry. The Scandinavian/Swiss model of using scientists as independent arbiters of the acceptability of new housing systems following rigorous testing procedures (Boe *et al.*, 1997) is an attractive one but is both expensive and slow, making it difficult to implement in a rapidly innovating industry. Scientists involved in such evaluation need to be fully aware of both the fundamental issues and the realities of commercial practice. The voice of scientists is already well represented on national and supranational advisory bodies (e.g. UK Farm Animal Welfare Council, EC Scientific Veterinary Committee) and at a more practical level in the development of industry and retailer based QA schemes. They must continue to offer informed and impartial advice to facilitate the best future legislative decisions. The implications of any fundamental welfare decision, such as the banning of a production system, must be fully realized and the industry must be given time to adapt. Scientists can assist in evaluating the impact of a decision, including world market implications and the best way in which alternative systems can be evolved, within a workable capital investment timescale.

However, scientists must also be more proactive in the processes influencing future legislation. They must present their research in such a way that manufacturers designing equipment can identify welfare benefits and transmit them on to product design. Scientists can help set performance design criteria, in order that designers and manufacturers can develop products relevant to the needs of the agricultural industry. In turn, building component designers must be far more receptive to research information on animal biology and behaviour. The setting of clearly stated performance design criteria leads to improved building and equipment design. A survey of livestock equipment manufacturers indicates a consistent gap between product design and customer need (Taylor, 1997). Scientists must also communicate to those working with animals the importance of attentive management and good attention to housing, including ventilation, repair and maintenance, in relation to animal health and welfare. Ventilation is a vital area for putting science into practice.

Perhaps above all, scientists must improve their communication with the general public. Well informed consumers should be able to decide for themselves the future acceptability of livestock housing systems, based on the greatest possible amount of impartial information. If consumers make irrational decisions through lack of information, rather than balanced judgement, scientists have failed in their duty to society.

Acknowledgements

SAC receives financial support from SOAEFD.

References

Al Homidan, A., Robertson, J. F. and Petchey, A. M. 1998. Influence of temperature, litter type and stocking densities on ammonia and dust production and broiler performance. *British Poultry Science* (In press).

Allen, V. And Hinton, M. 1993. Factors affecting the survival and growth of Salmonellas in the environment of broiler chickens. *Livestock Environment IV*, pp. 124-128. American Society of Agricultural Engineers, St Joseph, Michigan.

Barber, J., Brooks, P. H. and Carpenter, J. L. 1989. The effects of water delivery rate on the voluntary food intake, water use and performance of early-weaned pigs from 3 to 6 weeks of age. In: *The voluntary food intake of pigs* (ed. J. M. Forbes, M. A. Varley and T. L. J. Lawrence), pp. 103-104. British Society of Animal Production, occasional publication no. 13.

Berry, E. A. 1998. Mastitis incidence in straw yards and cubicles. *Veterinary Record* **142:** 517-518.

Blom, J. Y., Thysen, I., Madsen, P. S. and Petersen, E. E. 1985. *Udder health in dairy cows in relation to housing system. Report 588*, pp. 103-124. National Institute of Animal Production, Copenhagen.

Boe, K. E., Simensen, E., Myren, H. J. and Fridheim, D. F. 1997. Approval of housing systems for cattle and swine according to Norwegian regulations. *Proceedings of the ISAH Conference, Helsinki.*

Bruce, J. M. and Clark, J. J. 1979. Models of heat production and critical temperature for growing pigs. *Animal Production* **28:** 353-369.

British Standards Institute. *Buildings and structures for agriculture.* BS 550 2. BSI, Milton Keynes.

Commission of the European Community. 1989. *Alternative improved housing systems for poultry.* Report EUR 117111 EN.

Craig, J. V., Craib, J. A. and Vargas, J. 1986. Corticosteroids and other indicators of hens' well-being in four laying house environments. *Poultry Science* **65:** 856-863.

Dawkins, M. S. and Hardie, S. 1989. Space needs for laying hens. *British Poultry Science* **30:** 413-416.

Dumelow, J. 1993. Unbedded self cleaning sloped floors as alternatives to fully slatted floors for beef cattle housing. *Livestock environment IV*, pp. 209-216. American Society of Agricultural Engineers, St Joseph, Michigan.

Edwards, S. A. and Riley, J. E. 1986. The application of the electronic identification and computerised feed dispensing system in dry sow housing. *Pig News and Information* **7:** 295-298.

Edwards, S. A. 1992. Scientific perspectives on loose housing systems for dry sows. *Pig Veterinary Journal* **28:** 40-51.

Edwards, S. A. 1995a. Designing systems to meet behavioural needs: the 'Family Pen' system for pigs. In: *Animal behaviour and the design of livestock and poultry systems,* pp. 115-125. Northeast Region Agricultural Engineering Service, Indianapolis.

Edwards, S. A. 1995b. The application of behaviour to the design of new or improved animal production systems. In: *Animal science research and development: moving toward a new century* (ed. M. Ivan), pp. 471-484. CFAR, Ottawa.

Edwards, S. A. and Fraser, D. 1997. Housing systems for farrowing and lactation. *The Pig Journal* **39:** 77-89.

English, P. R. and Edwards, S. A. 1999. Animal welfare. In *Diseases of swine, eighth edition* (ed. B. Straw, S. D'Allaire, W. L. Mengeling and D. J. Taylor), pp. 1067-1076. Iowa State University Press, Ames, Iowa.

Farm Animal Welfare Council. 1996. *Report on the welfare of outdoor pig*s. MAFF. PB 2608.

Farm Animal Welfare Council. 1997a. *Report on the welfare of laying hens.* MAFF. PB 3221.

Farm Animal Welfare Council. 1997b. *Report on the welfare of dairy cattle.* MAFF. PB 3221.

Faure, J. M. 1994. Choice tests for space in groups of laying hens. *Applied Animal Behaviour Science* **39:** 89-94.

Fleming, R. H., Whitehead, C. C., Alvey, D. Gregory, N. G. and Wilkin, L. J. 1994. Bone structure and breaking strength in laying hens housed in different husbandry systems. *British Poultry Science* **35:** 651-662.

Grandin, T. 1980. Livestock behaviour as related to handling facilities design. *International Journal for the study of Animal Problems* **1:** 313-337.

Great Britain Parliament. 1987. *Welfare of battery hen regulations. Statutory instrument no. 2020.* Her Majesty's Stationery Office, London.

Great Britain Parliament. 1987. *Welfare of calves regulations. Statutory instrument no. 2021.* Her Majesty's Stationery Office, London.

Great Britain Parliament. 1991. *Welfare of pigs regulations. Statutory instrument no. 1477.* Her Majesty's Stationery Office, London.

Great Britain Parliament. 1994. *Welfare of livestock regulations. Statutory instrument no. 1226.* Her Majesty's Stationery Office, London.

Gustafsson, B. and Magnusson, M. 1994. Dairy animal welfare — the case of Sweden. *Proceedings of the third international dairy housing conference,* pp. 605-612. American Society of Agricultural Engineers, St Joseph, Michigan.

Hughes, B. O. 1990. Welfare in alternative housing systems for laying hens. *Proceedings of the eighth European poultry conference,* Barcelona, pp. 199-207.

Jarvis, S., van der Vegt, B. J., Lawrence, A. B., McLean, K. A., Calvert, S. K., Deans, L. A. and Chirnside, J. 1998. The effect of parity on the behavioural and physiological responses of parturient pigs to the farrowing environment. *Proceedings of the 32nd congress of the International Society for Applied Ethology, Clermont-Ferrand* (ed. I. Vassier and A. Boissy), p. 129.

Ketelaar-de Lauwere, C. C. and Smits, A. C. 1991. Spatial requirements of individually housed veal calves of 175 to 300 kg. In *New trends in veal calf production* (ed. J. H. M. Metz and C. M. Groenstein), pp. 49-53. EAAP publication no. 52, Pudoc, Wageningen.

Lagadic, H. and Faure, J. M. 1987. Preferences of domestic hens for cage size and floor types as measured by operant conditioning. *Applied Animal Behaviour Science* **19:** 147-155.

Lawrence, A. B., McLean, K. A., Jarvis, S. and Gilbert, C. L. 1997. Stress and parturition in the pig. *Reproduction in Domestic Animals* **32:** 231-236.

Logue, D. N., Offer, J. E., Chaplin, S. J., Knight, C. H., Hendry, K. A. K., Leach, K. A., Kempson, S. A. and Randall, J. M. 1995. Lameness in dairy cattle. *Proceedings of the 46th Annual Meeting EAAP, Prague.* Paper C4.4.

Mason, G. and Mendl, M. 1993. Why is there no simple way of measuring animal welfare? *Animal Welfare* **2:** 301-319.

Matthews, L. R., Temple, W., Foster, T. M. and McAdie, T. M. 1993. Quantifying the environmental requirements of layer hens by behavioural demand function. *Proceedings of an international conference of the International Society for Applied Ethology, Berlin.* pp. 206-209.

Metz, J. H. M. 1983. Food competition in cattle. In *Farm animal housing and welfare* (ed. S. H. Baxter, M. R. Baxter and J. A. MacCormack), pp. 164-170. Martinus Nijhoff, The Hague.

Ministry of Agriculture, Fisheries and Food. 1997. *Pig space requirements. Guidelines on Schedule 3 of the Welfare of Livestock Regulations 1994.* MAFF. PB 3225.

Morgernstern, R. and Lobsiger, C. 1993. Health of laying hens in alternative systems in practice. *Proceedings of the fourth European symposium on poultry welfare.* (ed. C. J. Savory and B. O. Hughes), pp. 81-86. UFAW, Potters Bar.

Norgaard-Nielsen, G., Vestergaard, K. and Simonsen, H. B. 1993. Effects of rearing experiences and stimulus enrichment on feather damage in laying hens. *Applied Animal Behaviour Science* **38:** 345-352.

Perez, E., Noordhuizen, J. P. T. M., van Wuijkhuise, L. A. and Stassen, E. N. 1990. Management factors related to calf mortality and mortality rates. *Livestock Production Science* **25:** 79-93.

Petherick, J. C. 1983. A biological basis for the design of space in livestock housing. In *Farm animal housing and welfare* (ed. S. H. Baxter, M. R. Baxter and J. A. MacCormack), pp. 103-120. Martinus Nijhoff, The Hague.

Redbo, I. 1990. Changes in duration and frequency of stereotypies and their adjoining behaviours in heifers, before, during and after the grazing period. *Applied Animal Behaviour Science* **26:** 57-67.

Robertson, J. F. 1994. Ventilation capacity of naturally ventilated buildings and ventilation requirements of beef cattle: problems associated with calf pneumonia. *Proceedings of an international winter meeting of the American Society of Agricultural Engineers, Atlanta.* Paper 944588.

Robertson, J. 1998. Environment/disease interactions in pigs. In *Progress in pig science* (ed. J. Wiseman, M. A. Varley and J. P. Chadwick), pp. 543-560. Nottingham University Press, Nottingham.

Rushen, J. 1993. Exploration in the pig may not be endogenously motivated. *Animal Behaviour* **45:** 183-184.

Sherwin, C. M. 1994. *Modified cages for laying hens.* UFAW, Potters Bar.

Spoolder, H. A. M., Burbidge, J. A., Lawrence, A. B., Simmins, P. H. and Edwards, S. A. 1995. Provision of straw as a foraging substrate reduces the development of excessive chain and bar manipulation in food restricted sows. *Applied Animal Behaviour Science* **43:** 249-262

Spoolder, H. A. M., Corning, S. and Edwards, S. A. 1999. The specification of stocking density in relation to the welfare of finishing pigs. In *Farm animal welfare — who writes the rules?* (ed. A. J. F. Russel, C. A. Morgan, C. J. Savory, M. C. Appleby and T. L. J. Lawrence), pp. 150-151. British Society of Animal Science, occasional publication no. 23.

State Veterinary Service. 1998. *Audit report of the Meat Hygiene Service, June 1996 to March 1997*. Veterinary Public Health Unit.

Stolba, A. and Wood-Gush, D. G. M. 1984. The identification of behavioural key features and their incorporation into a housing design for pigs. *Annales de Recherches Vétérinaire* **15:** 287-298.

Taylor, I. A. 1997. Opportunity awaits livestock equipment manufacturers. *Livestock environment V*. American Society of Agricultural Engineers, St. Josephs, Michigan.

Terlouw, E. M. C., Lawrence, A. B. and Illius, A. W. 1991. Influences of feeding level and physical restriction on development of stereotypies in sows. *Animal Behaviour* **42:** 981-991.

Turner, S. P and Edwards, S. A. 1999. Methods of assessing adequacy of drinker provision in group housed pigs. In *Farm animal welfare — who writes the rules?* (ed. A. J. F. Russel, C. A. Morgan, C. J. Savory, M. C. Appleby and T. L. J. Lawrence), pp. 152-154. British Society of Animal Science, occasional publication no. 23.

Vipond, J. and Hosie, B. D. 1997. Welfare aspects of sheep production systems. *Proceedings of the 48th annual meeting EAAP, Prague.*

Webb, N. and Nilsson, C. 1983. Flooring and injury — an overview. In *Farm animal housing and welfare* (ed. S. H. Baxter, M. R. Baxter and J. A. MacCormack), pp. 226-281. Martinus Nijhoff, The Hague.

Webster, A. J. F., Saville, C., Church, B. M., Gnanasakthy, A. and Moss, R. 1985. The effect of different rearing systems on the development of calf behaviour. *British Veterinary Journal* **141:** 249-264.

Wemelsfelder, F. and Birke, L. I. A. 1997. Environmental challenge. In *Animal welfare* (ed. M. A. Appleby and B. O. Hughes), pp. 35-47. CAB International, Wallingford.

Zayan, R. 1985. *Social space for domestic animals*. Martinus Nijhoff, Dordrecht.

Farm animal welfare — who writes the rules?
Occasional Publication No. 23 — British Society of Animal Science 1999
edited by A. J. F. Russel, C. A. Morgan, C. J. Savory, M. C. Appleby and T. L. J. Lawrence

Information and technology transfer in farm animal welfare

P. J. Goddard

Macaulay Land Use Research Institute, Craigiebuckler, Aberdeen AB15 8QH

Abstract

Considerable information is available on which to base practical recommendations for enhanced animal welfare. There is evidence of a reasonable flow of information between researchers, farmers, producers' organizations, legislators and the public, although more readily assimilated forms of information are required. New approaches to welfare assessment may allow the public to evaluate production systems in a more balanced way. As the urbanization of society increases, the rôle of education becomes more important to provide information about the reality of on-farm practices. Increasing use will be made of information technology to implement technological advances. Using interactive methods of on-farm assessment of welfare and decision support tools, it would seem possible to engage the producer to a greater extent in the process of improving standards. Measures of public willingness to pay for enhanced welfare provide valuable information about the utility value of animal welfare, influence the views of politicians and producers and ultimately determine production systems.

Introduction

This paper will consider the methods currently used to produce information, explore the uses to which this information is put and determine whether there are real advances to be made in the transfer of technology in relation to animal welfare. There is a considerable amount of information available which has a bearing on the welfare of animals in production systems (e.g. transport conditions for sheep: Cockram *et al.*, 1996 and 1997; Knowles *et al.*, 1995 and 1996). However, it is not always easy to identify the ways in which such information and the technology related to animal welfare are shared between the most important interested parties: researchers, farmers, producers' organizations, legislators and the public. In addition, it is not always immediately clear how information, i.e. the knowledge about an issue which empowers the

recipient, becomes translated into technological changes, which enable tasks to be performed differently, although the two are often closely linked. Neither is it clear whether there are widespread or significant advances to be made through the transfer of technology in relation to animal welfare.

What classes of information are available

Findings from research
The classes of information which exist and which are accessible and how this is exchanged between interested parties, are illustrated in Figure 1. It is often thought that the majority of factual information is provided by research scientists, as scientific papers and reports. Behavioural and physiological studies, undertaken according to the best contemporary scientific methods, provide a potential identification of problem areas, e.g. sheep provided with hay and water on a vehicle during a 3-h stationary period may become dehydrated (Cockram *et al.*, 1997), exposure of red deer to unfamiliar species may prove aversive (Abeyesinghe and Goddard, 1998). Such studies can be used to assess the relative effects of system changes, e.g. certain head restraints in a cattle slaughter crate may cause distress (Ewbank *et al.*, 1992). However, they may not always provide a great insight into the motivational or subjective state of the animal, aspects which are assuming greater importance from a theoretical viewpoint (Dawkins, 1990; Duncan and Petherick, 1991; Duncan, 1993). While scientific papers can be accessed by the general public, their impact is chiefly upon other scientists and legislators. Nor is there a widespread dissemination of this information: reports and popular summaries arising from this work (e.g. Hanlon, 1997) are not always available, yet this style of information would be more readily accessible and understood by both public and producers.

Product information and quality assurance schemes
Information generated by farmers and cooperative producers' organizations is generally in the form of product labelling and advertising, with the desire to alert the purchasing public to the producer's

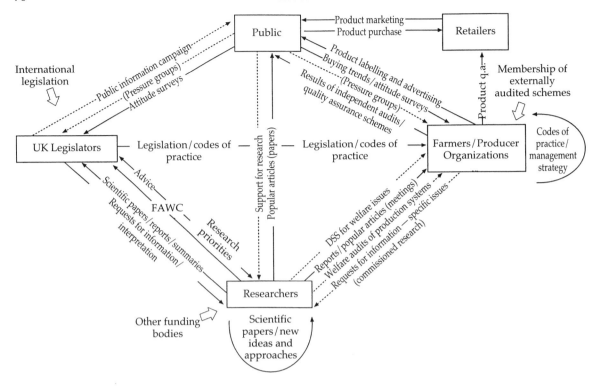

Figure 1 Animal welfare information.

adherence to relevant quality assurance schemes. These schemes attract additional credibility if there is a clear demonstration of independent audit and a high integrity of quality control. For example, those who participate in the RSPCA 'Freedom Food' scheme clearly see an advantage in addressing welfare issues. Similarly, retailers seek to enhance product description as a form of marketing. Perhaps farmers and producer's organizations should consider better ways to bridge the increasing gap in understanding of contemporary farm practices as the population becomes more urbanized. Paxman (1986) recognized that advertising has a potent effect and that retailers may tend to suppress product information if labelling one product with a positive attribute (e.g. free range) draws attention to alternative products which have a different status.

Consumer surveys/public opinion
A limited, although increasing, amount of information is available from published consumer surveys on attitudes towards animal welfare issues and major retailers deduce similar information from customers' purchasing practice. Clearly farmers and producers' organizations require to know about buying trends and the attitudes of the public towards

products. In addition, pressure groups may seek to exert an influence at various levels, including the point of production. Knowledge about public opinion is clearly important to legislators and government departments and information from attitude surveys, focus groups and individual contacts plays an increasing part in the way national governments build up a view of the public mood for animal welfare legislation and standards.

Legislation
Legislators, influenced by both national and international pressures, generate legislation and codes of recommendations which are targeted at producers and distributors. Legislators seek to embody contemporary public opinion and may draw from the type of surveys noted above, which assess public willingness-to-pay (WTP) for animal welfare. The level of WTP may allow policy makers to gauge the strength of feeling in a quantitative way but, as Paxman (1986) pointed out, factors which influence consumer buying trends, of which welfare concerns are but one, are exceptionally complex and numerous. In the United Kingdom (UK), primary legislation (e.g. statutory instruments) and codes of practice are used to provide for underpinning

minimum standards to be attained by producers, hauliers, abattoirs etc. It is, of course, important that proposed changes will improve animal welfare; this may only be determined from an animal-centred perspective and not simply from an anthropomorphic viewpoint. It is also essential that practical responses accompany or precede legislative changes (Ewbank *et al.*, 1992). Producers' organizations may provide some form of 'interpretation' for their members and may generate their own codes to be followed. Bennett (1996) and Bennett and Larson (1996) assessed the utilitarian concept of public WTP for welfare legislation: the value is related to the utility individuals derive from satisfying their wants. Dichotomous choice methods can be used which involve asking people whether they would be willing to pay a specified amount to support such legislation and then asking if they would be prepared to pay a higher specified amount if the answer was 'yes' or a lower amount if 'no'. A survey by Bennett (1998) focused on one particular production system, egg production and indicated a high level of public WTP for eggs not produced in a battery system. This method of analysis (contingent valuation) is useful when evaluating issues such as welfare which have no direct market price but for which respondents may ascribe a nominal monetary value. Responding in a way which is perceived to be socially desirable may be a problem in these types of survey but more importantly there is a lack of precise information not only about specific production systems (e.g. battery cages) but also about the alternatives. This lack of awareness may prove to be a limiting factor in the usefulness of such surveys. However, these types of survey are valuable ways for providing information about public opinion. Most studies which consider welfare from an economic perspective, have concentrated on systems such as veal production using crates, or egg production using battery cages and the ability to address other issues remains to be determined.

How does the information flow?

The key loci in the generation and receipt of information are researcher scientists, legislators, the public, farmers and producers' organization (Figure 1). Retailers also have an important rôle to play, together with a number of allied groups, e.g. hauliers, market and abattoir stockmen etc. It is important to consider how each of these groups participates in information flow.

Researcher scientists

From a research scientist's perspective, the use to which information is put is an important (but possibly inadequately considered) issue as requests for the popularization of research results increase. The majority of information probably circulates within the research community. Not only in animal welfare but also in other rapidly advancing areas such as genetic engineering (European Biomedical Research Association, 1997), there is a need systematically to bridge the information gap and stimulate a dialogue between research, industry and the public. That information which does escape from the research environment often reaches the public by way of popular reports or summaries (e.g. Hanlon, 1997). This is also the way much of the information reaches the 'user' community. When welfare audits of particular production systems have been conducted there is clearly intense dialogue between the parties. Similarly, when there has been specifically commissioned research, there is appropriate feedback.

It is likely that the use of decision support systems (DSS) will increase the scope for researchers to become involved in practical welfare audits of specific production systems, extending into on-farm welfare assessment (e.g. Bracke *et al.*, 1997).

Researchers also provide information to those responsible for legislation. Groups, such as the UK Farm Animal Welfare Council (FAWC), keep under review the welfare of farm animals and advise agriculture ministers of any legislative changes that may be necessary. FAWC can consider any topic falling within its remit and seek advice from leading experts in research and development (e.g. FAWC, 1993). Legislators, like producers, may make requests of researchers for specific information.

Farmer and producer organizations

In addition to receiving digests of recent research, producers may receive information from those responsible for a range of quality assurance schemes, many of which have a specific 'welfare' component. These schemes may be developed internally, although an additional degree of scrutiny can be introduced through external audit (e.g. the Freedom Food scheme). This quality assurance information is of value to the public directly and via retailers, through product marketing and advertising.

The public

There is considerable feedback to producers on public buying trends. Large retailers and farmer organizations are increasingly influenced by the results of consumer surveys. Similarly, this information affects legislators and generates pressure to act when market forces are deemed to be ineffective. Public pressure groups seek to influence primarily producers and legislators and the public have an influence on the direction of research, particularly that commissioned by government departments.

Legislators

Primary legislation and codes of practice and recommendations are drawn up to ensure minimum standards are adopted by producers, in response to a demand by society at large (see Ekesbo (1998) for a European perspective). Legislators in the UK can seek advice from the FAWC, which may advise on research priorities. This may result in the commissioning of research. Government departments are also responsible for informing the public at large and for responding to the need to translate relevant internationally binding legislation into appropriate practices within the UK.

What mechanisms are there to ensure that technological advances have a wide impact?

Figure 2 maps the flow of technological information. While the ultimate safeguards for minimum standards are usually embodied in legislation and codes of practice and recommendations, many producers, hauliers and markets aspire to higher standards for which, in some cases, a premium price is asked. To increase the skill of producers, hauliers,

slaughtermen and numerous others, advisory and other bodies have played a key rôle. For example, the Humane Slaughter Association has played an important part in improving slaughterhouse practice, in addition to the requirements for the licensing of slaughtermen, embodied in recent UK legislation. Similarly, improvements in the standard of transporting of animals will be achieved through appropriate accreditation of those responsible, following an assessment of their practical expertise in handling, transport and general care of animals (Ministry of Agriculture, Fisheries and Food (MAFF), 1998). Guidelines from organizations offering external standards and quality control for animal welfare are often of a practical nature and may incorporate information generated from a research environment. The decline of demonstration farms as a mechanism for demonstrating practical systems has reduced the impact of advances in management techniques. However, the potential for DSS to be applied to animal welfare audits in the future is an exciting possibility and may be one way to bridge the technology transfer gap from scientists to producers.

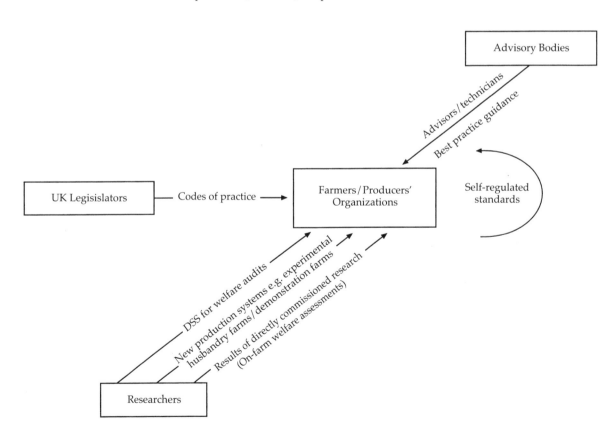

Figure 2 Animal welfare technology transfer.

Does technology transfer occur?

Technology transfer is a complex process and there are likely to be many interrelated factors which are involved. To increase the rate of uptake, incentive schemes run by producers' groups or cooperatives are valuable ways to ensure that members adhere to pre-set standards (e.g. Farm Assured Scots Livestock run by the Scottish Quality Beef and Lamb Association; the British Deer Farmers Association's Quality Assurance Scheme). Using modern marketing techniques, farmers whose products possess desirable attributes can increase market impact. Product quality is tending to become more important than quantity as the population become more affluent. These qualities include 'green' or organic attributes and, of relevance to the present debate, animal welfare attributes. For example, in the county of Vorarlberg in Austria, an animal welfare index has been developed to help implementation of legally binding standards and to provide subsidies for improved husbandry systems aimed at the production of local, quality animal products (Schmid, 1998). Ritson (1997) suggested that there were three (sequential) reasons why farmers were likely to adopt more welfare-friendly policies: because products from these systems attracted a higher price; because, if they did not, then they would be penalized (through lack of sales); and because they believe in the system. Thus there is movement from a market meeting consumer demand for a uniformly cheap commodity, to one where there is producer-driven concern about production techniques, where product differentiation occurs at source, although it may be led by the retailer (Ritson, 1997).

Jones (1995) asked the question 'why is technology transfer so hard?' It is clear that in some fields, such as computing and information technology, technology transfer is thought to occur readily but even in these fields technology evaluation and transfer are generally not very rapid processes. In the biological sphere, transfer occurs less readily, although in fields such as clinical medicine and some other areas of health care, there is increasing use of expert information systems. Even when a research paper clearly demonstrates that beneficial changes in practice could be made, it is still not clear how this is to be achieved. Consider, for example, the study of Hunter et al. (1997) who conducted a postal survey of producers in relation to pig management and ease of subsequent handling at the abattoir. The survey linked rearing, finishing and loading environments with subsequent ease of handling, which itself could affect pig welfare prior to slaughter. During rearing and finishing, access to a less varied environment (in terms of natural light and straw in rearing phases and walking shorter distances between the later finishing phases) resulted in a reduction in the subsequent ease of handling. But what is the best way to cause a change in practice and how do we detect any possible cost-benefit of doing so? Since the study in question was funded by the Humane Slaughter Association, the findings are likely to be incorporated into their publications for the industry but in other cases even this indirect link may not occur.

To achieve successful uptake of scientific advances, Betz (1994) noted the use of incentives and suggested that inclusion of industry partners when planning research was likely to facilitate subsequent transfer of advances. Since support for research depends increasingly on the relevance of the research to society's needs and public benefit, government officials recognize the need for a market focus in technology commercialization. Technology will be more readily taken up if the impetus for its development comes from not just the developers of innovative new technology but also from the commercial sector (Piper and Naghshpour, 1996) and bodies such as the Humane Slaughter Association which can publicize relevant findings. For example, work on the commercial transport and handling of pigs has indicated ways to reduce mortality and derive other direct and indirect welfare benefits related to *ante-mortem* stress (Guise and Penny, 1989; Guise, 1991; Hunter et al., 1994).

Technology transfer can often occur through education, e.g. extension courses or postgraduate training for professionals, together with specific training courses and certification for technicians (e.g. as we see for those wishing to use organophosphate sheep dips (National Proficiency Tests Council, 1994), training for slaughtermen (MAFF, 1995) or for those who transport animals on long journeys (MAFF, 1998)). It is widely recognized that ensuring freedom from disease is a key way to improve animal welfare. Over the first 25 years of its existence, more than 1100 students from 108 countries have attended courses run by the Centre for Tropical Veterinary Medicine in Edinburgh and thus the CTVM acts as a conduit for recent research findings (Scott and Smith, 1996). Indeed, in many countries the veterinary profession has been responsible for providing leadership in issues relating to welfare and the veterinary profession has often taken on the rôle of preparing various codes and regulations regarding animal welfare. Thus veterinarians have 'interpreted' both the available scientific information and the public mood in order to provide clear guidance. In this context, the World Veterinary Association recognizes its responsibility in promoting (amongst other things) animal welfare and the consequent need to have appropriate training for veterinarians.

Use of DSS may enhance technology transfer in the future. These systems are being developed to assist a number of on-farm processes (e.g. Bouche *et al.*, 1997) and could be designed to incorporate a welfare element. Similarly, aspects of the complex regulation of animals in extensive environments (e.g. 'HillDeer'; Milne, 1997) which has implications for animal welfare, are made more accessible by DSS technology. Such programmes have the additional potential to address environmental issues. Bracke *et al.* (1997) have developed a computerized DSS for welfare assessment. This tries to make explicit the scientific basis for the quantification process of components of farming systems (e.g. housing). It also uses an approach which recognizes the subjective nature of animal welfare — the conscious experiences animals have, which often translate into needs. On-farm assessment of animal welfare can be used as a tool for improving management and raising standards by identifying management weaknesses (Sandøe *et al.*, 1997). Improvements can be demonstrated on a year-by-year basis through changes in appropriate indicators e.g. fearfulness of animals towards humans. By using such approaches the relevance of welfare assessment to the producer at least may be increased and he/she may feel more directly in control of welfare-related improvements in management. Such systems, which are recognized to be in the early stages of development, may also find considerable public acceptance.

Current issues
Method development
Alternative ways of generating and presenting welfare-related information may allow for better understanding by farmers and the public. The use of cost-benefit dominance analysis has been proposed as one way of uniting a range of indices of welfare to provide an overall systematic assessment through qualitative rather than quantitative comparisons of a range of factors (e.g. simply asking is 'a' better than 'b'?). Using this method it is not necessary to know about which levels of welfare-relevant factors are preferable to others (Taylor *et al.*, 1995). It is an approach which allows decision-makers to effectively compare individual management systems in a practical way using a range of welfare-relevant factors. It is also likely that enhanced methods to assess the public willingness to pay for high welfare status goods will be developed. It is important to recognize that non-consumers of animal products have an interest in the adoption of appropriate welfare standards as part of the net benefit to society.

How can information and technology transfer be enhanced?
It is not clear which are the best ways to deliver animal welfare information to the various user groups, in particular to those whose daily activities impact directly on the welfare of animals. It is important to define the best way to present information since it is not known whether public meetings, mailshots or computer software approaches are most effective for the different user groups (or different classes of individual within the groups). Similarly, it is not known whether legislative or demand-led approaches result in better uptakes of new techniques by those responsible for animal care, although the latter may produce more rapid results.

From a welfare perspective, the proliferation of individual quality assurance schemes tends to fragment any message in the consumer's mind and consumers may find it more helpful to be presented with a small number of generic schemes or assessments. To capitalize on this 'demand side' approach, clear and distinctive labelling to associate products with an understandable production system are necessary. It may help to have an independently awarded welfare 'score' on each product. Given our present level of understanding, the time may not yet be right for making such an assessment in a widespread way, yet the animal welfare index proposed by Schmid (1998) is one example of how this may be done.

Another important issue is the selection and training of stockmen. It is clear that there are opportunities to train stockmen, particularly in the light of an increasing knowledge of human-animal interactions, to ensure high standards of animal welfare (Hemsworth *et al.*, 1994a). While most work has been conducted in relation to pig husbandry, there may be similar opportunities in relation to other species (e.g. poultry: Hemsworth *et al.*, 1994b; dairy cows: Hemsworth *et al.*, 1995; cattle: Boivin *et al.*, 1998). There may also be scope for improving selection procedures for stockmen in the light of likely human-animal interactions.

Further important and more wide-reaching educational opportunities exist. Better education of school children about animal welfare, possibly sponsored by government departments, would enable them to assimilate information about welfare that they subsequently receive, particularly as the urbanization of society increases. In a move, presumably aimed at boosting consumer confidence and understanding, the European Commission has created a new scientific committee to provide expert advice to DG XXIV on animal health and welfare, with a sub-committee covering each topic. At the Council of Europe Committees, the International Society for Applied Ethology (ISAE) provides summaries of relevant scientific information and sometimes suggests the text for recommendations.

Conclusions

The increasing amount of information available, which has a bearing on the welfare of animals in production systems, needs to be made more easily accessible by the general public. The desire of the public for enhanced standards can be measured by variety of techniques and both legislation and consumer choice are used to satisfy this demand. New methods of on-farm assessment of welfare need to be further developed to make them more relevant and to encourage elements of best practice to be more widely and more rapidly adopted. The current inability to relate the welfare attributes of different production systems in a systematic way needs to be overcome through advances in understanding and methodology. The practical impact of training and advisory bodies, which seek to ensure widespread adoption of high standards, is more likely to be successful if producers become more involved in the initiation and development of new welfare-friendly production methods.

References

Abeyesinghe, S. M. and Goddard, P. J. 1998. The preferences and behaviour of farmed red deer (*Cervus elaphus*) in the presence of other farmed species. *Applied Animal Behaviour Science,* **56:** 59-69.

Bennett, R. M. 1996. People's willingness to pay for farm animal welfare. *Animal Welfare,* **5:** 3-11.

Bennett, R. M. 1998. Measuring public support for animal welfare legislation: a case study of cage egg production. *Animal Welfare* **7:** 1-10.

Bennett, R. and Larson, D. 1996. Contingent valuation of the perceived benefit of farm animal welfare: an exploratory survey. *Journal of Agricultural Economics* **47:** 224-235.

Betz, F. 1994. Basic research and technology transfer. *International Journal of Technology Management* **9:** 784-796.

Boivin, X., Boissy, A., Chupin, J. M. and Le Neindre, P. 1998. Herbivores, caretakers and range management. In: *Animal health and welfare in extensive system* (ed. P. J. Goddard), *proceedings of an EU workshop, Aberdeen.*

Bouche, R., Choisis, J. P., Casabianca, F. and Dubeuf, B. 1997. Designing negotiation aids for milk quality in the Corsican dairy sheep sector. In: *Livestock farming systems — more than food production* (ed. J. T. Sørensen), *proceedings of the fourth international symposium on livestock farming systems, Foulum, Denmark,* pp. 183-189.

Bracke, M. B. M., Metz, J. H. M. and Udink ten Cate, A. J. 1997. Assessment of animal welfare in husbandry systems. In: *Livestock farming systems — more than food production* (ed. J. T. Sørensen), *proceedings of the fourth international symposium on livestock farming systems, Foulum, Denmark,* pp. 231-237.

Cockram, M. S., Kent, J. E., Goddard, P. J., Waran, N. K., McGilp, I. M., Jackson, R. E., Muwanga, G. M. and Prytherch, S. 1996. Effect of space allowance during transport on the behavioural and physiological responses of lambs during and after transport. *Animal Science* **62:** 461-477.

Cockram, M. S., Kent, J. E., Jackson, R. E., Goddard, P. J., Doherty, O. M., McGilp, I. M., Fox, A., Studdert-Kennedy, T. C., McConnell, T. I. and O'Riordan, T. 1997. Effect of lairage during 24 h of transport on the behavioural and physiological responses of sheep. *Animal Science* **65:** 391-402.

Dawkins, M. S. 1990. From an animal's point of view: motivation, fitness and animal welfare. *Behavioural and Brain Sciences* **13:** 1-19.

Duncan, I. J. H. 1993. Welfare is to do with what animals feel. *Journal of Agricultural and Environmental Ethics* Special Supplement **2:** 8-14.

Duncan, I. J. H. and Petherick, J. C. 1991. The implications of cognitive processes for animal welfare. *Journal of Animal Science* **69:** 5017-5022.

Ekesbo, I. 1998. European animal welfare legislation and codes of practice. In: *Animal health and welfare in extensive system* (ed. P. J. Goddard), *proceedings of an EU workshop, Aberdeen.*

European Biomedical Research Association. 1997. The ethics of the genetic manipulation of animals. *EBRA Bulletin,* February 1997, p. 7.

Ewbank, R., Parker, M. J. and Mason, C. W. 1992. Reactions of cattle to head-restraint at stunning: a practical dilemma. *Animal Welfare* **1:** 55-63.

Farm Animal Welfare Council. 1993. *Report on the priorities for animal welfare research and development.* Ministry of Agriculture, Fisheries and Food, London.

Guise, J. 1991. Humane animal management — the benefits of improved systems for pig production, transport and slaughter. In: *Farm animals: it pays to be humane* (ed. S. P. Carruthers), *C.A.S. paper no. 22,* pp. 50-58. Centre for Agricultural Strategy, Reading.

Guise, H. J. and Penny, R. H. C. 1989. Factors influencing the welfare and carcass and meat quality of pigs. 1. The effects of stocking density in transport and the use of electric goads. *Animal Production* **49:** 511-515.

Hanlon, A. J. 1997. The welfare of farmed red deer. I. Recent research. *Deer Farming* **53:** 14-16.

Hemsworth, P. H., Breuer, K., Barnett, J. L., Coleman, G. J. and Matthews, L. R. 1995. Behavioural response to humans and the productivity of commercial dairy cows. *Proceedings of the 29th international congress of the ISAE, Exeter, UK,* pp. 175-176.

Hemsworth, P. H., Coleman, G. J. and Barnett, J. L. 1994a. Improving the attitude and behaviour of stockpersons towards pigs and the consequences on the behaviour and reproductive performance of commercial pigs. *Applied Animal Behaviour Science* **39:** 349-362.

Hemsworth, P. H., Coleman, G. J. , Barnett, J. L. and Jones, R. B. 1994b. Behavioural responses to humans and the productivity of commercial broiler chickens. *Applied Animal Behaviour Science* **41:** 101-114.

Hunter, E. J., Riches, H. L., Guise, H. J. and Penny, R. H. C. 1997. The behaviour of pigs in lairage in relation to their post-weaning management: results of a postal survey. *Animal Welfare* **6:** 139-144.

Hunter, E. J., Weeding, C. M., Guise, H. J., Abbott, T. A. and Penny, R. H. C. 1994. Pig welfare and carcase quality: a comparison of the influence of slaughter handling systems at two abattoirs. *Veterinary Record* **135:** 423-425.

Jones, C. 1995. Why is technology transfer so hard? *Computer, June 1995,* pp. 86-87.

Knowles, T. G., Brown, S. N., Warriss, P. D., Phillips, A. J., Dolan, S. K., Hunt, P., Ford, J. E., Edwards, J. E. and Watkins, P. E. 1995. Effects on sheep of transport by road for up to 24 hours. *Veterinary Record* **136:** 431-438.

Knowles, T. G., Warriss, P. D., Brown, S. N., Kestin, S. C., Edwards, J. E., Perry, A. M., Watkins, P. E. and Phillips, A. J. 1996. Effect of feeding, watering and resting intervals on lambs transported by road and ferry to France. *Veterinary Record* **139:** 335-339.

Milne, J. A. 1997. Decision support systems to aid management of the vegetation of the uplands of Scotland. *Scottish Forestry* **51:** 108-109.

Ministry of Agriculture, Fisheries and Food. 1995. *The welfare of animals (slaughter or killing) regulations 1995.* MAFF, London.

Ministry of Agriculture, Fisheries and Food. 1998. *Assessment of practical experience in the handling, transport and care of animals.* MAFF, London.

National Proficiency Tests Council. 1994. *Certificate of competence in the safe use of sheep dips.* National Proficiency Tests Council, Kenilworth, UK.

Paxman, P. J. 1986. Consumer reaction to cost and health consequences of free range systems for veal and poultry production. *Proceedings of the Society of Veterinary Epidemiology and Preventive Medicine,* pp. 116-121.

Piper, W. S. and Naghshpour, S. 1996. Government technology-transfer — the effective use of push and pull marketing strategies. *International Journal of Technology Management* **12:** 85-94.

Ritson, C. 1997. Marketing, agriculture and economics: presidential address. *Journal of Agricultural Economics* **48:** 279-299.

Sandøe, P., Munksgaard, L., Bådsgård, N. P. and Jensen, K. H. 1997. How to manage the management factor — assessing animal welfare at the farm level. In: *Livestock farming systems — more than food production* (ed. J. T. Sørensen), *proceedings of the fourth international symposium on livestock farming systems, Foulum, Denmark,* pp. 221-230.

Schmid, E. 1998. Minimum care for maximum welfare. In: *Animal health and welfare in extensive system.* (ed. P. J. Goddard), *proceedings of an EU workshop, Aberdeen.*

Scott, G. R. and Smith, A. J. 1996. Technology-transfer in tropical animal health and production. The Centre for Tropical Veterinary Medicine (CTVM). *Tropical Animal Health and Production* **28:** 60-67.

Taylor, A. A., Hurnik, J. F. and Lehman, H. 1995. The application of cost-benefit dominance analysis to the assessment of farm animal quality of life. *Social Indicators Research* **35:** 313-329.

Farm animal welfare — who writes the rules?
Occasional Publication No. 23 — British Society of Animal Science 1999
edited by A. J. F. Russel, C. A. Morgan, C. J. Savory, M. C. Appleby and T. L. J. Lawrence

Development of acceptable standards

W. J. M. Black

Institute of Ecology and Resource Management, King's Buildings, West Mains Road, Edinburgh EH9 3JG

Abstract

UK welfare standards have evolved and are continuing to develop, as our knowledge increases and with the greater interest of a larger proportion of the general public. The government issues official 'codes of practice' on animal welfare, one for each of the major categories of farm livestock, addressed personally to every registered farmer in the country. UK legislation is continually updated, so that those with responsibility for keeping livestock have a basic set of rules which are relatively specific and which are enforced by random inspection, usually by the State Veterinary Service. The Farm Animal Welfare Council (FAWC) is responsible to the Minister and, with an element of independence, is asked to assist with the development of animal welfare standards in the UK FAWC is made up of 23 independent members, with a wide variety of skills, knowledge and experience, who, usually in working groups of about six people (with MAFF advisers and secretariat support), are commissioned to investigate and report on particular areas where farm animal welfare standards require attention or revision. The way in which FAWC operates is described using, as examples, recent reports on sheep and laying hens, to demonstrate how the government makes use of FAWC reports in revising codes of practice and legislation. Reference is also made to the way in which quality assurance schemes are being developed. These add a further dimension to the 'rules' which affect UK farm animal welfare standards.

Introduction

I was a member of the Farm Animal Welfare Council (FAWC) for almost 10 years, up to the end of 1997, closely involved in its working groups on laying hens, research and development and with a particular involvement in the sheep group as chairman.

I have therefore obtained a working knowledge of how FAWC works in practice and as a recently retired member I can perhaps express my views on FAWC in a relatively uninhibited way. The usual disclaimer applies: any opinions expressed are solely mine and must not be assumed to be those of the Council.

FAWC constitution and personnel

FAWC is an independent and authoritative body, reporting direct to the Minister of Agriculture and to the Secretaries of State for Wales and Scotland. It has a wide range of individuals as members of the 23 strong Council which is made up of people from quite different backgrounds. I believe that this is an important element in the FAWC constitution, where there is a cross-section of interests ranging from people with a practical knowledge of commercial animal industries, through those with an interest in the ethics of animal welfare and people concerned with consumer affairs, to a selection of academics with a range of specialisms.

It is important to be clear that all members are individually appointed and are not attending as representatives of any organization. When matters requiring a debate occur, every member can make their individual contribution without the need to be constrained by any 'party' line.

The full Council of FAWC meets three times per year to discuss matters of important general principle and to evaluate and eventually approve reports on particular topics prepared by the working groups.

These groups are normally set up by the FAWC to address particular topical issues, and are 'short-life', involving members of Council (usually five or six people) together with an expert adviser and a representative from the State Veterinary Service (SVS). I have personally been involved with six of these groups and have acted as chairman of two: Welfare of Hens in Colony Systems (1991) and Welfare of Sheep (1994). It is proposed to make use of experiences with developing FAWC documents relating to laying hens and sheep, which will perhaps illustrate how eventually FAWC contributes to the development of standards.

FAWC reports

FAWC has a clear remit to produce detailed reports, to be sent, first, direct to Ministers, and then made use of by the Ministry of Agriculture, Fisheries and Food (MAFF) and secondly, published widely and thus made available to everyone. The MAFF Animal Welfare Division has a representative attached to FAWC meetings and therefore had an early involvement in the production of detailed reports. In the past, FAWC has not been involved directly in the production of official MAFF codes of practice, or indeed in any changes to legislation, but it is, however, clear that MAFF has relied upon FAWC reports, suitably amended and modified by further wide consultations.

MAFF has the ultimate responsibility for the 'rules' and takes a great deal of care to send out drafts very widely, aiming to ensure that what is proposed is considered by most organizations to be both soundly based and enforceable in practice. Recently the FAWC secretariat has been involved in more detailed development of codes of practice, and indeed a new Code for Sheep is soon to be published in which they have had an increased involvement.

In this way, the effects of FAWC working group reports, approved by FAWC and then considered in detail by MAFF, extend direct to the 'Codes of Practice' which are issued to all farmers and form the basis of practical animal welfare standards.

Development of standards and reaching agreed policy

In my experience, FAWC has always had an important internal debate, both within working groups and also at the main council, about the effects of enhancing standards of practical welfare of animals in relation to the continued viability of commercial production systems.

It is impossible for FAWC to operate in total isolation to the practical and commercial realities of the animal industry. The internal debate is very commonly resolved with the production of an agreed report which conventionally proposes a progressive improvement in welfare standards which the industry is capable of accommodating without revolution.

An extreme form of this debate took place at the FAWC working group and main council in 1991 in the preparation of the report on the colony housing systems for laying hens. The working group had great difficulty in reaching agreement on specifications for colony laying hen accommodation, with a minority of members arguing for a more liberal approach to improving welfare. The available scientific evidence had been reviewed and interpretation differed regarding matters such as space, perch length and amount of littered area. The majority of the group were mindful of the practical and economic consequences of the generous approach and opted for a more moderate and a gradualist approach to changes of specification proposed to improve welfare.

The two factions within FAWC might be regarded as 'idealistic' or 'realistic' and personally, as an academic and agricultural practitioner, I tend towards the latter views but I do have sympathy for those who want to make rapid progress in improving welfare. The FAWC main council finally approved the 'realistic' view but also agreed to publish, at the same time, the 'idealistic' view as a minority report, prepared by five or six FAWC members, led by Mrs Ruth Harrison. In the event, the recommendations of the main report, whilst never established by MAFF as formal rules as codes or legislation to date, have since been widely implemented by the industry. The minority report remains available, perhaps as a set of standards to be aimed for in the longer term.

This was an extreme form of the debate, between the 'realists' and the 'idealists', which resulted in a published formal difference of opinion. Normally, working groups, comprising a wide range of interests, learn a great deal about both the theoretical and practical aspects of any welfare problem and, when it comes to producing a report, a set of standards emerge which can be formally agreed to go forward to the ministers and to MAFF to become part of the 'rules'. This inevitably requires a balance of interests and it is usually possible to reach a compromise. As a past chairman of working groups, it is essential, in my opinion, to have a relatively disparate team of members on a working group in order to encourage debate and promote the production of a balanced view in the recommendations which are published.

When I first became a member of FAWC, I was concerned that agreement might be hard to reach. In the course of a whole range of discussions the debate can be finally concluded, with the chairman having to work relatively hard to achieve agreement or an element of compromise, both at working group level and also at the main Council.

Working group activities

FAWC working groups undertake exhaustive investigations. Usually a postal survey of known experts is carried out initially, asking for written responses to questions, contacting a wide range of organisations involved with the topics concerned. The consultation lists include the farming and other commercial organizations (e.g. auctioneers, abattoir owners, hauliers) as well as the relevant animal protection societies. Also, university and research organizations are asked to comment at an early stage and indeed it has often been the case that academics are asked to amplify their published results in order to clarify detailed points when the working group is developing recommendations.

The consultation process is fascinating. Over my years in FAWC it was interesting to observe the trend towards a greater awareness of the need to improve animal welfare standards by commercial organizations. As the FAWC working groups proceed towards a final publication, it is standard practice to discuss broad conclusions with interested parties to ensure that FAWC is seen to be involving everyone who is interested, from commercial to welfare organizations.

I believe that this helps FAWC to be aware of the trends in public concern about the welfare of animals and membership of working groups normally includes at least one member who has a specific welfare interest or involvement. As animal welfare standards improve generally I believe that our UK 'rules' do relate to the needs of animals and to the industry in which they are involved.

The sheep working group
As chairman of the sheep working group of FAWC about 7 years ago, I had to work very hard to convince farmers at meetings and to suggest to them that an officially recognised code stipulating sheep welfare standards would be of benefit to them, providing an agreed baseline which would help to protect them from criticism. At that stage, quite a lot of farmers considered that FAWC was a variety of Government body with a clear remit to give them a hard time and cause them both physical and economic problems.

Our consultation process with the industry was always educational, both for farmers and members of the working group, some of whom had a relatively unclear understanding of how welfare standards could be developed and applied to the benefit of everyone.

It seemed to me that it was important that the FAWC working group should, in collecting evidence, cast a wide net across both geographical locations and production systems operating with the type of animal concerned. In the sheep working group of six

to eight people, I was concerned that the nucleus of individuals with practical experience of sheep should be balanced by the other views represented in FAWC; we added a member of a welfare organization and someone concerned with a consumer organization to provide a balance.

As the working group carries out visits and hears evidence, I believe that it is essential to have people on the group who ask fundamental questions and want to know why and how existing husbandry systems are the way they are. Without this questioning approach, it would be relatively easy for a group of technical experts to produce a report which could be comfortable for the industry and not be sufficiently concerned with improving welfare standards. The questions 'why?' and 'what for?' are essential to the working of a FAWC working group.

As is normal, a working group takes some time, commonly 12 to 24 months, gathering information and visiting a range of locations in the UK, both to see and to be seen. This latter is important in terms of the public image of FAWC, demonstrating that those who have a part in formulating the 'rules' do take the trouble to get out to meet those who may have to live with the rules in due course.

For our sheep working group, we went as far south as Dartmoor, and visited a range of locations in England, right up to Northumberland; we spent 2 days in Wales meeting farmers and members of the veterinary profession; we also visited Scotland, seeing some really extensive Blackface sheep production in mountainous areas.

As is also normal on FAWC visits, we tended to see only well-run efficient sheep enterprises, coping relatively well with the vagaries of climate, which is particularly important to hill sheep farmers. On the sheep itinerary we did visit, by prearrangement, a farm where there were real problems of animal welfare and the SVS representative who accompanied us made a subsequent return visit to make sure that the farmer appreciated the importance of keeping to the Code of Practice. This particular visit was of considerable value to the group in seeing what happens when too many sheep are being kept under poor conditions with inadequate facilities and staff.

Normally, fact-finding visits are planned for FAWC by the SVS or the Agricultural Development and Advisory Service (ADAS) and conditions are usually above average. It is, however, essential for a group to appreciate that animals are kept in practice under a very wide range of conditions so that any ideas for welfare improvements should be related to the real world in which the rules would have to operate and be enforced.

During the period of activity of the FAWC working group, there is a continual need to check on the scientific information which relates to the various practices observed, and that is where the group studies relevant published information. Many data are collected during the course of a working group life and we have always consulted with experts, both in writing and by visits, when an issue has arisen where clarification is required. Research findings are of considerable value to FAWC in formulating proposals but there is a wealth of animal behaviour research which is well conducted and very interesting but of relatively little value in the practical formulation of acceptable procedures aimed at developing codes of practice. We have often wished for more research to be done, to answer a particular question. Frequently this question will be posed in the FAWC working group report and will, if sufficiently important, be stated as a problem to be addressed in the FAWC regularly published list for further research required. Obviously MAFF, who are party to the FAWC activities, can, and do, extract ideas for further research to be put forward in their list of potential contracts.

As an example of how a FAWC working group can become involved in research interpretation and in making suggestions for future work, I propose to detail some of the background to discussions about the age and techniques for castration of lambs which took place within the sheep working group.

We received representations from hill sheep farmers asking that we should consider changing the requirements that lambs, if castrated by rubber rings, must be done before 7 days of age. Extensive farmers have had difficulty with this requirement, indicating to us that very young lambs may not survive such an operation at this very young age, which may be compounded by losing their mothers during the gathering process.

This is a real practical difficulty which the group appreciated and therefore undertook to evaluate the scientific literature. We accumulated the most up-to-date information and eventually ended up having detailed discussions with the two main. groups of workers in the field at the time, which were in New Zealand, led by David Mellor, and in Edinburgh, with Vince Molony. We had correspondence with both and met both groups (without going to New Zealand) to clarify their perception of our dilemma.

The scientific data on pain suffered by lambs was originally in favour of early castration (< 7 days)

compared with waiting until perhaps 6 weeks of age. The newer research information requires careful interpretation but we considered, after considerable evaluation and with the support of a number of academics, expert in the field, that we could recommend that rubber rings could be used up to 6 weeks of age without markedly increasing pain.

This was included in our report presented to ministers. However, after further detailed consideration, MAFF Animal Welfare Division were not able to recommend acceptance of allowing lamb castration by rubber rings up to 6 weeks of age.

Further research was called for and I believe that a contract is currently in progress at the University of Bristol. It would be my hope that eventually we might see the rule on castration by rubber rings changed. Perhaps this example helps explain how the 'rules' are developed and established. The new sheep welfare code, which is currently in preparation, will not show this proposed 'relaxation'.

However, we have to remember that the introduction to the revised sheep welfare code indicates that all farmers should consider very carefully if sheep require to be castrated at all. Total absence of any 'mutilation' could be welfare-friendly unless there are subsequent husbandry problems, which I believe can be severe in some practical situations. We await the research results from Bristol and FAWC will in due course re-examine the data in relation to castration techniques and recommended ages.

New codes and legislation

The FAWC involvement in drawing up the new sheep code has been greater that in past years. The FAWC working group report formed the basis of the new codefl but many people had a subsequent input.

The process of consultation goes out very widely and eventually a new book of 'rules' will emerge in 1998/ 99, having begun in 1990! I believe that the process of improving animal welfare in the UK will continue to progress in this way, ensuring that new, better standards evolve following improvements in our knowledge and also because of the continuing development of public interest and opinion. We have made much progress in the past in the UK, with a set of welfare codes of practice which are widely acknowledged to be beneficial to animal welfare.

In the last 5 years or so, I believe that commercial interests have been going along with improvements to welfare which have been emerging but FAWC have had repeated representations from the industry:

please will the UK Government not impose higher (and probably more expensive) standards on British producers, which will disadvantage them compared to our EU commercial competitors!

I am aware that much Government effort goes into EU negotiations and this culminated in the UK presidency of the EU in the first 6 months of 1998, pressing forward for EU directives for similar basic welfare standards across the whole of Europe. This will obviously help British producers to accept higher welfare standards as administered by the SVS and with the potential for EU inspectors to enforce new directives across the whole of Europe.

Quality assurance schemes

It is interesting to observe how the big multiple stores are now moving to set up their own individual standards which may move welfare standards further forward beyond that required officially. Indeed, the supermarkets have tried also to deal directly with FAWC in setting up their quality assurance schemes which will be used to promote sales as well as improve animal welfare.

FAWC has not the power to approve commercial schemes and has resisted providing a 'seal of approval', tending to respond to potential schemes by stating that 'we are in approval of any proposals to enhance animal welfare'. It may be, however, that the proliferation of quality assurance schemes, operated either by producer organizations or by multiple stores, will provide the impetus for further

improvements to welfare, almost short-circuiting the relatively slow process of government backed schemes. It could be, however, that this is a short-term phenomenon, at a time when supermarkets are being forced to adopt a whole range of measures to ensure that their operations are competitive in a market which is currently extremely cut-throat.

FAWC has, over the years, developed a good reputation, I believe, for the production of balanced reports which can be of considerable value in improving animal welfare. The area of continuing interest to me is how FAWC can retain the balance between preparing reports which are of practical value in drawing up codes of practice (or 'rules') and preparing interesting scientific reviews and recommendations which might be difficult to use for practical and economic reasons.

The drawing of a line between what is a welfare decision and what is a political matter is sometimes difficult. I believe we and FAWC have to base the 'rules' on practical welfare considerations.

References

Farm Animal Welfare Council. 1991. *Report on the welfare of laying hens in colony systems.* FAWC, Hook Rise South, Tolworth, Surbiton.

Farm Animal Welfare Council. 1994. *Report on the welfare of sheep.* FAWC, Hook Rise South, Tolworth, Surbiton.

Farm Animal Welfare Council. 1997. *Report on the welfare of laying hens.* FAWC, Hook Rise South, Tolworth, Surbiton.

Farm animal welfare — who writes the rules?
Occasional Publication No. 23 — British Society of Animal Science 1999
edited by A. J. F. Russel, C. A. Morgan, C. J. Savory, M. C. Appleby and T. L. J. Lawrence

Framing legislation: a legislator's viewpoint

J. C. Milne

Scottish Office Agriculture, Environment and Fisheries Department, Pentland House, 47 Robb's Loan, Edinburgh EH14 1TW

Abstract

Well balanced and effective legislation is required to protect animals and to address the concerns of organizations with interests in animal welfare. The principal aim of animal welfare legislation is the protection of animals by the prevention of suffering, pain and distress. This can be achieved by identifying animals' needs and by the prohibition of procedures having a detrimental effect on welfare. Welfare policy and legislation are determined by many factors, including the results from government-funded research, advice from bodies such as the Farm Animal Welfare Council and other interested organizations and pressure groups, and compliance cost assessments. The mechanisms and processes of consultation and drafting legislation, and of the passage of a bill through parliament, are lengthy procedures and take a considerable time to complete. Although animal welfare issues in Scotland will be devolved to the Scottish Parliament, it is not envisaged that there will be a divergence of policy within the UK as a whole. The legislation itself is clearly important but it is also imperative that it is actively and effectively enforced by all the relevant authorities. All aspects of animal welfare legislation are continually reviewed on both a UK and an EU basis.

Introduction

Welfare of animals covers a wide range of interests from the protection of wildlife, scientific experimentation, the keeping of pets and zoo animals and, of course, farmed livestock. Over the last few decades, the number of species farmed in Britain has increased to include species as diverse as shellfish, mink and ostriches.

Why do we need legislation?

There are understandably differing opinions on the need for welfare legislation. On the one hand many producers are of the view that everything in the garden is rosy and that legislation is irrelevant. Some of the more extreme welfare groups maintain that animals are abused and suffer in all farming systems, that it is morally unacceptable to exploit animals for food and that very strict rules should be implemented. The real position lies, I believe, somewhere in between these two extremes; consequently, well balanced and effective legislation is required to protect animals and to address the concerns of the range of organizations with interests in animal welfare.

One of the biggest problems is that animal welfare means different things to different people. Even members of the scientific community view it in different ways.

To some, welfare is only compromised if the ability to survive and reproduce is impaired; others believe that fear, anxiety and boredom are as important as physical problems. There is no simple way of measuring welfare and the various parameters used, such as plasma cortisol levels, heart rate etc., do not always produce consistent results and their relative importance is difficult to interpret. Some livestock systems can be judged as having poor welfare standards if they are associated with high levels of physical injuries such as lameness or skin lesions.

A large amount of research, including that funded by government, is currently being undertaken with a view to increasing our understanding of various welfare issues and also to develop a recognized method for measuring stress. This is clearly required in what is a subjective and highly emotive area.

What are the aims of welfare legislation?

The principal aim of animal welfare legislation is the protection of animals by the prevention of suffering, pain and distress. This can be achieved by identifying an animal's needs, e.g. space, diet or ventilation, and producing legislation which obliges producers to provide these minimum requirements. Alternatively, legislation can be used to prohibit procedures that are known to have a detrimental effect on animal welfare, e.g. short tail docking of sheep, hot branding of cattle, transport of animals likely to give birth during the journey.

Legislation can also be used as a tool to drive up welfare standards within a species. An example of this is the Welfare of Livestock Regulations (1994) which bans the use of tethers in pigs from 1 January 1999. It is recognized that such action needs to be taken on a European and ideally at a world level to avoid market distortion by the introduction of such measures. Put simply, improved welfare practice in one country alone may reduce the competitiveness of the industry. If the measures are not introduced on at least a pan-European basis, this may affect the economics of the industry and products may be imported from countries with far lower welfare standards. Obviously this is undesirable but we must also guard against the possibility of reducing our own standards to the lowest common level. To this end considerable efforts are made to encourage other member states and third countries to raise welfare standards.

The law can also act as a deterrent. This is particularly true of the Protection of Animals (Scotland) Act 1912 under which individuals can be banned from keeping animals.

Finally, welfare legislation also provides a mechanism by which means individuals who do not care for their animals in an acceptable manner and who cause pain, suffering or distress, can be prosecuted and, if guilty, punished. This option is not undertaken lightly as the imposition of heavy fines can in themselves result in further difficulties with owners possibly being unable to afford the measures needed to remedy the situation. This consideration should never prevent action being taken to protect animals that are seen to be suffering.

Interestingly, it could be argued that the welfare legislation currently in force provides animals with a higher level of protection than that provided for people.

Policy determination and the drafting of legislation

Government policy decisions are subject to a number of influences. Ministers are obliged to implement European legislation. In addition, the views of other government departments have to be borne in mind. Economic interests have to be considered both from a government finance point of view and also the cost

to the industry. Relevant research also needs to be taken into account; this may already be available or may be specifically funded when a policy issue arises.

The government funds considerable amounts of strategic animal welfare research with a view to addressing the issues raised during the framing of new legislation, both on the domestic front and also to enhance our arguments at a European level. It is essential that accurate high quality scientific data are available to demonstrate that any change in legislation will result in an improvement in animal welfare. Many proposals have initially appeared attractive but on further scientific examination have proved to yield little or no welfare benefit and on occasions would have actually had a detrimental effect on animal welfare. It is also important to demonstrate that proposals will result in real improvements in animal welfare particularly when some of the measures cause producers considerable expense to implement.

Practical advice and observations are obtained from the Farm Animal Welfare Council and the views of the various lobby groups, both from the industry and also the welfare organizations, have to be taken into account.

Interested organizations can apply pressure in a variety of ways, e.g. written correspondence. Agriculture Ministers receive more correspondence on animal welfare than on any other issue.

Pressure groups can also organize demonstrations and high profile media campaigns. They have an important part to play in highlighting welfare issues and are usually well informed, although on occasions their actions can be misguided, such as the recent release of mink in the New Forest.

The government also regularly consults the various interested parties on an ongoing informal basis and also, more formally if there are proposals for a significant change in policy or new legislation. The objective of consultation on any subject is to inform the public of government thinking, to test reactions to proposals or ideas and to persuade the interested organisations of the need for the proposed measures. It is also important that officials are open to constructive criticism to ensure that any resulting decisions are effective, workable and enforceable.

Consultation can occur at several stages of the policy-making process. New ideas are often proposed in a 'green paper'. This is purely a discussion document and does not commit the government to any further action. Following public discussion, the government may choose to offer further explanation, modify the proposals or abandon them altogether. A 'white paper' is issued as a statement of intent and its contents form the basis of legislation which usually follows soon after.

Further consultation can occur during the drafting of legislation and for difficult and complex legislation, such as the Welfare of Animals (Transport) Order (1997), consultation may occur at several stages.

Government must have proper regard to the overall impact of regulations on businesses and individuals. It must strike the balance between essential protection for the public, and in this case animals, and over-zealous, intrusive and expensive controls aimed at the elimination of all conceivable risk. To this end, all government departments must produce a compliance cost assessment (CCA) when evaluating policy proposals that could have an impact, however slight, on business. Its purpose is to inform Ministers and officials of the likely costs to businesses of complying with new or amended legislation.

CCAs should be completed as early as possible when forming proposals. They are often produced with the help of industry and should accompany consultation documents sent to interested outside bodies, such as industry representative organisations, to gauge reaction to the proposals.

The decision to draft a particular piece of welfare legislation may result from the need to: implement European legislation, e.g. Welfare of Animals (Transportation) Order; implement party policy; implement proposals from Department Ministers; address public representations which may result from a report by a Committee or Commission; or implement an accumulation of proposals for improving existing law.

One of the main obstacles to introducing new primary legislation is the lack of parliamentary time. The legislative programme is determined by the government, based on advice from the Cabinet Office, for each parliamentary session and government departments are usually required to submit proposals for legislation a year in advance. Good ideas may have to be dropped or postponed simply because Parliament doesn't have the time to consider them.

Ministers are responsible for the content of a bill, but major decisions are usually taken by a Cabinet committee or the full Cabinet, usually before a white paper is published.

A 'bill team' is assembled to oversee and co-ordinate the production of the bill and the bill itself is drafted by a Parliamentary draftsman. This is a complicated procedure which can take several months even for a bill of moderate length. Following agreement of the text of the bill, it is usually presented to the House of Commons although, on occasion, bills can be introduced through the House of Lords.

At this first reading stage, the Speaker simply reads out the formal title of the bill, the appropriate Minister rises and nods and the bill is ordered to be printed. This is followed by a second reading which is the first full debate on the principles of the bill at which time amendments are not made. The bill then goes to a Committee where there is a clause by clause examination. This is where much of the detailed work is done and is the main stage for amendments to be tabled and considered. The bill, with amendments, is then reprinted and a report made to the House at which stage further amendments can be made.

The third reading is usually a formal or short debate, a summing up, without the opportunity for amendments. The bill is then presented to the House of Lords and follows similar procedures to the House of Commons. Following passage through the House of Lords, any amendments made there need to be agreed by the Commons before the bill is finally approved. If the Commons do not agree with the Lords amendments, the bill is passed back and forward until agreement is reached.

Another mechanism for introducing minor or non-controversial changes is to use a Private Member's bill. A recent example was the bill on the welfare of animals in quarantine. These bills are often inspired by government and supported by government through their various stages. Alternatively, and more within the spirit of the Private Member's bill process, MPs come under considerable pressure from outside organizations to support their causes in a Private Member's bill. Gaining support in controversial areas does not guarantee change as a Private Member's bill can be blocked by parliamentary tactics, e.g. the proposed ban on hunting with hounds.

What are the implications of devolution?

All animal welfare issues have been devolved and will be the responsibility of the Scottish Parliament. The intention is that elections will be held in May 1999 and the Parliament should be up and running by July 1999. A lot of work has gone into producing the Devolution Bill and steering it through parliament. Without doubt, there remains much still to be done before we have a new Scottish Parliament up and running and with all the procedures and infrastructures in place.

At this stage, it is not envisaged that there will be a wide divergence of policy and practice north and south of the border in England, Wales and Scotland. Strong links will be maintained between departments, and indeed the UK is a single entity as far as the European Union is concerned. The criteria of proper welfare do not change merely because of a line on the map. But there are regional differences and it is not possible to predict how the new body of the Scottish Parliament will opt to use its legitimate democratic powers.

Implementation and enforcement

The law is just a piece of paper; it is how it is implemented and enforced that determine its effectiveness. Increasingly detailed guidance is being provided with complex legislation but, whilst this can be useful, it should be remembered that only a court can interpret the law.

Active and effective enforcement is required by all relevant enforcement authorities. Consistency is also important, both between different enforcement authorities and between different parts of the country. Consequently, good liaison between the State Veterinary Service, local authorities and such organizations as the Scottish Society for the Prevention of Cruelty to Animals is essential.

There are major differences in the legal system in Scotland compared with that in England and Wales, e.g. only the Procurator Fiscal can take a prosecution in Scotland. The enforcement authorities and others provide the Procurator Fiscal with a report and it is his judgement which decides if the case is taken to the court. Also, the rules of evidence are different and the Police and Criminal Evidence Act does not apply. Corroboration is also required for all evidence.

Some welfare legislation is specific to Scotland, e.g. the Protection of Animals (Scotland) Act (1912),

whereas other legislation, such as the Agriculture (Miscellaneous Provisions) Act (1968), is Great Britain based.

The power to confiscate animals that are suffering under the authority of an incidental warrant issued by the Sheriff under the Criminal Justice (Scotland) Act 1995 is unique to Scotland and is used from time to time in serious cases of neglect to provide appropriate care pending a welfare case coming to court.

Current and future issues

Over the next few years, all aspects of animal welfare legislation will be reviewed. As part of our rolling review programme the departments will jointly address the market and transport legislation and a consultation paper will be available shortly. It is also expected that we will take a look at the Welfare at Slaughter legislation, although no details are available as yet. The recent UK Presidency of the EU was successful in getting agreement on the general Farm Animal Welfare Directive for Farm Animals 95/58/EC and we will have to consider further how to implement this by 31 December 1999. Also, the new rules in staging posts and higher vehicle standards will need to be implemented by 1 January and 1 July 1999 respectively.

Looking ahead on the EU front, there is a proposal on laying hens. This Government is committed to phasing out battery cages but discussions under our presidency would indicate that this will have to be a long term goal. There are also further proposals on vehicle construction standards and on the movement of pigs through staging posts.

Within the next 5 years, the Commission is likely to bring forward proposals for species specific requirements for cattle, sheep and goats, chickens and ratites.

On the domestic front, we intend to continue the revision of the MAFF *Welfare Codes of Practice* which are based on recommendations made by the Farm Animal Welfare Council.

Farm animal welfare — who writes the rules?
Occasional Publication No. 23 — British Society of Animal Science 1999
edited by A. J. F. Russel, C. A. Morgan, C. J. Savory, M. C. Appleby and T. L. J. Lawrence

Too cramped for comfort?
Constraints on the Government's room to manoeuvre

M. Radford

School of Law, University of East Anglia, Norwich NR4 7TJ

Abstract

Traditionally, the UK parliament has been legislatively supreme: it can pass or repeal whatever measure it wishes. Membership of the European Community and the World Trade Organization has fundamentally changed this situation. Parliament and government are both constrained in what they may do if their action would conflict with the principle of free trade, to the extent that, under EC law, the domestic courts may override the will of Parliament. Provisions which allow nations to introduce restrictions in order to protect public morality, or the life and health of animals, have not been effective in providing a basis for the introduction of animal protection measures. Amendments to the Treaty of Rome, recognizing the sentiency of animals, is an advance, but what difference it will make in practice is as yet unclear. The apparent inability of a nation state to give effect to the will of its citizens raises important constitutional issues: it has serious implications for democracy and the rule of law and undermines the legitimacy of the political process.

Parliamentary supremacy

Evolving from the constitutional struggles of the seventeenth century, the fundamental principle of modern British legal and political practice has been that ultimate power resides with Parliament. This power has manifested itself principally through the doctrine of parliamentary legislative supremacy. In short, this recognizes Parliament's authority to enact or repeal any measure it wishes. It also defines the rôle of the courts as being subservient to that of the legislature. The judges' duty is to apply the law and, where its meaning is ambiguous or uncertain, to interpret it consistently with the declared or perceived will of Parliament. Traditionally, consideration of the validity or desirability of an Act's provisions is no part of the judicial function.

Such a situation is in sharp contrast to that in most modern liberal democracies, where the source of governmental power is to be found in a formal, written and legally enforceable constitution. In this case, the relationship between courts and legislature may be very different, with the latter constrained both by the terms of the constitution and the way in which it is interpreted and applied by the courts.

The significance of Parliament's legislative supremacy is that there is no legal constraint on the ability of Members of Parliament to respond to the wishes of the electorate. They may decline to do so on other grounds but that is essentially a *political* decision, rather than due to any limitation on their power to act. Domestic law does not, however, exist in a vacuum. It operates against the backdrop of the United Kingdom's international obligations and the combined effect of membership of the European Community and, latterly, the World Trade Organization (WTO) has been significantly to restrict Parliament's - and therefore the government's - room to manoeuvre.

The European Community

The European Economic Community (EEC) was established in 1957 by the Treaty of Rome, Article 2 of which stated:

'The Community shall have as its task, by establishing a common market and progressively approximating the economic policies of Member States, to promote throughout the Community a harmonious development of economic activities, a continued and balanced expansion, an increase in stability, an accelerated raising of the standard of living and closer relations between the States belonging to it.'

Article 3 specified those activities which the Community was empowered to undertake in order to further its purposes. These included:

● the elimination, as between Member States, of customs duties and other quantitative restrictions on the import and export of goods, and of all other measures having equivalent effect;

- the abolition, as between Member States, of obstacles to freedom of movement for persons, services and capital;
- the adoption of a common policy in the sphere of agriculture; and
- the institution of a system ensuring that competition in the common market is not distorted.

The underlying concern was therefore economic, particularly the promotion of free trade between Member States, and the term 'progressively approximating' indicated that, from the outset, it was accepted that the Community would not remain static; that the project had an inherent momentum which was intended to carry it forward towards its ultimate goal. As part of this process, the Treaty of Rome has been subsequently amended by the Single European Act (1986) and by the Treaty on European Union (the 'Maastricht Treaty', 1991), and further changes are pending as a result of the Treaty of Amsterdam (1997). Together, these have created the single market, provided for the introduction of a single currency, established the European Union, extended the competence of the European Community, introduced new institutions, and altered the powers and procedures of those already in existence. These changes to the fundamental rules are extremely important but in themselves they are not sufficient to ensure the success of the undertaking. Although the principal aims can be set down in treaties, their implementation require the establishment of appropriate mechanisms and institutions to initiate and develop policy; and in order to ensure that such policy is implemented and applied uniformly across the Community, means of enforcing and interpreting it are also needed. Accordingly, the Treaty also established Community institutions charged to exercise executive, legislative and judicial functions. Furthermore, in case Member States fail to fulfil their obligations, Article 3 of the Treaty of Rome empowered these institutions to secure 'the approximation of the laws of Member States to the extent required for the proper functioning of the common market'.

The comparison is not entirely accurate, but the Treaty of Rome is somewhat analogous to a written, legally enforceable constitution, but in this case it operates at a supra-national level. The Treaty established the EEC, now known as the European Community (EC), which is part of, but not the same as, the European Union (EU); specified the extent of its competence (that is, the purposes for which it exists and the matters which fall within its province); provided for rules to further its objectives which are common to, and binding on, Member States; established the institutions to carry out these functions, including defining the extent of their

powers and their relationship with each other, and with Member States; and affirmed that the rules of the Community were to have a higher status than the domestic law of Member States.

The major institutions of the European Community

All of the institutions are constrained by the terms of the Treaties: they may only do that which they are authorized to do.

The Council of Ministers

It is the Council of Ministers (not the European Parliament) which is the principal decision and law-making body of the Community, in that it has the final power of decision on most secondary legislation. This it does by approving, modifying or rejecting proposals put forward by the Commission (having consulted as required with the European Parliament and other bodies). The Council cannot itself initiate new legislation; it may only act in response to a proposal from the Commission but it is able to set the process in motion by asking the Commission to study an issue and present it with proposals. The Council of Ministers consists of one minister from each Member State but the individual membership varies according to the subject matter under discussion. Although some decisions require unanimity, most are decided by a qualified majority, by which the votes of each Member State are weighted very generally according to the size of its population. Under this arrangement, there is no power of veto and, if outvoted, a Member State is bound by the decision, regardless of the views of its government, legislature, or electorate.

The European Commission

The Commission acts as the executive and administrative body of the Community. It initiates and prepares legislative proposals to the Council; supervises the implementation of decisions and policy agreed by the Council, and policies delegated to it by the Council, such as the common agricultural policy (in which it has substantial autonomous powers); has a general responsibility to ensure that the Treaties' provisions are properly carried out; supervises implementation of, and compliance with, EU law by Member States; and negotiates international agreements on behalf of the EC. The Commission is presently made up of 20 Commissioners, nominated by the Member States and approved by the European Parliament.

Because, in most cases, the Commission has the sole right to initiate legislation, it represents the most important force for change within the Community, but in driving the project forward it is merely fulfilling its basic rôle as provided for in the Treaties.

It may act on the basis of submissions by other EU institutions or by interest groups and individuals or on its own initiative.

The European Parliament

The Parliament grew out of what was originally known as the Assembly, a non-elected body whose remit was essentially advisory rather than legislative. However, in reaction to growing concerns about the lack of democratic accountability of the other Community institutions, its power, influence and authority has developed considerably since 1979 when the first direct elections for Members of the European Parliament (MEPs) were held. On each occasion that the Treaty of Rome has been amended, the position of the Parliament has been strengthened. It is now made up of directly elected representatives of the citizens of the Community and, although its legislative powers are very different from those of the United Kingdom Parliament, its debates and views are becoming increasingly important in the legislative process, although it remains subservient to the Council of Ministers. However, by debating the programmes and reports of the Commission and Council it adds an element of democratic supervision of those bodies and can achieve publicity for its views which, in turn, may influence the policy-making process. MEPs may also obtain information by tabling written and oral questions to the Commission and the Council of Ministers. MEPs have traditionally shown considerable interest in animal welfare issues and, despite their limited powers, the Parliament has become a focus for the debate in the Community about the proper treatment of animals.

The European Court of Justice

If ultimate political power resides with the Council, ultimate legal power lies with the European Court of Justice (ECJ). Its decisions, from which there is no appeal, are binding across the Community. The rôle of the Court is to ensure that the terms of the Treaty are observed and, as the supreme authority on all matters of Community law, to provide in cases of dispute a conclusive interpretation of the meaning of the Treaties and secondary legislation made under their authority. In this respect, its function is not unlike that of the constitutional court of a nation state. Accordingly, the Court may:

● hold a Member State to account for failing to meet its obligations under Community law;

● quash as invalid legislative or executive measures adopted by the Commission or the Council if it considers them to be incompatible with the terms of the Treaty;

● provide, at the request of a national court from any Member State which is unsure of the legal position, a 'preliminary ruling' on the meaning of Community law. It is called a 'preliminary ruling' because the Court states what the law is, and it is then left to the governments and courts of the Member States to apply and give effect to the decision. The purpose of this procedure is to ensure uniform interpretation and application of Community law throughout the Community, and decisions are therefore binding on all Member States regardless of which particular country sought the assistance of the Court. In other words, the British government and the courts of England, Wales, Scotland and Northern Ireland, are just as much bound by a decision of the ECJ which originated in another Member State as it is by one which was referred by a court in the United Kingdom.

European Community law

There are three sources of Community law:
● primary legislation;
● secondary legislation; and
● decisions of the European Court of Justice.

Primary legislation

Primary Community legislation consists of the Treaty of Rome, as amended by the Single European Act, the Treaty on European Union, and (when it comes into force) the Treaty of Amsterdam. It is created directly by agreement between the Member States.

Secondary legislation

Secondary legislation is created by Community institutions acting under the authority of the Treaties. In the case of uncertainty as to what is permitted, it falls to the ECJ to determine their scope. There are three types of secondary legislation:
● regulations;
● directives; and
● decisions.

Regulations

These are 'directly applicable'. This means they automatically become part of the law of each Member State without the need for further legislation at a national level. Accordingly, they lay down the object to be attained and the means by which it is to be achieved, both of which are binding on all Member States. If there is any conflict with national law, the regulation will prevail. Regulations are used for measures which require uniform application throughout the Community.

Directives

These are the most common form of Community legislation. Their terms are also binding, their purpose being to require Member States to harmonize their national law with the provisions of the directive. They prescribe the object to be attained but it is left to individual governments to decide for themselves how this should be achieved. Unlike regulations, therefore, a directive is not directly applicable. It will generally require domestic legislation to be enacted to accomplish its implementation, unless appropriate provisions are already in place. A directive is in effect a mandatory instruction to each Member State to ensure that its own law conforms with the directive's provisions. If a government fails in this regard, it may be referred to the ECJ by the Commission, another Member State, or brought before the courts in its own country by an aggrieved party. Cases do arise where Member States have deliberately failed to implement all or part of a directive, but many cases come before the ECJ as a result of genuine uncertainty or disagreement over the meaning, due to ambiguous or obscure wording. Such a situation may result in Member States interpreting and applying the provisions of a directive in different ways, and it is then for the ECJ to make an authoritative and binding ruling on the matter.

Decisions
These are binding instructions relating to specific issues which may be addressed to a Member State, an enterprise, a section of the economy, or even an individual. They are used primarily for the administrative implementation of Community law.

Jurisprudence of the ECJ
The decisions and reasoning of the Court is binding on all Community institutions and all Member States, including their domestic courts.

Government liability
Failure to meet its obligations under Community law may leave a government liable for a claim for damages by an injured party.

The relationship between Community law and domestic law

'By contrast with ordinary international treaties,' observed the ECJ in 1964, the Treaty establishing the Community had created its own legal system which became 'an integral part of the legal systems of the Member States and which their courts are bound to apply.' According to the Court, the terms of the Treaty represented 'a transfer of powers from the states to the Community,' to the extent that Member States 'have limited their sovereign rights, albeit within limited fields, and have thus created a new body of law which binds both their nationals and themselves.' On the basis of this analysis, the Court declared that 'the law stemming from the Treaty' — that is, the terms of the Treaty itself and any secondary legislation made under its authority, such as regulations and directives — 'could not ... be

overridden by domestic legal provisions, however framed, ... without the legal basis of the Community itself being called into question.' In consequence, said the Court, acceding to the Treaty involves 'a permanent limitation' of each Member State's sovereign rights, 'against which a subsequent unilateral act incompatible with the concept of the Community cannot prevail' (*Costa* v *ENEL* [1964] ECR 585).

The supremacy of Community law over the domestic law of Member States was recognized by the UK Parliament in the European Communities Act 1972. Section 2(1) provides that all rights, powers, liabilities, obligations and restrictions created or arising by or under the Treaties, together with all remedies and procedures, 'shall be recognised and available in law, and be enforced, allowed or followed accordingly.' Furthermore, s.3(2) lays down that the domestic courts, confronted by any question as to the meaning or effect of Community law, shall have regard to the Treaties, the *Official Journal* and any decision or expression of opinion of the ECJ. The effect is to incorporate EC law into the law of the UK, so that, first, it is binding on those to whom it is applicable; secondly, it is enforceable in the domestic courts; and, thirdly, in respect of issues with a Community law dimension, the courts are required to take account of, and give effect to, the objects of the Treaties, the purpose underlying secondary Community legislation, and the jurisprudence of the ECJ.

The supremacy of Community law has been consistently reasserted by the ECJ. It is a principle of particular legal and political potency. On the one hand, it means that a Community measure has an impact on the law of 15 nation states, a factor that makes lobbying for change at a Community level especially attractive to pressure groups. On the other hand, the principle poses a fundamental challenge to the functioning of representative democracy within the nation state. The requirement laid down by the ECJ that 'every national court must, in a case within its jurisdiction, apply Community law in its entirety and protect rights which the latter confers on individuals and must accordingly set aside any provision of national law which may conflict with it, whether prior or subsequent to the Community rule' (*Amministrazione delle Finanze dello Stato* v. *Simmenthal SpA* [1978] ECR 629) has the effect not only of restricting the autonomy of legislatures and governments but may also serve to frustrate the popular will of the people. In the case of the UK, the precedence of Community law over national law also goes to the heart of traditional constitutional arrangements, namely the legislative supremacy of Parliament. Whereas the traditional rôle of the courts has been to identify and enforce the will of Parliament, they may now be in a position where they are required to ignore the provisions of an Act of Parliament, or prevent its implementation (*R* v. *Secretary of State for Transport, ex parte Factortame Ltd (No 2)* [1991] 1 AC 603). Accordingly, notwithstanding that a policy may have widespread public support, and Parliament seeks to give effect to it by passing legislation, or the government responds by adopting an appropriate policy, both may be overridden by the national courts if they are incompatible with national law.

Article 36

Article 36 of the Treaty of Rome does countenance interference with free trade on grounds which include public morality, public policy and the protection of the health and life of animals, provided that any restrictions do not constitute 'a means of arbitrary discrimination or a disguised restriction on trade between Member States.' Animal welfare campaigners have argued that it permits national governments to give priority to animal welfare over trade but this argument has had little practical impact. The ECJ has ruled, for example, that the UK acted unlawfully in refusing to grant licences for the export of sheep to Spain between 1990 and 1993 in the belief that the Spanish were not adequately complying with Directive 74/577 on stunning animals before slaughter (Case C-5/94, *R* v. *Ministry of Agriculture, Fisheries and Food, ex parte Hedley Lomas (Ireland) Ltd* [1996] 2 CMLR. 391). According to the ECJ, a Member State 'may not unilaterally adopt, on its own authority, corrective or protective measures designed to obviate any breach by another Member State of rules of Community law' (at 446). The Court is clearly conscious of the formal mechanisms available within the Community's legal order to bring complaints against alleged contraventions of EC law.

The legal status of animals under Community law

As we have seen, two of the original objectives of the EC were the establishment of a common market and the adoption of a common agricultural policy, developments which necessitated the introduction of Community-wide rules and minimum standards. In consequence, the way in which farm animals were treated became a relevant consideration. To that extent, the Commission was correct to observe, as it did in 1993, that the protection of animals 'has always been taken into account in Community legislation, particularly the Common Agricultural policy' (Commission of the European Communities, 1995). Taking the protection of animals into account

is, however, rather different from giving the matter the attention it merits. Moreover, the impetus for the introduction of animal protection measures in agriculture and other areas has been predominantly to facilitate the working of the internal market, rather than for the benefit of the animals themselves. Nevertheless, despite its shortcomings and weaknesses, the body of EC legislation relating to animals is testimony to those campaigners, politicians and officials whose efforts over many years have achieved some success in changing attitudes and persuading a sufficient number of the relevant decision-makers that this was a subject on which it was necessary for them to act.

The scale of this challenge has been a consequence of different cultural attitudes to animals among the Member States, together with the priority accorded to commercial considerations. It has also been due to the fact that under the Treaty of Rome, on which all subsequent Community legislation is based, live animals were specifically defined as 'agricultural products'. There was no recognition that their nature was any different from that of inanimate commodities, and hence no special provisions which recognized their particular needs. Such welfare measures as have been agreed are essentially on the basis that they further the objective contained in Article 39, 'to increase agricultural productivity by promoting technical progress and by ensuring the rational development of agricultural production.'

In response to this situation, persistent efforts have been made since the early 1980s by pressure groups, MEPs, and some national governments, to amend the Treaty to recognize the sentiency of animals. An acknowledgement of the particular needs of animals was achieved as part of the negotiations leading up to the Treaty on European Union with the result that a Declaration was appended to the Treaty which 'calls upon the European Parliament, the Council and the Commission, as well as Member States, when drafting and implementing Community legislation on the common agricultural policy, transport, the internal market and research, to pay full regard to the welfare requirement of animals.' The Declaration represented the most that was politically possible to achieve at the time. Although welcome both as recognition of the issue and a statement of intent, it is not formally incorporated into the Treaty of Rome, does not have the status of law, and is not therefore legally enforceable. It is aspirational rather than mandatory, and thereby failed to meet the original objectives of the campaign, which continued - and to some effect.

The Treaty of Amsterdam, formally signed by Member States on 2 October 1997 (but which will not

come into force until it has been ratified by each Member State) provides for the Treaty of Rome to be amended to include the following Protocol:
THE HIGH CONTRACTING PARTIES [i.e. the Member States]
DESIRING to ensure improved protection and respect for the welfare of animals as sentient beings
HAVE AGREED upon the following provision which shall be annexed to the Treaty establishing the European Community.
In formulating and implementing the Community's agriculture, transport, internal market and research policies, the Community and Member States shall pay full regard to the welfare requirements of animals, while respecting the legislative or administrative provisions and customs of the Member States relating in particular to religious rites, cultural traditions and regional heritage.

For the first time, the sentiency of animals is formally acknowledged and an explicit duty to have regard to their welfare imposed upon Community institutions and Member States. This is a significant achievement. To have succeeded in having the founding Treaty amended highlights the influence of the animal welfare lobby and the political significance now attached to the issue. At a practical level, the Protocol has the potential to make a real difference by changing attitudes and affecting the substantive law. When the Treaty comes into effect, EC law will recognize animals as sentient beings. This new status will clearly need to be taken into account when formulating future legislation, and it will be incumbent on Member States to take account of it when transposing directives into national law. The Protocol will also become a factor in the deliberations of the ECJ. Furthermore, in relation to EC legislation, it will be enforceable in the domestic courts of Member States as well as the ECJ.

However, while the implications may be far-reaching, what the Protocol means in practice, and therefore the degree of protection it affords animals, will ultimately be determined by the courts. Clearly, how liberal an interpretation they will apply to the caveat relating to practices in individual Member States will be an important factor. Moreover, it may be argued that a duty 'to pay full regard to the welfare requirements of animals' does not amount to an overriding duty to give effect to them. They must be considered, but that does not necessarily prevent them being qualified by competing considerations, such as other objectives contained in the Treaties, or international obligations such as, for example, the rules of the WTO.

There are considerable opportunities for differing views as to the weight to be attached to the Protocol.

It is probably inevitable that animal welfare campaigners will challenge the way in which the Commission and Member States interpret and apply the Protocol; it does not take a great leap of imagination to envisage a situation where the wording of a directive, or its transposition into national law, does not go as far as campaigners would wish, and they will then turn to the courts on the basis that the terms of the Protocol have not been met.

The World Trade Organization
The WTO, based in Geneva, was established on 1 January 1995. The successor to the General Agreement on Tariffs and Trade (GATT), the WTO is the legal and institutional foundation of the international trading system in respect of goods, services and intellectual property. It is 'dedicated to open, fair and undistorted competition', reflecting the prevailing commercial orthodoxy that 'liberal trade policies which allow the unrestricted flow of goods, services and productive inputs multiply the rewards that come with producing the best products, with the best design, at the best price' (WTO, 1995). Each country which belongs to the WTO is obliged to ensure that its laws, regulations and administrative procedures comply with the obligations arising from its membership. Countries must accept the rules; no reservations or exceptions are permitted.

Unlike GATT, which was little more than a set of rules, the WTO is a permanent institution with an international legal personality, which allows it to act independently of individual nation states. The WTO has its own secretariat and procedures which enable it to fulfil its functions. These include:
● administering and implementing the multilateral and plurilateral agreements which together make up the WTO;
● providing the machinery to resolve trade disputes between its members;
● overseeing national trade policies of its members.

In the event of a dispute between WTO members which cannot be settled by means of conciliation, a panel is established by the WTO's Dispute Settlement Body to examine the matter, whose conclusions and recommendations are normally binding. One or both parties may appeal to the standing Appellate Body, composed of seven persons broadly representative of the WTO's membership who are required to be of recognized standing in the field of law and international trade, and not affiliated to any government. If the Appellate Body upholds the panel's recommendations, they must be implemented. Failure to do so may result in the recalcitrant member having to pay compensation, or being the subject of retaliatory measures authorized by the Dispute Settlement Body.

The WTO therefore has the power and authority to prevent an individual nation state from determining its own trading policies and to punish it should it decide to ignore WTO rules. This may be considered desirable in securing one of the organization's principal objectives: preventing 'a self-defeating and destructive drift into protectionism,' (WTO, 1995). However, it raises the important question of whether a country can refuse to import a product because of moral or ethical concerns about the way in which it has been produced: for example, the terms and conditions of the workforce, the environmental impact, and, of course, issues of animal welfare. In particular, it is not permitted to distinguish between the products of different countries on the basis of the way they are produced, unless the respective methods make a discernible difference to the character of the article. This poses a major obstacle to the proponents of higher welfare standards because, in most cases, there is no perceptible difference (at least in the eyes of the WTO) between meat from intensely or extensively reared animals, or eggs which come from respectively free-range or battery-caged hens.

It is provided that 'nothing' in the WTO Agreement 'shall be construed to prevent the adoption or enforcement by any contracting party of measures
● necessary to protect public morals;
● necessary to protect human, animal or plant life or health;
● or relating to the natural conservation of exhaustible natural resources.'

However, such exceptions may not be used to discriminate arbitrarily or unjustifiably between members, or as a disguised restriction on international trade. It is also a requirement that a restriction introduced on any of these grounds should be based on scientific evidence. Experience suggests that these potential exceptions to the free-trade orthodoxy are going to be interpreted very narrowly.

Under the WTO Agreement, the manner in which animals are treated is not, in itself, recognized as a legitimate basis on which to impose restrictions. Measures introduced to ensure standards of animal welfare will be compatible with the WTO regime only if it can be shown that they comply with the basic principles of non-discrimination between WTO members, and non-discrimination between imports and domestically produced goods and services. In practice, this will generally mean that they cannot be used as a basis to prevent the export or importation

of goods to or from countries where the standards are lower. Not only does such a situation raise important issues of principle concerning the respective weight to be attached to unrestricted trade on the one hand, and questions of public morality on the other, it also has far-reaching implications for the stringency of domestic regulation: measures to protect animal welfare can add significantly to the cost of a product, and additional domestic regulation can therefore have a serious effect on the competitiveness of home-produced goods.

Conclusion

The effect of European Community law and the rules of the WTO is to turn the traditional doctrine of parliamentary legislative supremacy on its head. In relation to those matters which fall within their province, the will of both the government and parliament may be overridden, and the domestic courts are specifically charged with the duty to give effect to Community law. The apparent inability of a nation state to prevent practices which are widely regarded as unacceptable by its citizens raises an important constitutional issue. One of the abiding impressions of the controversy over transport during 1994/5 was the UK Government's powerlessness. The Minister of Agriculture, William Waldegrave, conceded that 'we really are, in Britain, more or less on the same side of this argument,' and yet he was unable to act on his own initiative to resolve it: 'we really should be directing our anger and our national efforts towards getting things changed in Europe' (The Observer, 5 February 1995). Indeed, the most the Government could do was to trifle at the margins of the problem, introducing, for example, additional measures relating to hauliers' journey plans.

If law does not command widespread assent, its legitimacy is undermined, particularly when it appears in conflict with the moral consensus. If such a law cannot be changed, it is dangerous for both democracy and the rule of law. In such circumstances, it is unsurprising that people take to the streets when making their views known by constitutional means appears useless. In the context of protests against the live export trade, the High Court has repeated the well established position that any activity is unlawful which disrupts the rights of others to go about their lawful business (R v. Coventry City Council, ex parte Phoenix Aviation [1995] 3 All ER 37, at 41). But what if the body politic is impotent to redefine what constitutes lawful business? The bleakness of this situation was well summed up by the Court itself:
'It may, indeed, be doubted whether there remains any logic in protesting at the ports: the only body properly able to ban this lawful trade is Parliament

itself — unless indeed the Secretary of State is rightly advised that even that would be unlawful under Community law, in which event the only solution lies across the Channel' (at 64-5).

The ECJ has recently confirmed that the Secretary of State was rightly advised (Case C-1/96, *R* v. *Minister of Agriculture, Fisheries and Food, ex parte Compassion in World Farming*). There is a lesson here, with serious implications for representative democracy: while the Government and Parliament were unable to respond to popular sentiment, commercial undertakings — the ferry operators — could, and did. As the rising power of the consumer coincides with the declining power of national politicians, it will not be surprising if pressure groups and their supporters think less in terms of MP, and rather more of PLC, in campaigning to further their objectives.

References

Commission of the European Communities. 1995. *Background report: animal welfare.*

World Trade Organization. 1995. *Trading into the future.* WTO, Geneva.

Farm animal welfare — who writes the rules?
Occasional Publication No. 23 — British Society of Animal Science 1999
edited by A. J. F. Russel, C. A. Morgan, C. J. Savory, M. C. Appleby and T. L. J. Lawrence

Perception of farm treatment of various livestock in Zaragoza (Spain)

G. A. María, J. L. Olleta and M. L. Mocé

Animal Production Department, University of Zaragoza, Miguel Servet 177, 50013 Zaragoza, Spain

Introduction

Livestock production in intensive conditions has resulted in considerable criticism by various segments of society. The animal rights movement has developed rapidly in northern Europe and North America. The strong social claim in favour of animal welfare has produced important changes in the European legislation controlling livestock industries in the EU. As a consequence of these changes it will be necessary to introduce important modifications in the production systems which could affect production costs. The question is to determine whether people in southern European countries such as Spain will accept the increment in the price of the products in order to improve farm animal welfare. The objective of this study was to assess the perception of farm animal treatment of various livestock of people with urban backgrounds.

Material and methods

The human attitude and perception of farm animal treatment of various livestock were examined in a selected sample of 956 people living in Zaragoza (700 000 inhabitants city in NE Spain) during the years 1995, 1996 and 1997. The study used the 'feeling thermometer' with a scale ranging from 0 to 100, with 0 being a very cool or negative response and 100 being a very warm or positive response (Jamison, 1992). The survey included the following questions. (1) Do you eat animal products? (yes, no). (2) What is your 'feeling' about animal treatment or animal welfare in the farms? (very good, good, fair, bad, very bad). (3) Using a scale from 0 (very bad treatment) to 100 (very good treatment), give a score to the following livestock: horses, sheep, beef cows, dairy cows, goats, veal calves, swine, rabbits, turkeys, broilers and layers. People were also asked about their willingness to pay more for an animal product in order to improve farm animal welfare.

For the analysis, animals were assembled in two groups: group 1 (ruminants and horses) and group 2 (swine, rabbits, and poultry). Descriptive statistics were calculated and the fixed effects of sex (2 levels: male and female), age (3 levels: < 30; 30-45 and > 45 years old), occupation (4 levels: student, worker, professional and housewife), and animal group (2

Table 1 *Two-way frequency table by sex, age and occupation of people perception on farm animal treatment and the willingness to pay more for an animal product to improve the welfare of the animals*

	View on the farm animal treatment					Pay more for a product to improve animal welfare	
Variables	Very good	Good	Fair	Bad	Very bad	Yes	No
Overall frequency %	2·90	25·20	45·10	17·20	9·00	72·80	26·50
Gender							
male %	3·42	27·78	43·16	17·52	7·69	62·39	37·18
female %	2·47	22·63	46·91	16·87	10·29	82·99	16·18
Age							
< 35 %	1·11	21·08	48·20	18·28	10·53	74·65	25·07
35-45 %	8·33	37·50	29·17	14·58	8·33	60·42	39·58
> 45 %	8·82	33·82	39·71	13·24	1·47	72·06	25·00
Occupation							
Student %	0·00	14·29	42·86	21·43	21·43	85·71	14·29
Worker %	4·81	28·85	35·58	10·58	19·23	67·31	32·69
Professional %	6·10	24·39	34·15	30·49	3·66	67·07	30·49
Housewife %	9·68	32·26	54·84	3·23	0·00	80·65	19·35

Table 2 *Mean scores on farm animal treatment of various livestock by sex, age and occupation and the overall mean score (± s.d.)*

Livestock	Overall mean	Gender		Age			Occupation			
		Males	Female	<35	35-45	>45	Student	Worker	Professional	House-wife
Group 1										
Horses	76 ± 20	77	75	75	77	81	76	73	78	79
Sheep	56 ± 22	50	56	54	57	66	39	54	55	69
Beef	52 ± 23	54	51	49	58	68	44	50	53	72
Dairy	59 ± 24	60	58	56	62	72	39	57	58	75
Goat	53 ± 22	56	51	51	57	64	46	52	54	65
Veal	55 ± 22	55	54	51	58	71	43	52	53	74
Average	58 ± 18	59	58	56	62	70	48	57	59	72
Group 2										
Swine	42 ± 24	42	40	38	44	53	31	42	39	50
Rabbit	41 ± 24	42	40	38	43	57	25	41	40	59
Turkey	45 ± 25	46	43	42	50	55	28	43	46	52
Broiler	36 ± 25	37	35	33	42	50	24	35	35	54
Layer	42 ± 27	43	41	39	44	58	25	43	39	52
Average	40 ± 22	42	38	37	44	53	29	39	39	52

levels) were analysed using a factorial model (Statistical Analysis Systems Institute, 1988).

Results

Frequencies showing the distribution by sex, age and occupation of the answers about farm animal treatment and the willingness to pay more for an

Table 3 *Significance probabilities for fixed effects from the analysis of variance of the scores*

Livestock group	Source of variation			
	Gender	Age	Occupation	Animal
Group 1				
Horse		***	*	NM
Sheep		***	***	NM
Beef cow	*	***	***	NM
Dairy cow		***	***	NM
Veal calf		***	***	NM
Goat	***	***	***	NM
Average group 1		***	***	NM
Group 2				
Swine		***	**	NM
Rabbit		***	***	NM
Turkey	*	***	**	NM
Broiler		***	***	NM
Layer		***	***	NM
Average group 2	*	***	***	NM
Average 1 + 2	*	***	***	***

NM: not in the model.

animal product to improve animal welfare are presented in Table 1. The distribution of the answers along the treatment classes (very good, good, fair, bad and very bad) were similar in males and females. Nevertheless, women seem to be more predisposed to pay more for the product in order to improve animal welfare. Differences between age classes were more evident. The answers of young people seem to be more biased to the negative extreme (bad treatment) than those observed for middle age people, which were less willing to pay an extra charge for the animal products. Between the occupation classes the answers of the students and professionals (qualified workers) were more biased to the negative (more critical) than those observed for non-qualified workers.

Overall mean score and the mean score assigned to each livestock by sex, age and occupation are presented in Table 2. In general, livestock of the first group (ruminants and horses) are scored higher than those included in the second group. It is evident that the greater the perception of intensity and industrialization of the production (group 2), the more negative the perception.

Significance probabilities for fixed effects from the analysis of variance of the scores are presented in Table 3. The effects of age and occupation were highly significant for the scores assigned to the livestock and the livestock group. No significant effect of sex was observed. The first group (ruminants and horses) received a significantly higher score than the second group (swine, poultry and rabbits), in agreement with the observation described in Table 1. Similar results were observed by Jamison (1992). The comparison of the results obtained by this author with our results, indicate that people in Spain are less sensitive to farm animal welfare concerns than in USA.

Conclusions
A high proportion of the people in Spain seemed to be ready to pay more for the product, if this greater price would guarantee better welfare for the animals (all of them depending in their economic capacity). The higher the perception of industrialization of the production, the more negative was the perception. Furthermore, the belief that the animals have the same feeling and emotions as humans (anthropomorphism) was perceived in the answers. Young and old people, students and professionals were more in favour of animal welfare than middle age people and non-qualified workers. There was a trend indicating a warm or positive response in women. In general, people did not understand the animal production systems because of their urban background and they need to be informed and educated.

Acknowledgements
This study was supported by the *Comisión Interministerial de Ciencia y Tecnologia* (CICYT) of Spain.

References
Jamison, W. 1992. The rights of animals, political activism, and the feed industry. In *Biotechnology in the feed industry,* (ed. T. P. Lyons), pp. 121-138. *Proceedings of the Alltech eighth annual symposium,* Alltech Technical Publications, Nicholasville, KY.

Statistical Analysis Systems Institute. 1988. *SAS/STATS user's guide (release 6.03).* SAS Institute, Inc., Cary, NC.

Farm animal welfare — who writes the rules?
Occasional Publication No. 23 — British Society of Animal Science 1999
edited by A. J. F. Russel, C. A. Morgan, C. J. Savory, M. C. Appleby and T. L. J. Lawrence

Revealing public preferences for farm animal welfare

D. E. B. Burgess, W. G. Hutchinson and J. Davis

Department of Agricultural Economics, The Queen's University of Belfast, Newforge Lane, Belfast BT9 5PX

Farm animal welfare is an issue of great public concern, illustrated by the sheer volume of letters sent to both MPs and MEPs and the amount of press coverage given to the issue. This is not in doubt. However, the question which has yet to be answered is how much does the public actually VALUE farm animal welfare? How much will the public be prepared to pay to increase the welfare of animals?

If the public are prepared to pay for improving animal welfare, then this finding would justify research into animal welfare. Alternatively, if the public are unwilling to pay for improvements, does this mean that research into animal welfare is seen as irrelevant to the public? The value of animal welfare is based on the preferences of the public and such preferences may indicate areas of greater and lesser welfare concern and of willingness to pay. However, how valid are these preferences for animal welfare? Are the public able to order their preferences rationally over this very emotive subject? If the public are unable to order preferences rationally, this casts doubt on their ability to value animal welfare and to contribute towards decisions made on animal welfare matters.

In order to determine how much the public value animal welfare, a survey will be undertaken to reveal both the public's willingness to pay and their preferences between several potential welfare improvements. If the preferences are ordered rationally, then consistency will be present — internally and externally. Preferences are consistent internally when given three choices (A, B or C). A is preferred to B, B is preferred to C and A is preferred to C. External consistency occurs when different elicitation methods reveal the same preference order.

The study is based on four welfare improvement schemes. In the first programme, the welfare of the dairy cow is improved by changing the winter housing of cattle from cubicles to straw yards in order to reduce lameness. The second scheme involves changing from fast-growing breeds of broiler chickens to slower growing breeds to improve leg quality. The third and fourth programmes enlarge and enrich the cages and pens of laying hens and pigs respectively, in order to enable the expression of their natural behaviours.

Figure 1 An example of a contingent valuation questionnaire.

The implementation of the welfare improvement schemes will incur costs. It is proposed that to cover these costs, a levy (similar to VAT) is placed on food items. As a result, everyone's food bill will increase by the amount of the levy.

i) The government has decided to introduce ONLY the scheme that improves the welfare of laying hens by enlarging and enriching their cages, while all other farm animals remain in their existing conditions.
Would you be prepared to support the levy, if your food-bill rose by _____ a month?

Yes	❏
No	❏

ii) The government has decided to introduce ONLY the scheme that improves the welfare of broiler chickens, by using slower growing breeds, while all other farm animals remain in their existing conditions.
Would you be prepared to support the levy, if your food bill rose by _____ a month?

Yes	❏
No	❏

iii) The government has decided to introduce ONLY the scheme that improves the welfare of the dairy cow by changing their winter housing from cubicles to straw yards, while all other farm animals remain in their existing conditions.
Would you be prepared to support the levy, if your food bill rose by _____ a month?

Yes	❏
No	❏

iv) The government has decided to introduce ONLY the scheme that improves the welfare of pigs, by enlarging and enriching their living conditions, while all other farm animals remain in their existing conditions.
Would you be prepared to support the levy, if your food bill rose by _____ a month?

Yes	❏
No	❏

Animal welfare is valued by employing the contingent valuation method (Mitchell and Carson, 1989), a technique frequently used in valuing environmental goods. It is a direct survey instrument which involves the setting up of a realistic, hypothetical market. In this market, all the welfare improvement programmes are specified. The respondents are then asked how much they would be prepared to pay for each of the proposed improvements (see Figure 1). While this method derives the estimates of the value that is placed on animal welfare by the public, it also reveals their preference ordering. As individual values are produced for each improvement programme, the estimates reveal the order in which the schemes are preferred.

While the contingent valuation method produces an order of the preferences for the animal welfare improvement schemes, it cannot test for inconsistency alone. In order to test for consistency, other methods have to be used. Two other techniques employed are paired-comparisons and matching. Both produce the order in which the welfare programmes are preferred, enabling external consistency to be checked. Additionally, they test for internal consistency, through the way the preferences are revealed. If the respondents are

Figure 2 An example of matching.

The implementation of the welfare improvement schemes will incur costs. It is proposed that to cover these costs, a levy (similar to VAT) is placed on food items. As a result, everyone's food bill will increase by the amount of the levy.

Through this levy, suppose that a large government fund was to be made available to improve the welfare of farm animals. This fund has been initially allocated to improve ONLY the welfare of laying hens in the UK through enlarging and enriching their cages, as outlined in the information booklet. This will result in 10 million laying hens having their welfare improved, while all other farm animals remain in their existing conditions.

However, this fund could be used instead to improve the welfare of dairy cows through changing their winter housing from cubicles to straw yards, as outlined in the information booklet. How many cows would have to have their welfare improved for you to prefer the money to be spent on cows rather than laying hens?

Answer _____

internally inconsistent, a unique order of their preferences cannot be produced.

In paired comparisons (Edwards, 1957), the respondents are presented with the welfare improvement schemes in pairs and have to select their preferred option. All potential combinations are shown randomly. Respondents must state which of the pair they prefer, any other answers i.e. 'don't mind' are not allowed. Matching (Tversky et al., 1988) is similar to paired-comparisons, as respondents are offered pairs of schemes. However, additional information about the numbers of animals affected through implementing only one of the programmes is given. The respondent has to state the number of animals which would have to have their welfare improved in the alternative scheme, for that scheme to be chosen instead of the initial programme (see Figure 2). The number given by the respondent indicates which option is preferred, i.e. if the response is less than the original figure, then the alternative is favoured over the first proposed. In both paired comparisons and matching, a valid order of preferences can only be revealed if the respondent is internally consistent. External consistency can be checked by comparing the orders of preferences revealed by each of the methods.

The contingent valuation produces a value for the willingness of the public to pay for specific animal welfare improvements, while all the different methods reveal the order of the public's preferences for the different animal welfare schemes. As a variety of techniques is used, different orderings of preferences could potentially occur, indicating inconsistency. Any inconsistencies that are present challenge the validity of the values gained from the contingent valuation, and possibly the public's ability to articulate rationally their preferences on these issues.

References

Edwards, A. L. 1957. *Techniques of attitude scale construction.* Appleton-Century-Crofts, Inc., New York.

Mitchell, R. C. and Carson, R. T. 1989. *Using surveys to value public goods: the contingent valuation method.* Resources for the Future, Washington DC.

Tversky, A., Slovic, P. and Sattath, S. 1988. Contingent weighting in judgement and choice. *Psychological Review* **95:** 371-384.

Farm animal welfare — who writes the rules?
Occasional Publication No. 23 — British Society of Animal Science 1999
edited by A. J. F. Russel, C. A. Morgan, C. J. Savory, M. C. Appleby and T. L. J. Lawrence

Who are the consumers of farm animal welfare?

R. M. Bennett and R. J. P. Blaney

Department of Agricultural and Food Economics, University of Reading, Reading RG6 6AR

Introduction

There are inextricable linkages between the disciplines of animal science, moral philosophy and economics when studying the welfare of farm animals. The task facing economists is to translate farm animal welfare into an economic concept and so be able to analyse it within an economic framework. Within economic theory farm animals may be viewed as no more than agricultural products, which represents the ethical position that animal welfare is only important as far as it impacts on human welfare. Thus, the following approach is appropriate: people are faced with choices which they may act upon individually or collectively and one choice to be made is about the level of farm animal suffering perceived to be acceptable. This may be characterized as a trade-off between farm animal products and perceived farm animal welfare. The value of farm animal products can be indicated by their prices but the value of farm animal welfare to society may not be fully recognized. Although consumers may respond to their farm animal welfare concerns by buying products perceived to be associated with higher levels of animal welfare they may stop buying some animal products altogether. Therefore, their preference for a high level of farm animal welfare will not be taken into account by the market. This under-recognition of people's true values can lead to poor farm animal welfare. Therefore, to optimize the production of various farm animal products within society the true value of farm animal welfare must be estimated. This involves taking account of the values to both consumers and non-consumers of farm animal products (Bennett, 1995). To enable measurement of society's valuation of farm animal welfare various economic tools can be used, one of which is contingent valuation. Although this methodology has theoretical and practical problems, its application to farm animal welfare issues has been explored (Bennett and Larson, 1996) and may provide a useful input to the farm animal welfare debate. The aim of this experiment was to determine how people's attitudes and moral beliefs concerning farm animal welfare affect the value they place on farm animal welfare improvements.

Material and methods

A contingent valuation survey of 120 undergraduate students at the University of Reading was conducted during the 1998 summer term. The students were from the Department of Economics and the Department of Psychology and were given the contingent valuation questionnaire to complete in class. The questionnaires consisted of three sections and the farm animal welfare scenario chosen to elicit valuations was pig slaughtering. The first section asked the students questions about their age, sex, nationality, and their existing purchasing behaviour with regard to animal products. It then asked them to score on a scale of 0 to 10 the importance of six farm animal welfare issues, with 10 being 'very important'. The second section provided information about the existing pig slaughtering techniques used in the UK, including some of the potential animal welfare problems and alternative 'humane' slaughter techniques. The students were then asked whether they would support government legislation to make it compulsory for slaughterhouses to use the 'humane' pig slaughter techniques (i.e. the head-to-back system). They were then asked the amount of money they would be willing to pay, as an increase in their weekly food bill, to support this legislation (a single-bounded dichotomous choice format was used, with amounts ranging from 25p to £2). The third section asked the students eight related attitudinal questions, which they were asked to score on a scale of 0 to 10, with 10 being 'very much like my way of thinking'. These attitudinal questions also included questions about the morality of the pig slaughtering techniques. Finally, the students were asked to state their considerations behind the scores they gave.

Results

Of the two groups sampled, 64 psychology students and 48 economics students completed the questionnaires. The age range of the students was 18 to 35 years; 8% of the students were from outside the UK and 5% were vegetarian. The gender profile was 60% female, 40% male. The mean expenditure on food consumption was £24·78 per week. In response to the question: to what extent are you concerned that farm animals may be mistreated or may suffer in the process of producing food/agricultural products?' the mean score of 'concern' was 2·7 (s.d. 0·94) on a scale of 0 to 4, indicating that they were only somewhat concerned. However, when asked whether they agreed that: 'it is morally wrong to cause harm animals any pain or injury for the purposes of producing food' the mean score on the agreement scale of 0 to 10 was 6·8 (s.d. 2·35), indicating agreement with the statement that it is morally wrong.

The most important animal welfare issues were identified as hens kept in battery cages, pig slaughter without adequate stunning, and live exports (Table 1).

Just over 61% of the sample population supported the proposed pig slaughter legislation and 15% were against, with a mean willingness to pay (WTP) to support the legislation of 60p per week (i.e. 0·60, s.d. 0·69). This is equivalent to a 2·4% increase in food expenditure. The WTP was higher for females (0·72 v. 0·44; s.e.d. 0·09; $P < 0.05$), psychology students (0·77 v. 0·46; s.e.d. 0·10; $P < 0.05$), and those already avoiding some animal products because of animal welfare concerns (0·77 v. 0·41; s.e.d. 0·09; $P < 0.01$). About 20% of the sample population avoid buying some animal products because of their concerns about the welfare of the farm animals involved in those products. Spearman correlation analysis indicated correlations between WTP and age-group ($P < 0.05$), belief that it is morally wrong to cause farm animals any pain ($P < 0.01$), belief that pigs have a right to as painless death as possible ($P < 0.001$), belief that the current pig slaughter techniques are wrong ($P < 0.001$), belief that public opinion is that current pig slaughter techniques are wrong ($P < 0.05$) and concern about other farm animal welfare issues ($P < 0.001$ to 0·05). Of the attitudinal questions the most significant was: 'pigs have a right to die in as painless way as possible', which had a mean score (on a scale of 0 to 10) of 8·4 (s.d. 2·3), indicating strong agreement with the statement. The considerations the students stated were behind their scoring indicating that they had followed a reasoned and logical approach.

Conclusions

A higher valuation of pig welfare was associated with gender, age and course studied. This is in line with other studies that have shown that females are more ethical than males, that moral development is a function of age and that economics students are less concerned with moral issues than non-economists (Frank et al., 1993; Baron, 1994; Eckel and Grossman, 1998). A higher valuation of pig welfare was also associated with a high degree of perceived moral importance of farm animal welfare (and pig welfare in particular), other farm animal welfare concerns and a belief that there is consensus in society that current pig slaughter techniques are wrong (Table 2). These results support the validity of the contingent valuation methodology and the preliminary findings suggest that there is a positive link between attitudes and moral beliefs concerning farm animal welfare and the value people place on improvements in farm animal welfare.

Table 1 *'Importance' scoring of farm animal welfare issues*

Animal welfare issue	Rank	Mean score†	s.d.
Hens kept in battery cages	(1)	7·4	2·64
Pig slaughter without adequate stunning	(1)	7·4	2·51
Live export of farm animals from the UK	3	6·8	3·11
Nose-ringing pigs to limit field damage	4	5·0	2·68
Castration of lambs with rubber rings	5	4·8	2·69
Use of high-yielding breeds of dairy cows	6	4·7	2·85

† Note: the scoring was on a scale of 0-10, with 10 indicating a 'very important issue', and 0 indicating 'not an important issues'. Thus, a mean score of 5 indicates 'neither an important nor unimportant issue'.

Table 2 *The most significant factors influencing students' valuations of pig welfare*

Factor influencing valuation	High valuation	Low valuation
Gender	Female	Male
Course being studied	Psychology	Economics
Age	23	18
Ethical purchasing behaviour	Avoid some animal products	None
Farm animal welfare issues	Concerned	Not concerned
Moral importance of pig welfare	Very important	Not important

Acknowledgements

R. J. P. Blaney is grateful to MAFF for the provision of a Ph.D. studentship.

References

Baron, J. 1994. *Thinking and deciding, second edition.* Cambridge University Press.

Bennett, R. M. 1995. The value of farm animal welfare. *Journal of Agricultural Economics* **46:** 46-60.

Bennett, R. M. and Larson, D. 1996. Contingent valuation of the perceived benefits of farm animal welfare legislation: an exploratory survey. *Journal of Agricultural Economics* **47:** 224-235.

Eckel, C. and Grossman, P. 1998. Are women less selfish than men? Evidence from dictator experiments. *The Economic Journal* **108:** 726-735.

Franc, R., Gilovich, T. and Regan, D. 1993. Does studying economics inhibit co-operation? *Journal of Economic perspectives* **7:** 159-171.

Farm animal welfare — who writes the rules?
Occasional Publication No. 23 — British Society of Animal Science 1999
edited by A. J. F. Russel, C. A. Morgan, C. J. Savory, M. C. Appleby and T. L. J. Lawrence

Animal health and welfare issues on organic livestock farms in the UK: results of a producer survey

S. Roderick, M. Hovi and N. Short

Veterinary Epidemiology and Economics Research Unit, Department of Agriculture, University of Reading, Earley Gate, PO Box 236, Reading RG6 6AT

Introduction

Organic farming methods place paramount importance on the health and welfare of farm animals. Standards have been clearly established that put the needs of animals first. Although the proportion of organic farms in the UK occupies less than 0·5% of the total land area, a rapid increase in consumer demand is being partly met by an increase in the number of farms currently in a state of conversion. Standards for animal health management emphasize reduced dependence on prophylactic treatments, particularly antibiotics. The philosophy of organic farming emphasizes the need to produce food in an 'integrated, humane, environmentally and economically sustainable agricultural production system' (Lampkin and Measures, 1995). Concerns have been expressed about the potential impact on animal health and welfare (Andrews, 1991). Conversely, it has been argued that organic livestock systems offer opportunities to introduce improved husbandry methods that have long been recognized to be of general benefit to animal health and welfare (Vaarst, 1995). It has been suggested also that, while there has been a general increase in research into organic farming, little attention has been directed to animal health and welfare issues (Borgen, 1995). In 1995 a study of organic livestock systems in the UK was conducted with the objectives of describing health and welfare practices and identifying research priorities.

Material and methods

Postal questionnaires were sent to 270 Soil Association registered organic farmers. These contained questions relating to farm type and details of animal health practices for each livestock enterprise, including producer perception of disease. Open-ended questions referring to organic practices were also included. Producers' perceptions of disease was based on a subjective assessment of a range of common conditions, with respondents asked to score each from 1 (no problem) to 5 (serious problem).

Results

One hundred and sixty (59%) questionnaires were returned, of which 139 (52%) were considered to be useful returns. Most respondents kept more than one species of livestock, most commonly beef cattle and sheep.

Dairy systems

Thirty-four respondents kept dairy herds, of which 13 (38%) had herds of more than 50 cows. The majority of farmers reared all their own replacement stock. The farms were evenly divided between those that wean calves at less than 1 week and those that wean at more than 1 week. A small minority removed calves after 12 weeks of age. The most important culling decisions were related to age (37%), infertility (37%) and mastitis history (37%). A minority of farmers used routine prophylactic vaccinations against lungworm (27%) or leptospirosis (19%), with only one farmer using both. The majority of producers relied on clean grazing (54%) and/or mixed grazing strategies (50%) to control worms in young stock. Thirty-three percent used routine anthelmintic treatments. A small minority (8%) did not use any of these strategies. Seventy-seven percent of dairy farmers used some form of footrot control strategy. The majority (62%) adopted foot-trimming, with a third of these also using a footbath.

The highest problem-ranked disease was mastitis (Table 1). A combination of antibiotics (62% of farms) and homeopathic remedies (65% of farms) were used to treat mastitis. Approximately a quarter of producers were using cold water massage with 19% using uddermint. All conditions pertaining to calf and heifer rearing received a low average ranking with little difference between diseases. Some conditions, such as lungworm respiratory diseases did receive high rankings on individual farms.

Beef systems

A total population of 8506 beef animals were surveyed on 112 farms. Eighty-nine percent of farms were single suckler units, 13% had multiple-suckler

Table 1 *Farmer perception of animal health problems in organic farms: dairy cows (23 herds)*

Disease	Average score	Distribution of score (%)				
		No problem	Not common	Slight problem	Occasional problem	Serious problem
Mastitis	3·3	4	15	52	26	4
Infertility	2·7	11	33	41	11	4
Lameness	2·4	22	41	30	7	0
Milk fever	2·3	11	52	30	7	0
Calving problems	1·9	41	44	15	0	0
Abortion	1·7	56	33	4	7	0
BSE	1·6	67	22	7	4	0
Bloat	1·5	59	26	15	0	0
Ketosis	1·4	59	37	4	0	0
Grass staggers	1·3	81	7	7	4	0

Key for disease perception score: 1 = no problem; 2 = not common; 3 = slight problem; 4 = continuous problem; 5 = serious problem.

systems and 10% bucket-reared calves. Many also kept sheep and the majority (46%) practised mixed or clean (61%) grazing to control internal parasites. Twenty-eight percent of beef producers used anthelmintics, mainly integrated with controlled grazing practices. Generally, health issues among adult beef animals were not given high problem rankings (Table 2). External parasites, diarrhoea and mineral deficiencies, although receiving low rankings, were considered the most important conditions in young, growing stock.

Sheep systems
Sixty-four percent of the 90 sheep systems covered were classed as lowland, 19% were upland and 11% were hill flocks. A small percentage operated a combination of these. The farms were evenly divided into those lambing outdoors, indoors and both. Most flocks were wintered outdoors. Thirty-eight percent of farms sold lambs direct to an abbatoir, 32% through a livestock auction, 21% via farm shop and

28% through unspecified means. Cull ewes were generally sold through traditional auction yards (62%). Forty-one percent of the farmers surveyed vaccinated against clostridial diseases and 28% against pasteurella. A number of these (24%) used both vaccination regimes. The majority (64%) used anthelmintics, to varying degrees. Many of these were using anthelmintics in combination with other methods. Sixty-nine percent used clean grazing practices and 55% mixed grazing. A proportion was obviously using a combination of these methods. Six percent of farmers were using homeopathic remedies to control worms. The use of garlic was also common. Only 2% responded that they did not have a control policy. Almost half of organic farmers (48%) either used anthelmintics on lambs infrequently or never. Thirty-two percent wormed every 3 to 6 months, whilst 12% wormed every 2 months and 8% wormed every month. Footrot was perceived to be the most important adult sheep condition (Table 3). Twenty percent felt that this was

Table 2 *Farmer perception of animal health problems in organic suckler beef herds (89 herds)*

Disease	Average score	Distribution of score (%)				
		No problem	Not common	Slight problem	Occasional problem	Serious problem
Infertility	1·9	40	37	18	5	0
Calving difficulties	1·8	43	37	17	2	0
Mastitis	1·7	52	32	14	1	1
Lameness	1·6	53	33	13	0	0
Grass staggers	1·3	77	15	6	1	1
Fluke	1·2	84	8	7	1	0
Bloat	1·2	83	15	2	0	0
BSE	1·1	92	7	0	0	1

Key for disease perception score: 1 = no problem; 2 = not common; 3 = slight problem; 4 = continuous problem; 5 = serious problem.

Table 3 *Farmer perception of animal health problems in organic sheep flocks: breeding ewes (85 flocks)*

Disease	Average score	Distribution of score (%)				
		No problem	Not common	Slight problem	Occasional problem	Serious problem
Footrot	2·7	14	30	29	23	5
Mastitis	2·1	23	47	28	2	0
Fly strike	2·1	26	43	26	5	1
Fluke/worms	2·0	37	29	27	7	0
Lambing difficulties	1·9	29	45	26	0	0
Twin lamb disease	1·7	46	38	16	0	0
Clostridial diseases	1·6	62	21	13	4	0
Pasteurella	1·5	63	27	5	4	1
Abortion	1·5	70	17	12	1	0
Sheep scab	1·2	90	5	2	2	0
Scrapie	1·1	95	1	4	0	0

Key for disease perception score: 1 = no problem; 2 = not common; 3 = slight problem; 4 = continuous problem; 5 = serious problem.

a continuous problem. The majority used either footbaths, foot trimming or a combination of the two for control. Antibiotics were not widely used. Of the diseases afflicting lambs, fly strike, worms and footrot received the highest rankings, although overall these were perceived as slight problems. Eleven percent did, however, regard fly strike as a continuous problem and 8% gave worms a similar ranking. The problem of fly strike was mainly tackled by a combination of the use of cyromazine (Vetrazin; Novartis) and management techniques such as dagging. There were too few goats covered in the survey to allow any meaningful analysis.

Pig systems
Only 24 organic pig farmers with a total of 6250 pigs responded to the questionnaire. More than half of these were kept on one farm. Most of the herds were classified as mixed breeding and fattening units, with pigs predominantly housed outdoors in arcs. The main outputs from these farms were pork and bacon weight animals for slaughter. A small sample and large between farm variation rendered data reflecting disease perception as less meaningful than data from ruminant systems. Lice infestation was the only condition given a mean ranking suggesting a slight problem. Disease control trends were of low inputs of chemotherapy and chemoprophylactic treatments.

Poultry systems
Only eight broiler producers responded, one of which had 5000 birds, accounting for 87% of the total broiler population. The mean flock size of the other seven producers was only 11 birds. Forty-seven respondents indicated that they kept laying hens. The average laying flock size was 42 hens. Only 22 producers completed detailed health and management questions and therefore only a limited analysis of organic poultry was possible. The trends were of low disease ranking and veterinary inputs.

Discussion
Generally, organic farmers do not perceive animal health issues as a major problem on their farms. The most significant disease problems identified by organic farmers are similar to those commonly seen in conventional systems. The view that organic farming constitutes a welfare concern was not the perception of the producers. The common misconception of organic farming being mainly reliant on 'alternative' medicines without the use of conventional veterinary inputs was not borne out by the results of this study. What was evident is that there is a reliance on a reduced input of the veterinary services combined with integrated alternative treatments and appropriate husbandry. A number of producers commented that they would like more practical information on homeopathy from veterinarians trained in its use.

Many of the comments received were concerned with welfare issues, particularly those pertaining to housing and transport. There was particular concern with regards to a marketing and infra-structure that limit the achievement of high welfare standards. A fundamental component of the organic philosophy relates to the avoidance of animal suffering. The Soil Association (1989) states 'if, despite appropriate and humane husbandry, animals fall ill and drug use is deemed necessary, it must not be withheld'. Respondents frequently commented on the importance of this flexibility in organic standards as a rigid set of rules may have some negative welfare impact.

Acknowledgements
We would like to thank the Animal Health Trust for supporting this study.

References
Andrews, T. 1991. Suffering animals in a green landscape. *Dairy Farmer* **38**: 26-28.

Borgen, M. 1995. *Ecoguide 1995/96*. Organic Service Centre, Copenhagen.

Lampkin, N. and Measures, M. 1995. *Organic farm management handbook 1995/96*. University of Wales, Aberystwyth.

Soil Association 1989. *Organic farming and animal welfare*. Soil Association, Bristol.

Vaarst, M. 1995. Sundhed og sygdomshadtering I danske okologiske malkekvaebesaetninger. *Ph.D. thesis. The Royal Veterinary and Agricultural School, Copenhagen.*

Farm animal welfare — who writes the rules?
Occasional Publication No. 23 — British Society of Animal Science 1999
edited by A. J. F. Russel, C. A. Morgan, C. J. Savory, M. C. Appleby and T. L. J. Lawrence

The effect of cow-calf separation in dairy cattle on animal behaviour

J. K. Margerison[1], C. J. C. Phillips[2] and T. R. Preston[3]

[1]*Department of Agriculture and Food Studies, Seale-Hayne Faculty, University of Plymouth, Newton Abbot, Devon TQ12 6NQ*
[2]*Department of Clinical Veterinary Medicine, University of Cambridge, Madingley Road, Cambridge CB3 0ES*
[3]*Department of Agriculture and Forestry, University of Ho Chi Min, Ho Chi Min City, Vietnam*

Introduction

The abrupt separation of cows and calves has been found to affect both cow and calf behaviour (Hopster *et al.*, 1995). This abrupt separation is typical in artificial calf rearing systems which are common practice in the majority of beef and dairy production programmes. The artificial rearing of calves is characterized by individual penning, which facilitates accurate measurement of food intakes but limits calf contact. Cross-suckling behaviour has been found to occur frequently in artificially reared calves (Wood *et al.*, 1967; Lalande *et al.*, 1979) and individually penned calves have been found to perform stereotypic behaviours which are generally oral in nature. In contrast, calf rearing in developing countires is dominated by the use of suckling systems. The dairy production systems limit suckling to facilitate milk removal, which allows the calf and the cow to have continued but limited contact. In these systems cows have been found to give greater milk yields and calves reared by limited suckling seem to have greater milk conversion efficiencies (Ugarte and Preston, 1972; Gaya *et al.*, 1978; Knowles and Edwards, 1983) and lower mortality rates (Ugarte, 1989; Alvarez *et al.*, 1980) compared with calves reared artificially. However, the effect of abrupt separation of the cow and calf has been found to be relatively short lived with cows and calves showing increased cortisol levels and 'stress' for up to 6 to 8 h following separation (Hopster *et al.*, 1995). This may indicate that cows which are continually separated from their calves may be subjected to repeated periods of 'stress' each time the cow and calf are separated. The objective of this experiment was to compare the effect on cow and calf behaviour of abrupt cow-calf separation and continuous limited contact between cows and their own calf or a foster calf.

Material and methods

The experiment was completed in Colombia with the co-operation of a non-government organizations Centro Inter-institucional para la Producción de Agropecuaria en el Valle del Rio Cauca (CIPAV) and a commercial dairy farm, Hacienda Lucerna. At 4 days *post partum* 36 multiparous dairy cows were allocated to one of three treatments, where they remained for the following lactation (up to 305 days). The treatments used were: a non-suckling treatment (NS), where the cow and the calf were separated at 4 days *post partum* and the calves were reared artificially and separately from the dam and two limited suckling treatments where the cows were sucked for 15 min following mechanical milking. In the first treatment, 12 cows were sucked by their own calf (SM) and in the second experiment, 12 cows were sucked by a foster calf (SF). The calves were reared in their treatment groups and all the experimental cows were grazed together throughout the experiment. The behaviour study was conducted over 24 h at 30-day intervals, equivalent to three observation periods during the first 100 days of lactation or age. Behavioural observation periods began after morning milking and continued until the same time the following day. During these periods each animal was observed once every 5 min until dusk and then every 15 min until dawn. The cows and calves were observed on the same days. During the observation periods the times cows spent in various behaviours were recorded. A count of the number of acts of aggression were recorded, using 15-min recording periods. In calves the times spent lying, grazing, sucking, feeding on concentrate and standing were recorded. The incidence of walking, non-nutritive cross-sucking, allo-grooming, grooming others and agonistic behaviour were recorded, using 15-min recording periods during which the number of actual events were recorded. The duration of sucking and the incidence of cross-sucking was recorded by observing calves for 6 s every minute during and for 20 min following the ingestion of milk. Cross-sucking was defined as a calf performing sucking movements while having some part of another calf's body in its mouth. During this cross-sucking, new sucking events were recorded when: a calf stopped sucking one calf and sucked another calf; the calf changed to suck another part of the

Table 1 *Behaviour in suckled and non-suckled cows (min or incidence per 24 h)*

Activity	Non-suckled	Suckled (Foster)	Suckled (Maternal)	s.e.d.†
Grazing	348	360	348	25·5
Lying	150	145	148	18·0
Lying ruminating	440	437	442	24·1
Standing ruminating	120	116	119	10·1
Total ruminating	550	553	561	30·2
Feeding	59	59	61	25·5
Walking	111	105	109	12·0
Standing	212	218	213	9·6
Total	1440	1440	1440	–
Aggression	2·1	1·9	1·7	0·08

† All differences not statistically significant ($P > 0.05$).

body; or the calf stopped to perform another behaviour and then resumed sucking the same calf and body part. During cross-sucking events, the body area which was sucked and the calf performing the sucking and being sucked were recorded.

All the data were analysed using the Minitab software package. The behaviour data which were not normally distributed was transformed by adding 0·5 to each observation and then were analysed as with normally distributed data. The data were analysed using analysis of variance (ANOVA) with the generalized linear model (GLM) and a significant effect was determined from the 'P' value in the ANOVA table for three treatments, following which the treatments were paired and compared by Tukey's method for equal observations.

Results
The times spent in various behavioural activities during three 24-h periods by the cows are presented in Table 1. Behaviour was similar in all the treatment groups, with suckling treatment having no significant effect on grazing, lying, feeding, walking, standing or ruminating (either standing and lying) time in the long term.

The time spent and the incidence of various behavioural activities during 24 h by the calves are presented in Table 2. In all the treatment groups, the time spent lying and standing were similar. However, the time spent eating concentrate was significantly greater ($P < 0.05$) in calves reared artificially, compared with restrictedly suckled calves. The frequency of cross-sucking was greater in calves reared artificially, ($P < 0.05$) compared with calves which were restricted suckled. The number of incidents of walking, grooming and performing agonistic behaviour was similar in all the treatments groups.

During the experiment, a total of 96 instances of cross-sucking were recorded. In artificially reared calves the frequency of cross-sucking was greatest directly following the ingestion of milk and the frequency reduced slowly over the following 15 min, falling to negligible levels at around 12 min post feeding. In restrictedly suckled calves, the incidence of cross-sucking was significantly lower and the incidents occurred only after calves had been sucking the cows for 12 min.

Discussion
In this experiment the long-term behaviour in calves was similar irrespective of whether they had been sucked by calves with no significant effect of suckling treatment on grazing, lying, feeding, walking, standing or ruminating (either standing and lying) time. However, it has been found that cows and calves show increased cortisol levels and 'stress' in the short term, within 6 to 8 h following

Table 2 *Behaviour in suckled and non-suckled calves (min or incidence per 24 h)*

Activity	Non-suckled	Suckled (Foster)	Suckled (maternal)	s.e.d.	P
Time spent (min/day)					
Lying	970	968	965	110·0	
Standing	325	342	336	45·5	*
Feeding (concentrate)	70	33	39	13·5	*
Grazing	10	13	14	7·1	
Suckling	25	28	29	5·1	
Total	1400	1384	1383	–	
Incidents (no. per 24 h)					
Walking	26·4	30·4	32·0	6·5	
Grooming (self)	14·7	18·2	19·1	4·1	
Grooming (other)	2·3	5·1	3·5	1·7	
Agonistic	11·1	10·4	9·8	2·56	
Cross-suckling	1·80	0·52	0·14	0·231	*

separation (Hopster *et al.*, 1995) and these responses were observed over a longer period. It has been found also that cows respond to the calf when it is placed in an adjoining paddock (Hudson and Mullford, 1977). The cows in this experiment were grazed at least 300 m away from where the calves were housed and did not show any signs of response. The cows used in this experiment were multiparous and Hopster *et al.* (1995) found that multiparous cows only respond mildly immediately following cow-calf separation. The results indicated that the continuous limited suckling and repeated cow-calf separation had no significant effect on cow behaviour. The incidence of cross-sucking was found to be significantly greater in artificially reared calves compared with limited suckled calves. This cross-sucking has been found to occur in artificially reared calves (Wood *et al.*, 1967; Lalande *et al.*, 1979) particularly those reared in groups. In contrast, the incidence of cross-sucking in the limited suckled calves was negligible. In the artificially reared calves the frequency was found to be greatest following milk ingestion, which is similar to previous work with artificially reared calves (Hammel *et al.*, 1988; Passillé *et al.*, 1992; Lidfors, 1993). The ingestion of milk has been found to increase the motivational state (Toates, 1986) of the calf to perform sucking behaviour. Also the ingestion of only small quantities of milk has been found sufficient to stimulate cross-sucking (Brake *et al.*, 1982). The artificially reared calves spent significantly less time consuming milk, which left them with a high sucking motivation. As a consequence the incidence of cross-sucking was greater in calves reared artificially. In contrast, limited suckled calves spent longer sucking and consequently would return to a pen with a low motivational state which would result in a low incidence of cross-sucking.

References

Alvarez, F. J., Saucedo, G., Arriaga, A. and Preston, T. R. 1980. Effect on milk production and calf performance of milking crossbred European/Zebu cattle in the absence or presence of the calf, and of rearing their calves artificially. *Tropical Animal Production* **5:** 25-37.

Brake, S. C., Sager, D. J., Sullivan, R. and Hofer, M. 1982. The rôle of intra-oral and gastrointestinal ones in the control of suckling and milk consumption in rat pups. *Development Psychobiology* **15:** 529-541.

Gaya, H., Hulman, B. and Preston, T. R. 1978. Effect of two methods of restricted suckling on performance of cows and on the growth rate of calves. *Tropical Animal Production* **3:** 118-124.

Hopster, H., Connell, J. M. and Blokhuis, H. 1995. Acute effects of cow-calf separation on heart rate, plasma cortisol and behaviour in multiparous dairy cows. *Applied Animal Behaviour Science* **44:** 1-8.

Hammell, K. L., Metz, J. H. M. and Mekking, P. 1988. Suckling behaviour of dairy calves fed milk *ad libitum* by bucket or teat. *Applied Animal Behaviour Science* **20:** 275-285.

Hudson, S. and Mullford, M. M. 1977. Investigation of maternal bonding in cattle. *Applied Animal Ethology* **3:** 271-276.

Knowles, R. T. and Edwards, M. D. 1983. A comparison of the effects of restricted suckling and artificial calf rearing systems on dam and calf performance. *Malaysian Agricultural Journal* **54:** 1-9.

Lalande, G., Beauchemin, K. and Fahmy, M. M. 1979. A note on the performance of Holstein Friesian veal calves raised to weaning individually or in groups. *Annals of Zootechnia* **28:** 235-238.

Passillé, A. M. B., Metz, H. M., Mekking, P. and Wiepkema, P. R. 1992. Does drinking milk stimulate suckling in young calves? *Applied Animal Behaviour Science* **34:** 23-36.

Toates, F. 1986. *Motivational systems.* Cambridge University Press, Cambridge.

Ugarte, J. 1989. Restricted suckling in dual purpose systems. *Feeding dairy cows in the tropics. Proceedings of the FAO expert consultation. Bangkok, Thailand 7-11 July 1989,* pp. 199-207. Food and Agriculture Organization, Rome.

Ugarte, J. and Preston, T. R. 1972b. [Milk production and calf growth as affected by the length of the interval between milking and suckling.] *Revista Cubana de Ciencia de Agricultura* **6:** 331-336.

Wood, P. D. P., Smith, G. F. and Lisle, M. F. 1967. A survey of inter-suckling in dairy herds in England and Wales. *Veterinary Record* **81:** 396-398.

Farm animal welfare — who writes the rules?
Occasional Publication No. 23 — British Society of Animal Science 1999
edited by A. J. F. Russel, C. A. Morgan, C. J. Savory, M. C. Appleby and T. L. J. Lawrence

Initiation of suckling in suckler cows with natural and adopted calves

H. D. Randle

Department of Agriculture and Food Studies, Seale-Hayne Faculty, University of Plymouth, Newton Abbot TQ12 6NQ

Introduction

Wild bovines such as water buffalo have been observed to adopt orphans (Murphey *et al.*, 1991). Spontaneous adoption has also been reported in domestic bovines and occurs either as a result of the dams mismothering by poaching young or permitting young other than their own to suck, or due to the opportunistic tendencies of young calves. The bond between a beef cow and her calf is considered to be less flexible than that between a dairy cow and her calf (Le Neindre, 1989). This difference is attributed to beef cows having been selected for early calf recognition and strong bonding (Kiley-Worthington and de la Plain, 1983) and dairy cows having been selected for amenability to the removal of the calf and milk let down in its absence (Edwards and Broom, 1982). Nevertheless, it is possible to manipulate the beef cow into accepting a second calf in addition to her own, although there can be problems with this since calves are typically only fostered (tolerated and not treated as her own). A system in which calves are only fostered can be time consuming as the sucking may require human supervision. However, Kiley-Worthington (1976) developed a double-suckling system involving adoption in which the additional calf (the 'adopter') is treated by the (beef) cow in a similar way to her own calf (the 'natural'). The sucking behaviour of calves raised in this system is studied further in this paper.

Suckling has been found to play an important rôle in the reinforcement of the mother-young bond (Le Neindre, 1982). There are conflicting results regarding who controls the occurrence and length of suckling bouts. Lent (1991) reported that dams initiated the majority of suckling bouts in the first few weeks *post partum*, whilst earlier, Vitale *et al.* (1986) reported that calves initiated 87% of suckling bouts in this period. Clearly calves play an important rôle in the initiation of suckling. The objective of the studies reported in this paper was to compare the number of suckling bouts initiated by natural and adopted calves sucking beef cows.

Material and methods

A total of 13 trios were observed, each consisting of a South Devon cow, her homebred natural calf and an adopted calf. Adoptions were carried out using the method developed by Kiley-Worthington (1976). The adoptee was usually at least 3 days old at the time of adoption. The potential adoptee was fed and covered with amniotic fluid, before being introduced to the dam alongside her natural calf immediately after the natural calf had sucked for the first time. It was important to ensure that the adoptee was not hungry at the point of first introduction to the dam. For the first 2 to 3 days *post partum* the calves were separated from the dam. They were put into an adjacent pen which allowed visual, vocal and tactile contact between the dam and calves. The calves were then reunited with the dam simultaneously for suckling. Suckling was closely supervised as it was important that the dam learned to tolerate the adoptee and that the adoptee was not put off. The dam was tied up and the adoptee only allowed to suck for a maximum of 5 min (to prevent scouring and consequent separation of the dam and adopted calf). By day 4 if possible the dam was untied and the adoptees sucking was unrestricted. Typically by day 5 the two calves remained with the cow between suckling sessions. By day 7 the trio was turned out to pasture and observed periodically to check that the adoptee was permitted to suck the adoptive dam.

In group 1, six trios were observed for the 1st week of the adoption and week 3 post adoption. In group 2, seven trios were observed during the 1st week of the adoption and the 1st week of month 5 post adoption. During these observation periods all suckling bouts which occurred between 06.00 and 21.00 h were observed. Observations included all of the behaviours exhibited by the darn and both the natural and adopted calves. The identity of the initiator of the suckling bout was recorded (dam, natural, adoptee, human). The frequencies of the following behaviours directed by the dam towards both the natural and adopted calf were recorded: contact making, head throwing, head butting, stamping, leg lifting, weight shifting, smelling, licking, calling, head shaking and chasing. The frequencies of the following behaviours directed by the natural and adopted calf towards the dam were recorded: approaching, contact making, touching body, teat searching, smelling the udder, sucking, bunting, tail wagging, contact breaking, head shaking, following and calling. The sucking positions assumed and durations achieved in each position were also recorded for both calves, as were any necessary incidences of intervention by the human supervisor. All of these behaviours were recorded instantaneously from the point of initiation to the end of the suckling session.

At the end of the four observation periods the success of the adoptions were rated using the five-point system developed by Kiley-Worthington and de la Plain (1983): R — rejected, the calf was persistently attacked by the dam and not allowed to suck; F1 — level one fostering, the calf was tolerated, it was allowed to suck adjacent to the natural calf or from between the hind legs; F2 — level two fostering, as F1 but the calf was also allowed to suck on the opposite side to the natural calf; A1 — level one adoption, as F2 but could also suck alone if the dam was distracted; A2 — level two adoption, calf permitted to suck alone without the dam being distracted and there was evidence of the dam actively seeking the calf out and protecting it.

In this study, the majority (70%) of the suckling sessions in group 1, week 1 were initiated by the human supervisor. This was controlled to ensure acceptance of the adoptee calf as outlined above. In group 2, week 40% of the suckling sessions were initiated by the human supervisor.

Results
At the end of the 1st week of adoption 12 of the 13 adoptions carried out were considered to be successful, i.e. the cow had 'adopted' the second calf and no human intervention was necessary to ensure successful suckling (Table 1).

In total 409 suckling sessions were observed. In both groups the number of initiations performed by the humans decreased dramatically after the 1st week of the adoption (Figure 1). In all observation periods the natural calves initiated substantially more of the suckling sessions than the adopted calves. In both follow up observation periods (week 3 post adoption in group 1 and the 1st week of month 5 post adoption in group 2) dams initiated more suckling sessions than the adopted calves. In fact, adopted calves seldom initiated suckling sessions. It was found that adopted calves had developed an 'opportunistic' strategy which allowed them to suck.

Table 1 *The success rating† of the 13 adoptions studied at the end of week 1 of the adoption*

Group 1	dam						
	1	2	3	4	5	6	
	A1	A1	A1	A2	A1	A1	
Group 2	dam						
	1	2	3	4	5	6	7
	A1	A1	A1	A2	A2	A2	R

† R = rejection; A = adoption: 1 = calf sucks when dam is distracted; 2 = calf sucks without dam being distracted.

Adopted calves waited for their natural calf partner to commence sucking before they sucked the dam. This opportunistic strategy was still employed at 5 months post adoption. It can be seen in Figure 1 that in group 2 (5 months post adoption) there were some human interventions. However, these were all performed on the one trio in which adoption was not achieved and the calf was rejected.

Discussion
Double suckling with adoption
The double suckling with adoption method used was successful. One of the 13 adoptions failed, although the additional calf was allowed to suck if the dam was under close human supervision.

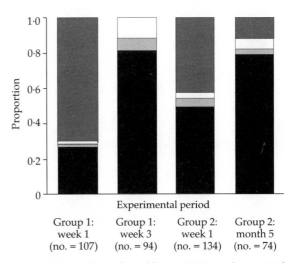

Figure 1 Proportion of suckling initiations by natural calves (■), adopted calves (❑), dams (▩) and humans (■) intervention.

Initiation of suckling

The sucking behaviour of all of the calves studied was typical of calves in a beef suckler system. The natural calves took responsibility for controlling suckling sessions (Vitale *et al.*, 1986; Veissier *et al.*, 1990) from week 1 post adoption and by the follow up observation periods (week 3 in group 1 and month 5 in group 2) the calves initiated most of the suckling sessions (Giovengo and Waring, 1990). Throughout the study the natural calves initiated substantially more suckling sessions than the adoptee calves. Adoption was achieved since adoptee calves were permitted to suck without human supervision, however they seldom initiated the suckling session and were rarely observed sucking without the natural calf. In order to suck and obtain milk, adoptee calves developed an opportunistic strategy, in which they waited for their natural counterpart to initiate suckling. The importance of the synchronization of suckling in ensuring that the two offspring will be able to suck successfully on one dam has been highlighted by Price *et al.* (1984) in beef cows rearing twins and Birgersson *et al.* (1991) in deer. This study demonstrated that the synchronization of suckling is equally important when the beef cow has adopted an additional calf to her own and that the adoptee develops an opportunistic strategy to ensure suckling success part of which involves waiting for the natural calf to initiate the suckling session.

Acknowledgements

This work was undertaken as part of a Ph.D. at the University of Exeter. The author is extremely grateful to Dr Marthe Kiley-Worthington and Mr Chris Rendle for the use of their cattle.

References

Birgersson, B., Ekvall, K. and Temrin, H. 1991. Allosuckling in Fallow deer, *Dama dama. Animal Behaviour* **42:** 326-327.

Edwards, S. A. and Broom, D. M. 1982. Behavioural interactions of dairy cows with their newborn calves and the effects of parity. *Animal Behaviour* **30:** 525-535.

Giovengo, S. L. and Waring, G. H. 1990. Social development of the American bison calf. *Proceedings of the Society for Veterinary Ethology summer meeting, 15-17 May, Edinburgh.*

Kiley-Worthington, M. 1976. Fostering and adoption of beef cattle. *Digest — British Cattle Breeders Club* **31:** 42-55.

Kiley-Worthington, M. and de la Plain, S. 1983. *The behaviour of beef suckler cattle* (Bos taurus). Birkhauser Verlag, Basel.

Le Neindre, P. 1982. Cow-calf relationships: the effects of management type. In *Welfare and husbandry of calves* (ed. J. P. Signoret), pp. 5-15. Martinus Nijhoff, London.

Le Neindre, P. 1989. Influence of rearing conditions and breed on social relationships of mother and young. *Applied Animal Behaviour Science* **23:** 117-127.

Lent, P. C. 1991. Maternal-infant behaviour in Muskoxen. *Mammalia* **55:** 3-23.

Murphey, R. M., Paranhos da Costa, M. J. R, de Souza Lima, L. O. and de Moura-Duarte, F. A. 1991. Communal suckling in Water Buffalo (*Bubalis bubalis*). *Applied Animal Behaviour Science.* **28:** 341-352.

Price, E. O., Martinez, C. L and Coe, B. L. 1984. The effects of twinning on mother-offspring behaviour in range beef cattle. *Applied Animal Behaviour Science* **13:** 309-320.

Veissier, I., Le Neindre, P. and Garel, J. P. 1990. Decrease in cow-calf attachment after weaning. *Behavioural Processes* **21:** 95-105.

Vitale, J. F., Tenucci, M., Papini, M. and Lovari, S. 1986. Social behaviour of the calves of semi-wild Maremma cattle, *Bos primigenius taurus. Applied Animal Behaviour Science* **16:** 217-231.

Farm animal welfare — who writes the rules?
Occasional Publication No. 23 — British Society of Animal Science 1999
edited by A. J. F. Russel, C. A. Morgan, C. J. Savory, M. C. Appleby and T. L. J. Lawrence

Sucking position and duration in natural and adopted calves

H. D. Randle

Department of Agriculture and Food, Seale-Hayne Faculty, University of Plymouth, Newton Abbot TQ12 6NQ

Introduction

It is possible for domesticated beef cattle to adopt an additional calf. A method of double suckling in which the additional calf is adopted by the cow was developed by Kiley-Worthington (1976). This method differs from those such as multiple suckling (e.g. Hudson, 1977) which are based on fostering and often require substantial amounts of human resources. It is well known that suckling plays a fundamental rôle in the reinforcement of the mother-young bond in cattle (Le Neindre, 1982). In the case of double suckling it is particularly important that the additional calf (the adoptee) is permitted to suck. However, to achieve this the adoptee must behave appropriately to ensure acceptance by the dam. Most cows will not allow calves other than their own natural calves to suck them (Price *et al.*, 1986). Once the natural calf starts sucking, milk is let down by the cow (Orihuela, 1990) and is potentially available to the adoptee. There is some evidence that adoptee calves employ an 'opportunistic' strategy in order to obtain milk. One aspect of this is the initiation of suckling bouts. Adoptees learn to synchronize their sucking with that of the natural calf, i.e. they wait for the natural calf to suck before starting to suck themselves. The typical position assumed by a single sucking, natural calf is 'parallel inverse', where the calf's head faces the mother's tail and there is maximum body contact between the dam and calf (Le Neindre, 1982). However, Spinka and Illman (1992) report that adopted calves do not assume this position. A typical suck position taken up by alien calves is between the cow's hind legs, a position frequently assumed by single sucking, natural, calves near the end of a sucking bout (Le Neindre, 1982). Sucking duration typically declines with increasing calf age (Le Niendre, 1982; Kiley-Worthington and de la Plain, 1983; Nakanshi *et al.*, 1993). The work reported in this paper aims to compare the sucking positions and durations achieved by adopted calves with those exhibited by the natural calves.

Material and methods

A total of 13 trios were observed, each consisting of a South Devon cow, her homebred natural calf and an adopted calf. Adoptions were carried out using the method developed by Kiley-Worthington (1976). For further details see Randle (1996b).

In group 1, six trios were observed for the 1st week of the adoption and week 3 post adoption. In group 2, seven trios were observed during the 1st week of the adoption and for the 1st week of month 5 post adoption. These observation periods covered all suckling sessions which occurred between 06.00 and 21.00 h. Observations included all of the behaviours exhibited by the dam and both the natural and adopted calves. These were recorded simultaneously. The full list of behaviours recorded during a suckling session is given in Randle (1999b) All of the different positions assumed by both the natural and adopted calves (for at least 5 s) throughout a suckling session were recorded. Sucking positions were categorized as inside — focal calf (where the focal calf was either the natural or the adoptee whichever was being recorded) on the inside of the other calf, parallel and adjacent to the dam, or outside — focal calf on the outside of the other calf, parallel but not adjacent to the dam, or sucking from between the dam's hind legs. The sucking duration exhibited by both calves in each position was also recorded.

At the end of the four observation periods the success of the adoptions were rated using the five-point system developed by Kiley-Worthington and de la Plain (1983). The detailed descriptions of R (rejected), F1 (level one fostering), F2 (level two fostering), A1 (level one adoption) and A2 (level two adoption) are given by Randle (1996b).

The proportion of sucking time spent in the inside sucking positions by naturals and adoptees was subjected to ANOVA. The durations of sucking by naturals and adoptees in the inside and outside positions were subjected to a two-way ANOVA. Two further three-way ANOVAS were performed in order to examine the influence of calf type (natural, adoptee), sucking position (inside, outside) and time (week 1, week 3 in group 1; week 1, month 5 in group 2) on sucking duration.

Table 1 *Proportion of sucking time spent in the inside positions by natural and adopted calves (upper) and mean suckling duration (min) exhibited by natural and adopted calves in the inside and outside sucking positions (lower) for both group 1 and group 2*

Sucking	Natural calves		Adopted calves		Significance
Proportion of time inside					
Group 1	0·92		0·33		***
Group 2	0·74		0·31		***
Duration of sucking	Inside	Outside	Inside	Outside	
Group 1	5·49	1·48	3·55	3·30	*
Group 2	4·99	2·05	3·13	2·62	*

Results

At the end of the 1st week of the adoption 12 of the 13 adoptions were considered to be successful, i.e. the cow had 'adopted' the second calf and no human intervention was necessary to ensure successful suckling (see Table 1: Randle, 1999b).

In total 409 suckling sessions were observed, in group 1, 107 during week 1, 94 during week 3 and in group 2, 134 during week 1 and 74 during the 1st week of month 5. In both groups the natural calves spent a significantly greater proportion of time sucking from the inside positions (inside the other calf, parallel and adjacent to the dam) than the adopted calves ($P < 0.001$) (Table 1). In both groups there was a significant interactive effect of calf type (natural, adoptee) and sucking position (inside, outside) on the duration of sucking ($P < 0.05$). The natural calves sucked for significantly longer when in the inside positions compared with adopted calves in either the inside or outside positions ($P < 0.05$), whilst the adopted calves exhibited significantly longer sucking durations when in the outside positions (outside of the natural calf, not adjacent to

the dam, or between the dam's hind legs) than the natural calves when they were in the outside positions ($P < 0.05$) (Table 1). There was a significant interactive effect of calf type (natural, adoptee), sucking position (inside, outside) and time (week 1, week 3) in group 1 but not in group 2 (Table 2). The adoptees achieved their longest, uninterrupted sucking durations in week 3 post adoption when suckling from the outside positions.

Discussion

Double suckling with adoption
The double suckling with adoption method used was successful. One of the 13 adoptions failed, although the additional calf was allowed to suck if the dam was under close human supervision.

Suckling positions and durations
The sucking behaviour of all of the calves studied was typical of calves in a beef suckler system. Since the adopted calves always sucked at the same time as the natural calves it can be concluded that the welfare of the adoptees was not compromised by being reared by an adoptive dam (Lidfors et al., 1993). At week 3 post adoption the differentiation of sucking positions assumed by natural and adoptee calves was pronounced. Natural calves sucked from the typical parallel, inverse, positions (Le Neindre, 1982) which afforded maximum bodily contact with the dam, whilst the adoptee calves sucked from positions resulting in less bodily contact with the dam, usually on the outside of the natural calf. It appears that the adoptees learnt that it was more effective to suck from the outside positions and utilized this as part of an opportunistic strategy (coupled with waiting for the natural calf to initiate the sucking, see Randle (1999b) to obtain milk. This suggestion is supported by the longer sucking durations achieved by adoptees when in the outside positions at week 3 post adoption when the trio was not subject to human supervision. The non-significant interaction between calf type, sucking

Table 2 *Mean sucking duration (min) exhibited by natural and adopted calves, in the inside and outside sucking positions in week 1 (groups 1 and 2) and week 3 (group 1) and the 1st week of month 5 (group 2) of the adoption*

Group	Natural calves		Adopted calves		Significance
Group 1					
Duration of sucking (min)	Week 1	Week 3	Week 1	Week 3	
Sucking in inside position	4·85	6·14	4·18	2·93	
Sucking in outside position	1·99	0·96	2·34	4·25	*
Group 2					
Duration of sucking (min)	Week 1	Week 1, month 5	Week 1	Week 1, month 5	
Sucking in inside position	4·74	5·24	3·75	2·51	
Sucking in outside position	2·62	1·48	2·67	2·57	

position and time (week 1 *v.* the 1st week of month 5 post adoption) in group 2 was likely to have been due to occurrences of cross sucking (Randle, 1999a).

Acknowledgements
This work was undertaken as part of a Ph.D. at the University of Exeter. Dr Kiley-Worthington and Mr C. Rendle are thanked for their help and guidance with this work.

References
Hudson, S. 1977. Multi-fostering of calves onto nurse cows at birth. *Applied Animal Ethology* **3:** 57-63.

Kiley-Worthington, M. 1976. Fostering and adoption of beef cattle. *Digest — British Cattle Breeders Club* **31:** 42-55.

Kiley-Worthington, M. and de la Plain, S. 1983. *The behaviour of beef suckler cattle* (Bos taurus). Birkhauser Verlag, Basal.

Le Neindre, P. 1982. Cow-calf relationships: the effects of management type. In *Welfare and husbandry of calves* (ed. J. P. Signoret), pp. 5-15. Martinus Nijhoff, London.

Lidfors, L. M., Jensen, P. and Algers, B. 1993. Temporal patterning of suckling bouts in free ranging beef cattle. *Proceedings of the 1993 Society for Veterinary Ethology congress, Berlin.*

Nakanshi, Y., Maehara, Y., Masuda, Y. and Umetsu, R. 1993. Some behavioural aspects of cow-calf relationships in a herd of beef cattle in semi-confinement. *Journal of the Faculty of Agriculture, Kyushu University* **37:** 219-226.

Orihuela, A. 1990. Effect of calf stimulus on the milk yield of Zebu type cattle. *Applied Animal Behaviour Science* **26:** 187-190.

Price, E. O., Smith, V. M., Thos, J. and Anderson, G. S. 1986. The effects of twinning and maternal experience on maternal-filial social relationships in confined beef cattle. *Applied Animal Behaviour Science* **15:** 137-146.

Randle, H. R. 1996a. Cross-suckling in beef suckler cows with natural and adopted calves. In *Farm animal welfare — who writes the rules?* (ed. A. J. F. Russel, C. A. Morgan, C. J. Savory, M. C. Appleby and T. L. S. Lawrence), pp. 122-124. British Society of Animal Science occasional publication no. 23.

Randle, H. R. 1996b. Initiation of suckling in suckler cows with natural and adopted calves. In *Farm animal welfare — who writes the rules?* (ed. A. J. F. Russel, C. A. Morgan, C. J. Savory, M. C. Appleby and T. L. S. Lawrence), pp. 116-119. British Society of Animal Science occasional publication no. 23.

Spinka, M. and Illman, G. 1992. Suckling behaviour of young dairy calves with their own and alien mothers. *Applied Animal Behaviour Science* **33:** 165-174.

Farm animal welfare — who writes the rules?
Occasional Publication No. 23 — British Society of Animal Science 1999
edited by A. J. F. Russel, C. A. Morgan, C. J. Savory, M. C. Appleby and T. L. J. Lawrence

Cross-suckling in beef suckler cows with natural and adopted calves

H. D. Randle

Department of Agriculture and Food, Seale-Hayne Faculty, University of Plymouth, Newton Abbot TQ12 6NQ

Introduction

Interactions beyond a single-suckling beef cow and her calf are rare in the early post-partum period (Le Neindre, 1982) which would suggest that the dam-calf bond is robust. However, there is evidence that the dam-calf bond can be disrupted by both the calf and the dam. Young calves have been known to exhibit non-specific following responses to any large, moving object (Kiley-Worthington and de la Plain, 1983) consequently leading to disruption of the mother-young bond (Gubanick, 1981). Illman and Spinka (1983) also observed non-specific following responses made by beef calves in the early post-partum period which resulted in attempts to suck alien dams. It is not surprising therefore that cross-sucking is common under group-housing conditions. Indeed, Edwards (1983) found that in group-housed dairy cows 6% of suckling was directed towards cows other than the natural mother (aliens) and that one-third of the calves sucked from an alien dam at some point during the first 6 days of life. Spinka and Illman (1992) successfully made use of this opportunistic tendency of calves, encouraging them to suck alien dams as their only source of milk in an extensive rearing system.

Cows do not always rear a single calf e.g. a cow may have twins and therefore rear two natural calves. Price *et al.* (1984) found that the bond between the dam and a twin calf was less robust than the bond between the dam and a single calf. Furthermore, cows suckling twins were generally more permissive to alien calves (calves other than their own) than cows suckling a single calf. Similarly, Kiley-Worthington (1976) found that double-suckling beef cows were also more permissive to alien calves than single-suckling beef cows. There is also evidence that twin calves are more persistent in trying to suck alien cows than single-suckled calves (Price *et al.*, 1984). The objectives of the work reported in this paper were first, to examine the cross-sucking activity of natural and adopted calves and secondly to compare the sucking behaviour of adoptees acting as adoptees and adoptees acting as aliens.

Material and methods

A group of 21 individuals, comprising seven trios (each consisting of a South Devon cow, her homebred natural calf and an adopted calf) were observed for a week at 5 months post adoption. Adoptions were carried out using the method developed by Kiley-Worthington (1976) (for further details see Randle (1999a)).

During the observation period all incidences of cross-suckling which occurred between 06.00 and 21.00 h were recorded. Observations included all of the behaviours that occurred between the dam and sucking calves (her natural, her adoptee and any others, 'aliens'). The full list of behaviours recorded during a suckling session is given in Randle (1999a). Data recorded also included the identity of the alien (the cross-sucking calf), the composition of the suckling group joined by the alien, the sucking position assumed by the alien (inside — on the inside of an already sucking calf, parallel and adjacent to the cow, or outside — on the outside of an already sucking calf or between the cow's hind legs) and the duration of sucking. The sucking positions and durations recorded for adopted calves sucking their adoptive dams were also utilized (Randle, 1999b).

At the end of the observation period the success of the seven adoptions was rated using the five-point system developed by Kiley-Worthington and de la Plain (1983). Randle (1999a) gives detailed descriptions of R (rejected), F1 (level one fostering), F2 (level two fostering), A1 (level one adoption) and A2 (level two adoption).

The proportion of cross sucking exhibited by natural and adopted calves was compared using the Fisher exact test. The proportions of successful and unsuccessful attempts made by alien calves on different types of already suckling groups were calculated. The sucking behaviour of adoptees when acting as adoptees (i.e. sucking on their adoptive dam) with that of adoptees acting as aliens (i.e. sucking on alien dams) was compared by means of two-way ANOVAs, on first, sucking position (inside *versus* outside) and secondly on sucking durations achieved.

Results

By the 1st week of month 5 post adoption six of the seven adoptions were considered to be successful, i.e. the cow had adopted the second calf and no human intervention was necessary to ensure successful suckling (see Table 1, Randle (1999a)).

Of the 74 suckling sessions observed in the 1st week of month 5 post adoption 38 (51%) consisted of the natural and adopted calves, 13 (18%) consisted of only the natural calf, 10 (13%) consisted of the natural and adopted calves and an alien calf and 13 (18%) consisted of the natural calf and an alien calf. Within the population of seven natural calves and seven adopted calves the mean proportion of sucking of alien dams was 0·30 (s.e. 0·27). This ranged from 0 to 0·78. Five of the seven adopted calves engaged in cross sucking activity, i.e. acted as an alien, compared with just one of the seven natural calves. This represented a significantly greater proportion of cross-sucking in adopted calves (Fisher exact test, $P < 0.05$). Of the 56 attempts made by alien calves to suck, 45 (80%) were successful. A calf attempting to cross-suck a dam is most likely to be successful if he/she attempts to suck on a cow already nursing two calves, the natural and either the adoptee or another alien, and least likely if he/she attempts to suck a cow already nursing just her natural calf (Figure 1).

A two way ANOVA performed on the frequency of adopted calves acting as adoptees and adopted calves acting as aliens, occupying the inside and outside sucking positions showed that there was no significant difference in the positions occupied by adoptees and aliens. A similar two-way ANOVA performed on the sucking durations achieved by adoptees acting as adoptees and adoptees acting as aliens demonstrated that both adoptees and aliens spent a greater proportion of time sucking from the outside positions than from the inside positions ($P < 0.01$).

Discussion

Adopted calves engaged in significantly greater levels of cross-sucking compared with natural calves. Within this system there was a relatively high proportion of cross-sucking. However this may be explained by the fact that the data were collected at 5 months post adoption. This is a time by which relations between the dam and young are weakening (Veissier et al., 1990).

There is evidence that calves which are acting as aliens in order to obtain milk from a dam other than their own (i.e. their own natural dam, or own adoptive dam) are extending the opportunistic strategy that they have developed in order to obtain milk from their adoptive dam (see Randle (1999a and b). The results obtained in this study show that the best strategy for a calf acting as an alien is to join a suckling group in which two calves (either the natural and adopted or natural and another alien calf) are already sucking. Price et al. (1984) concluded that the presence of the natural calf is very important if aliens are going to be able to suck. In their study they found that 82·9% of cross sucking occurred when the natural calf was already sucking and 5·7% when the natural was nearby. In this study it was found that the cow did not tolerate attempts by an additional calf if just her natural calf was sucking but would if she was already nursing her natural and one other (either her adoptee or another alien calf) It appears that once the cow is nursing two calves she is generally more permissive to additional calves (a characteristic of double-suckling cows noted by Kiley-Worthington, 1976). Comparison of the sucking behaviour of adopted calves sucking their adoptive dams and sucking other dams showed that they did not alter their strategy to obtain milk since they assume similar positions (typically outside — see preceding paper) and suck for similar durations.

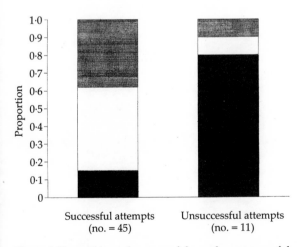

Figure 1 Proportion of successful and unsuccessful attempts made to cross-suck on dams already nursing her natural calf (■), her natural and adopted calf (□), and her natural and one other alien calf (▨).

Acknowledgements

This work was undertaken as part of a Ph.D. at the University of Exeter. Dr Kiley-Worthington and Mr C. Rendle are thanked for their help and guidance with this work.

References

Edwards, S. A. 1983. The behaviour of dairy cows and their newborn calves in individual or group housing. *Applied Animal Ethology* **10**: 191-198.

Gubernick, D. G. 1981. Parent and infant attachment in mammals. In *Parental care in mammals* (ed. D. G. Gubernick and P. H. Klopfer), pp. 117-169. Plenum Press, New York.

Illman, G. and Spinka, M. 1993. Maternal behaviour of dairy heifers and suckling of their newborn calves in group housing. *Applied Animal Behaviour Science* **36**: 91-98.

Kiley-Worthington, M. 1976. Fostering and adoption of beef cattle. *Digest — British Cattle Breeders Club* **31**: 42-55.

Kiley-Worthington, M. and de la Plain, S. 1983. *The behaviour of beef suckler cattle* (Bos taurus). Birkhauser Verlag, Basel.

Le Neindre, P. 1982. Cow-calf relationships: the effects of management type. In *Welfare and husbandry of calves* (ed. J. P. Signoret), pp. 5-15. Martinus Nijhoff, London.

Price, E. O., Martinez, C. L. and Coe, B. L. 1984. The effects of twinning on mother-offspring behaviour in range beef cattle. *Applied Animal Behaviour Science* **13**: 309-320.

Randle, H. R. 1999a. Initiation of suckling in suckler cows with natural and adopted calves. In *Farm animal welfare — who writes the rules?* (ed. A. J. F. Russel, C. A. Morgan, C. J. Savory, M. C. Appleby and T. L. J. Lawrence), pp. 116-119. British Society of Animal Science occasional publication no. 23.

Randle, H. R. 1999b. Sucking position and duration in natural and adopted calves. In *Farm animal welfare — who writes the rules?* (ed. A. J. F. Russel, C. A. Morgan, C. J. Savory, M. C. Appleby and T. L. J. Lawrence), pp. 119-121. British Society of Animal Science occasional publication no. 23.

Spinka, M. and Illman, G. 1992. Suckling behaviour of young dairy calves with their own and alien mothers. *Applied Animal Behaviour Science* **33**: 165-174.

Veissier, L., Le Neindre, P. and Garel, J. P. 1990. Decrease in cow-calf attachment after weaning. *Behavioural Processes* **21**: 95-105.

Farm animal welfare — who writes the rules?
Occasional Publication No. 23 — British Society of Animal Science 1999
edited by A. J. F. Russel, C. A. Morgan, C. J. Savory, M. C. Appleby and T. L. J. Lawrence

Temperature profile in double-decker transporters and some consequences for pig welfare during transport

L. Christensen and P. Barton Gade

Danish Meat Research Institute, Maglegaardsvej 2, DK-4000 Roskilde, Denmark

Introduction

Adequate ventilation during transport has been emphasized repeatedly in legislation and various welfare schemes to safeguard animal welfare during transport. One practical method of measuring the effectiveness of ventilation is to measure temperature inside the vehicle and compare this with outside temperatures, smaller differences being expected to be indicative of better ventilation. There are, however, no published data on how temperature varies within a vehicle for different outside temperatures. The aim of this work, which was part of a project to evaluate optimal tier heights, ventilation openings and stocking densities in double-decker pig transporters, was to investigate the temperature variation within the vehicle during experimental transports at different times of the year. In addition, heart rate (HR) was measured in randomly chosen pigs to evaluate the effect of transport on this parameter. Finally, some information from the routine journeys with the experimental vehicle was obtained.

Material and methods

A detailed description of the experimental vehicle is given in Christensen and Barton Gade (1996). Only a few aspects will be mentioned here. Each tier was divided into four compartments of 15 pigs at a stocking density of 286 kg/m², the Danish norm at that time. Ventilation openings ran along both sides of both tiers and could be varied continuously from 0 to 350 mm (lower tier) and 0 to 500 mm (upper tier). The vehicle was also equipped with mechanical ventilation, although this was not used during the experimental journeys to simulate current practice.

For routine journeys the mechanical ventilation systems were used, both when the vehicle was stationary (loading) and continuously during transport when environmental temperatures reached about 20°C. The vehicle also had a misting system that was used intermittently during transport when environmental temperatures reached about 25°C. Three experiments were carried out with a total of 16 individual journeys (Table 1).

In the August/September experiment, four different stocking densities: 200, 238, 263 and 286 kg/m² and standardized ventilation openings/tier heights were used; otherwise stocking density was 286 kg/m². The pigs were three or four breed crosses between Landrace, Large White, Duroc and Hampshire and had a live weight of 100 to 105 kg. Temperature was measured at five points in each compartment above the pigs (Table 2) and relative humidity (RH) at the centre of each compartment. Temperature and RH were also measured outside the vehicle, above the driver's cabin.

Measurements were recorded when both tiers were laden during transport to the abattoir. Rolling averages were calculated for temperatures at the various points in the vehicle and values obtained at constant intervals directly compared using correlation and regression analysis. In all journeys two pigs from each compartment were randomly chosen at loading and equipped with HR monitors (Schutte *et al.*, 1996). HR curves were first scanned visually and those with obvious defects rejected (9% of the total). When curves had intermittent loss of contact that allowed an evaluation of approximate

Table 1 *Temperature range and ventilation openings/tier heights used in the three experiments*

| Time of year | Temperature (°C) | | Ventilation openings/tier heights (mm) | | | |
	Mean	Range	Low tier		Upper tier	
January/February	3	(–4 to 6)	150/900	150/1100	350/ 900	350/1100
June	18	(14 to 23)	350/900	150/1100	350/1300	150/1300
August/September	19	(15 to 27)	350/900	350/1100	350/ 900	350/1300

Table 2 *Temperature measuring points in the experimental vehicle as viewed from above and nomenclature used*†

	Front compartment													Rear compartment			
Lower tier	111	112 114 115	113	121	122 124 125	123	131	132 134 135	133	141	142 144 145	143
Upper tier	211	212 214 215	213	221	222 224 225	223	231	232 234 235	233	241	242 244 245	243

† The first digit = tier, the second = compartment within tier and the third = measuring point within compartment

level this was inserted, after which rolling averages were calculated according to A. Schutte (1995, personal communication). In routine journeys, where ventilation openings were normally 350 mm on both tiers and tier heights 900 and 1300 mm for lower and upper tiers respectively, a number of details were registered over a 27-month period: numbers and placement of animals on the vehicle, number of pigs dead during transport and where the death occurred. In all 216 227 slaughter pigs were transported during this period to four different abattoirs. Journey times, i.e. time from loading the first pig to off-loading the first pig at the abattoir varied from 45 min to 3 h 5 min with an average time of 1 h 57 min.

Results

Temperatures inside the vehicle were not related to the tier heights / ventilation openings or stocking densities used but mainly to environmental conditions. A preliminary analysis on pooled data showed that measuring point 111 in the front lower compartment was affected by heat from the motor / transmission and that there were problems with cables to measuring point 5 in several compartments. The statistical analysis was therefore restricted to points 2, 3 and 4 in the eight compartments, 24 measuring points in all. There are many combinations between these measuring points and as the final aim of this analysis was to pinpoint possible

Table 3 *Relationship between temperatures measured at the centre in the front lower compartment and other points in the vehicle and calculated values at selected temperatures*

				Selected temperatures (°C)				
Regression equation		R^2	RMSE	5	10	15	20	25
°C 112 = −0·7303 + 1·0018	°C 114	0·96	1·3	4·3	9·3	14·3	19·3	24·3
°C 113 = 2·2306 + 0·8904	°C 114	0·83	2·6	6·7	11·1	15·6	20·0	24·5
°C 122 = −1·1995 + 0·9848	°C 114	0·95	1·4	3·7	8·6	13·6	18·5	23·4
°C 123 = −0·7136 + 0·9781	°C 114	0·97	1·2	4·2	9·1	14·0	18·8	23·7
°C 124 = −1·7868 + 1·0268	°C 114	0·96	1·3	3·3	8·5	13·6	18·8	23·9
°C 132 = −3·8423 + 1·0594	°C 114	0·95	1·5	1·5	6·8	12·0	17·3	22·6
°C 133 = −2·8407 + 1·0057	°C 114	0·94	1·6	2·2	7·2	12·2	17·3	22·3
°C 134 = −3·6544 + 1·0740	°C 114	0·96	1·5	1·7	7·1	12·5	17·8	23·2
°C 142 = −5·2695 + 1·0734	°C 114	0·94	1·8	0·1	5·5	10·8	16·2	21·6
°C 143 = −5·2707 + 1·0857	°C 114	0·94	1·8	0·2	5·6	11·0	16·4	21·9
°C 144 = −3·6836 + 1·0550	°C 114	0·94	1·7	1·6	6·9	12·1	17·4	22·7
°C 212 = −2·7656 + 1·0157	°C 114	0·93	1·7	2·3	7·4	12·5	17·5	22·6
°C 213 = −2·8648 + 1·0198	°C 114	0·93	1·8	2·2	7·3	12·4	17·5	22·6
°C 214 = −2·5201 + 1·0275	°C 114	0·93	1·8	2·6	7·8	12·9	18·0	23·2
°C 222 = −4·2272 + 1·0656	°C 114	0·93	1·8	1·1	6·4	11·8	17·1	22·4
°C 223 = −5·0671 + 1·0800	°C 114	0·93	1·9	0·3	5·7	11·1	16·5	21·9
°C 224 = −3·5878 + 1·0551	°C 114	0·93	1·9	1·7	7·0	12·2	17·5	22·8
°C 232 = −5·1460 + 1·0607	°C 114	0·93	1·9	0·2	5·5	10·8	16·1	21·4
°C 233 = −5·1114 + 1·0603	°C 114	0·92	2·0	0·2	5·5	10·8	16·1	21·4
°C 234 = −4·8307 + 1·0892	°C 114	0·91	2·2	0·6	6·1	11·5	17·0	22·4
°C 242 = −4·9187 + 1·0680	°C 114	0·91	2·1	0·4	5·8	11·1	16·4	21·8
°C 243 = −5·4500 + 1·0816	°C 114	0·89	2·4	0·0	5·4	10·8	16·2	21·6
°C 244 = −5·6160 + 1·1124	°C 114	0·90	2·4	−0·1	5·5	11·1	16·6	22·2

positions that could be used to indicate temperature levels in the whole vehicle in practice, it was decided to choose the compartment with the highest average temperature (the front lower compartment) as the basis for the comparison. The results (Table 3) showed that R^2 values between measuring point 114 and other measuring points were only exceptionally below 0·9 and that a single measurement in the front lower compartment could predict levels elsewhere in the vehicle ±2 to 5°C, depending on the actual measuring point itself (95% confidence level). Average temperature levels were highest on the front lower compartment and lowest in the rear upper compartments.

The relationships between temperatures within the vehicle and outside temperatures were slightly poorer than within the vehicle itself (R^2 values 0·83 to 0·95 and RMSE values 1·7 to 2·4, i.e. ± 3 to 5°C). Calculated values from the regression equations (Table 4) show that temperature differences were greatest in colder weather. With an outside temperature of 5°C, temperatures within the vehicle varied from 11 to 12°C in the front lower compartment to 7 to 8°C in the rear upper compartments. The differences were much smaller at higher environmental temperatures. RH was high (0·85 to 0·95) during transport for all experiments and irrespective of measuring point. This was partly due to the humidity produced by the pigs themselves and partly to the fact that the vehicle had not dried out after cleaning at the factory.

HR levels were, not unexpectedly, high just after placement of the belt, varying between 140 and 220 beats per min (b.p.m.) depending on animal. HR levels fell thereafter rapidly, as pigs became accustomed to the belt and recovered from the stress of loading. By 5 to 45 min after loading, again depending on animal, levels were of the order of 80 to 130 b.p.m. This time dependence meant that average HR was lower in pigs transported on the upper tier (average transport time 2 h 44 min) relative to those transported on the lower tier (average transport time 1 h 4 min), i.e. 123 to 126 v. 134 to 140 b.p.m. None of the ventilation openings / tier heights used had any effect on average HR,

despite large difference in environmental temperatures. Stocking density had no effect on average HR either, varying from 114 to 121 b.p.m. for pigs on the upper tier to 140 to 145 b.p.m. for pigs on the lower tier.

Twenty-six pigs died on the vehicle during the routine transports (0·012%). All of these were transported in the front lower compartment and eight came from the same producer.

Discussion

The results of this work show that there is a systematic variation in temperature within a fully laden vehicle during transport and that a single measurement in the front lower compartment can be used to give an indication of temperatures throughout the vehicle. RH was high during transport but critical combinations of temperature and RH, as described in the US livestock weather safety index (Grandin, 1992) were rarely encountered in the experimental journeys and then only for short periods. However, such high RH values mean that mechanical ventilation or other methods of cooling pigs (e.g. intermittent misting) would be advantageous at temperatures above about 25°C.

Mortality was low during routine journeys, although it is not possible to say whether it was lower than the national average (0·018% at that time). Not included in the mortality figures were two pigs which died during the experimental journeys, one during the January/February experiment (ventilation opening 150 mm, tier height 1100 mm) and one during the June experiment (ventilation opening 350 mm, tier height 900 mm). Both pigs originated from the same producer, both carried belts to measure HR and both died in the front lower compartment. Pigs from this producer had more cases of rapid post-mortem glycolysis and PSE-meat than pigs from other producers (P. Barton Gade and L. Christensen, 1996, unpublished material) i.e. typical signs of pigs carrying the halothane gene. The higher mortality in pigs transported in the front lower compartment was therefore probably caused by a combination of genotype and placement on the vehicle. Poorer

Table 4 *Average temperatures within the vehicle for different outside temperatures*

Temperature (°C)	Lower tier				Upper tier			
	Front			Back	Front			Back
5	11·9	10·4	8·7	7·8	9·9	9·0	8·0	7·3
15	19·5	18·4	17·2	17·2	17·7	17·1	16·3	16·3
25	27·1	26·3	26·3	25·6	25·5	25·5	24·6	25·2

ventilation seems to have been implicated, as the front lower compartment had the highest temperature. Nielsen (1981) also showed that an optimized ventilation system halved transport mortality in pigs.

Acknowledgements

The authors acknowledge financial support from EC-AIR3-Project CT92-0262 and the Federation of Danish Pig Producers and Slaughterhouses.

References

Christensen, L. and Barton Gade, P. A. 1996. Design of experimental vehicle and some preliminary environmental measurements. *Proceedings of an EU seminar 'New information on welfare and meat quality of pigs as related to handling transport and lairage' Mariensee. Germany, June 1995,* pp. 47-67.

Grandin. T. 1992. *Livestock trucking guide.* Livestock Conservation Institute, Madison, Wisconsin, USA.

Nielsen, N. J. 1981. The effect of environmental factors on meat quality and deaths during transport and lairage before slaughter. *Proceedings of a symposium 'Porcine stress and meat quality — causes and possible solutions to the problems', Jeløy, Norway, November 1980,* pp. 287-297.

Schutte, A., Broom, D. M. and Lambooij, E. 1996. Standard methods of estimating physiological parameters during pig handling and transport. *Proceedings of an EU seminar 'New information on welfare and meat quality of pigs as related to handling, transport and lairage' Mariensee, Germany, June 1995,* pp. 69-80.

Farm animal welfare — who writes the rules?
Occasional Publication No. 23 — British Society of Animal Science 1999
edited by A. J. F. Russel, C. A. Morgan, C. J. Savory, M. C. Appleby and T. L. J. Lawrence

Environmental conditions within livestock vehicles during the commercial transport of sheep

A. M. Jarvis and M. S. Cockram

Department of Veterinary Clinical Studies, University of Edinburgh, Easter Bush Veterinary Centre, Easter Bush, Roslin, Midlothian EH25 9RG

Introduction

The air temperature and relative humidity experienced by sheep during commercial road transport in the UK were recorded to assess whether it was likely that the sheep experienced thermal discomfort due to inadequate ventilation. When sheep are confined in a livestock vehicle, heat and water enter the air space. If the ventilation of the vehicle is inadequate the temperature and humidity could increase and this could affect the welfare of the sheep. When the ambient temperature is greater than about 25°C the rate of evaporative water loss by sheep in an attempt to maintain body temperature increases rapidly (Degen and Shkolnik, 1978). If the humidity is also high the ability of sheep to lose heat via evaporative water loss is impaired due to a decreased vapour pressure gradient between respired air and the environment.

Material and methods

Tinytalk™ PT-100 temperature loggers (accuracy ± 0·35°C at 25°C) and Tinytalk™ PT-100 humidity loggers (accuracy ± 3%) (Orion Components, Chichester Ltd) programmed to record at 12-min intervals were fitted to three-deck livestock transporters used by commercial hauliers for transporting sheep. The livestock transporters were between 12·8 and 13·3 m in length and 2·45 m wide. The deck height was between 0·80 and 0·97 m. The area of the ventilation slats on the vehicle sides ranged between 25 and 65 per cent of the floor surface area. The area of ventilation slats on each deck ranged between 2·10 and 4·98 m². A full load of about 300 sheep was transported on each journey. Data were collected during 10 journeys of between 2·5 and 11 h duration in the UK between the months of February and September. Five temperature loggers were attached inside the vehicle: at the mid point of each deck and at approximately 1 m from the front and back of the middle deck. Three humidity loggers were attached next to the temperature loggers on the middle deck. The loggers were attached to the roof (approx. 0·1 m above sheep head height) mid way between the sides of the vehicle. An additional temperature logger was

attached to the outside of the vehicle at the front of the livestock compartment at the level of the middle deck.

Results

Temperatures within the vehicle typically increased during loading, decreased after the vehicle began to move, remained relatively constant as the journey progressed and increased during stationary periods (Figure 1). Relative humidity typically increased during transport to reach 0·8 to 0·9 saturation after transport of 1 to 2 h and remained relatively high during stationary periods. When sheep with wet fleeces were loaded, the relative humidity within the vehicle was greater than 0·8. External temperatures recorded during the journeys ranged from –2 to 19°C. The maximum temperature recorded inside

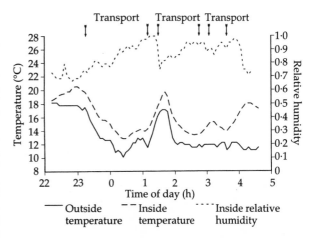

Figure 1 Air temperatures and relative humidity recorded during the commercial transport of sheep in the month of August. Relative humidity was recorded in the front section of the middle deck. Temperature was recorded outside of the vehicle, in the middle section of the lower and upper decks and in the front (F), middle (M) and back (B) sections of the middle deck. The journey involved three periods when the vehicle was moving. These are labelled transport and the arrows indicate the times when the vehicle started and stopped.

the vehicle during transport was 27°C (this occurred immediately after loading and decreased to 23°C within 0·5 h of the journey). A temperature of 22°C was recorded inside of the vehicle 1·6 h after it had stopped for repairs and was fully loaded (the outside temperature was 12°C). The temperature fell to 19°C 2·6 h later but the mean relative humidity during this time was 0·8 (Figure 2). The minimum temperature recorded during transport was –2°C. During transport, the mean temperature difference between inside and outside of the vehicle was 0·7°C on the lower deck, 0·5°C on the middle deck and 0·2°C on the upper deck. During transport, the mean temperature difference between inside and outside of the vehicle was 1·1°C on the front section of the middle deck, 0·5°C on the middle section of the middle deck and 0·9°C on the back section of the middle deck. When the vehicle was stationary and loaded with sheep, the mean temperature difference between inside and outside of the vehicle was 1·7°C on the lower deck, 3·3°C on the middle deck and 1·5°C on the upper deck. When the vehicle was stationary and loaded with sheep, the mean temperature difference between inside and outside of the vehicle was 3·0°C on the front section of the middle deck, 3·3°C on the middle section of the middle deck and 2·7°C on the back section of the middle deck.

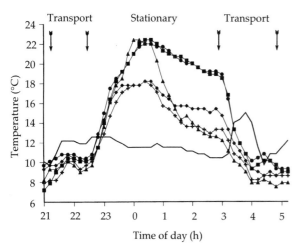

Figure 2 Air temperatures recorded during a commercial journey of sheep involving two periods of transport and one stationary period in the month of March. The arrows indicate the times when the vehicle started and stopped. Temperature was recorded outside of the vehicle, in the middle section of the lower and upper decks and in the front, middle and back sections of the middle deck: ——— outside; ——+— lower middle; ——◆— middle front; ——●— middle middle; ——■— middle back; ——▲— upper middle.

Discussion

Air movement during transport is caused by pressure differences between the inside and outside of the vehicle. However, when a vehicle without mechanical ventilation is stationary, air movement within the vehicle is dependent on the convection caused by the animals heating the air, the warmer air rising and cooler air entering through the side inlets and on any external air movement such as wind. Randall and Patel (1994) predicted that the most important factor influencing temperature within a stationary livestock vehicle was the area of the ventilation openings. The stocking density, vehicle size and construction were considered to be less important. The only circumstances in which a sheep may have experienced thermal distress during these journeys due to the air temperature being too cold would be if it had been recently shorn, unable to move away from any draughts or rain near the air inlets, had been starved for several hours or was lying on a cold floor. However, thermal distress during sheep transport can arise if either the temperature or temperature and humidity are too high (Alexander, 1974). During transport, air distribution as measured by air temperature appeared to be reasonably effective. This study did not however include many long journeys at high temperatures in vehicles with limited air inlets.

The most important finding in this study was the high relative humidity recorded during transport. This occurred particularly when sheep with wet fleeces were loaded and when the vehicle was stationary and fully loaded. This indicated that the ventilation was inadequate to remove the moisture produced by the sheep. Although relative humidity decreases within the vehicle as temperature rises, if the moisture load produced by the sheep was combined with high temperatures it could result in the sheep becoming thermally distressed. When environmental temperature rises sheep can increase evaporative heat loss by increased respiration and sweating (Hales and Brown, 1974). The ability to lose heat by this route could be impaired in hot environments when humidity is high and the body temperature and respiration rate of the sheep could rise markedly and panting is likely to occur (Bligh, 1963). Further work is required to evaluate whether sheep exposed to the combinations of temperature and humidity that occur during transport experience thermal distress.

Acknowledgements

AMJ was supported by a grant from the Royal Society for the Prevention of Cruelty to Animals (RSPCA) and the work was undertaken as part of research projects funded by the Scottish Office Agriculture Environment and Fisheries Department and the RSPCA. We are grateful for the help and co-operation that we received from the management and staff of the haulage company.

References

Alexander, G. 1974. Heat loss from sheep. In *Heat loss from animals and man: assessment and control* (ed. J. L. Monteith and L. E. Mount), pp. 173-203. Butterworths, London.

Bligh, J. 1963. The receptors concerned in the respiratory response to humidity in sheep at high ambient temperature. *Journal of Physiology* **168:** 747-763.

Degen, A. A. and Shkolnik, A. 1978. Thermoregulation in fat-tailed awassi, a desert sheep, and in German mutton Merino, a mesic sheep. *Physiological Zoology* **51:** 333-339.

Hales, J. R. S. and Brown, G. D. 1974. Net energetic and thermoregulatory efficiency during panting in sheep. *Comparative Biochemistry and Physiology* **49A:** 413-422.

Randall, J. M. and Patel, R. 1994. Thermally induced ventilation of livestock transporters. *Journal of Agricultural Engineering Research* **57:** 99-107.

Farm animal welfare — who writes the rules?
Occasional Publication No. 23 — British Society of Animal Science 1999
edited by A. J. F. Russel, C. A. Morgan, C. J. Savory, M. C. Appleby and T. L. J. Lawrence

Evaluation of the effects of the positive 'befriending' of sows and gilts ('pleasant' treatment) prior to parturition and in early lactation on sow behaviour, the process of parturition and piglet survival

P. R. English, S. A. Grant, O. McPherson and S. A. Edwards

Department of Agriculture, University of Aberdeen, MacRobert Building, 581 King Street, Aberdeen AB24 5UA

Introduction

There is evidence that pleasant handling of pigs relative to aversive handling has beneficial influences on reproduction, growth, animal physiology and indices of welfare (Hemsworth *et al.*, 1986 and 1987). However, there are no objective data available on the effect of pleasant handling of sows prior to parturition on the progress and efficiency of the parturition process and on subsequent piglet survival. The response to pleasant, relative to aversive, handling of pigs has been shown to be an effect of reducing fear responses to humans and the alleviation of a chronic stress response which has been associated with aversive handling. In indoor pig production, normal pre-farrowing practice involves the transfer of sows from pregnancy to farrowing accommodation around 4 to 7 days before the calculated farrowing date. The most common type of indoor farrowing facility is a pen with crate system, the crate being deployed to accommodate and restrain the sow so as to reduce the risk of piglets being overlain. However, the confinement within the crate prior to parturition may have negative influences on the sow in some situations. Both Cronin *et al.* (1991) and Lawrence *et al.* (1993) have demonstrated higher corticosteroid levels, which are indicative of both acute and chronic stress, in crated sows without bedding relative to loose housed sows with bedding prior to parturition. Pre-farrowing stress can affect the efficiency of parturition through hyperactivity of the adrenal cortex, increased adrenalin secretion and depressed oxytocin secretion from the anterior pituitary gland. Prolonged parturition, an increased incidence of intrapartum stillbirths and a higher incidence of anoxia in live-born piglets (especially the later births) is likely to result.

There is evidence from studies on sows in an aversive housing system in pregnancy, *viz.* individual confinement in tether stalls, that pleasant handling can significantly reduce chronic stress levels relative to aversive and even minimal (neutral) handling treatments (Pedersen *et al.*, 1999). Thus, it is possible that pleasant handling applied to sows prior to parturition and continued during and for a period after parturition might help to reduce stress levels at this time with consequent benefits to the sow, the efficiency of parturition and piglet survival.

Moreover, it is possible that any stress in the sow around parturition is not induced solely by confinement within the crate. The process of removing the sow from her pregnancy accommodation, isolating her from her penmates and guiding her along unfamiliar passage ways and eventually into a farrowing crate could induce acute stress, and more especially (a) in the case of gilts due to farrow for the first time and (b) where a high proportion of negative behaviours may be deployed by some stockpeople in 'persuading' the sow or gilt to move from pregnancy to farrowing accommodation. Thus the influence of pleasant handling applied for a short period each day from late pregnancy to just after farrowing was evaluated both in gilts farrowing for the first time and in older sows relative to a 'minimal' or 'neutral' treatment as the control.

Material and methods

The study took place in a 500 sow commercial herd with hybrid sows. Parity 1 pregnant gilts were loose housed in pen groups of six to eight and were given food on the floor once daily. Sows in their second and later pregnancy were housed in individual stalls and were also given food once daily. In general, sows on this farm were handled carefully and gently by the stockpeople. However, the handling of gilts and sows during pregnancy could be described as 'minimal' since the daily food was dispensed from outwith the pen or stall and there had been no direct tactile contact with the sows since they were served. Pleasant handling of the sows was applied in the pregnancy accommodation from 7 days before transfer to the farrowing quarters and this continued up to farrowing and for 2 days subsequently. The pleasant handling or 'befriending' took the form of close contact, talking to the sows and hand contact to stroke or to rub them. Approximately 1 min was spent in such befriending per animal per day. In the case of the pregnant gilts, handling took the form of entering the pen and 'befriending' each of the gilts in turn. Thus the interaction with the gilts was of a tactile, visual, auditory and olfactory nature, and 6 to 8 min was spent in each pen daily according to the number of gilts accommodated in it. It was more difficult to achieve such close contact with the sows in the stalls. The experimenter knelt down in front of each stall for 1 min, making gentle hand contact with each sow as it approached the extended hand while talking quietly at the same time.

A block of adjacent sows in the stalls which were due to farrow at the same time was randomly allocated to either the pleasant (P) or control (C) treatment, while pens of gilts were also randomly allocated to treatment. Individual farrowing houses containing 12 or 16 pens contained only C or only P treatment sows. Sows were considered to be receptive to the befriending of the experimenter when they approached the stationary observer in the pen (gilts) or at the front of the stall (multiparous sows) and also on the basis of their vocalizations. In contrast, sows were considered to be nervous of the experimenter when they did not approach or retreated from the stationary observer and on the basis of their vocalizations. In the process of transferring sows from pregnancy to farrowing accommodation, each was handled in a standard manner by the experimenter. Each sow was scored subjectively for 'ease of handling' (easy, moderate, difficult), while an approach behaviour test to assess level of fear was carried out on each sow in a standard test arena en route between pregnancy and farrowing accommodation.

Monitoring and supervision of farrowings were carried out by farm staff according to their normal routine. The experimenter was opportunistic in monitoring the progress of farrowings, recording the timing of as many piglet births as possible so as to determine birth intervals. There were 33 C sows and gilts and 27 subjected to the P treatment, with the great majority being in parities 1 and 3.

Frequencies were compared using the Fisher exact probablity test. Other parameters were compared by analysis of variance using the sow as the experimental unit in all cases.

Results

When befriending of the gilts and sows was started 7 days before entry into the farrowing rooms, a very high proportion of the gilts (93·1%) were classified as

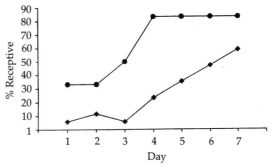

Figure 1 Trends in the percentage of gilts and parity 3 sows tested which were receptive to daily befriending by the stockperson (in pregnancy accommodation): —●— parity 3 (no. = 10); —◆— parity 1 (no. = 17).

Table 1 *Ease of handling and approach behaviour scores†*

	Control	Pleasant	χ^2
Easy to move (%)			
Parity 1	50	69	0·05
Parity 3	92	100	0·25
Approach time (s)			s.e.d.
Parity 1	54	46	33·5
Parity 3	65	32	36·5

† No differences were statistically significant ($P > 0.05$).

Table 2 *Proportion of sows making savaging attempts during parturition†*

	Control	Pleasant	χ^2
Parity 1	22·2	0	4·55
Parity 3	13·0	0	0·87
All parities	15·2	7·4	0·28

† No differences were statistically significant ($P > 0.05$).

being nervous/very nervous at being handled in the 'befriending' process (see Figure 1). However, fairly quickly both gilts and sows became receptive to the befriending process. Thus on the first day, only 5·9% of the gilts were receptive to the befriending process but by day 7, 58·9% of these gilts were receptive. The respective figures for parity 3 sows were 33·3% on day 1 and 83·3% on day 7. The proportion of gilts and sows which became receptive to daily befriending continued to increase in the farrowing accommodation prior to parturition.

In the transfer from pregnancy to farrowing accommodation, P sows achieved higher 'ease of handling' and 'approach behaviour' scores in a test arena but none of these differences approached statistical significance (see Table 1). During

Table 3 *Mean interval (min) between births of successive piglets*

	Control	Pleasant	s.e.d.
Parity 1	20·9	13·9**	2·3
Parity 3	21·7	17·9	6·0
All parities	20·7	15·6	3·4

Table 4 *The incidence of stillbirths and live-birth losses†*

	Control	Pleasant	s.e.d.
Stillbirths per litter	0·76	0·52	0·21
Live births per litter	11·18	10·74	0·69
Livebirth losses (%)			χ^2
Before fostering	1·1	0·7	
From fostering up to 14 days	3·9	2·6	1·12
Ill thriving pigs fostered off	11·2	11·3	0·66

† No differences were statistically significant ($P > 0.05$).

parturition, the proportion of sows which made savaging attempts on newborn piglets was consistently lower in the P group (see Table 2).

On the basis of 196 and 143 birth intervals observed in the C and P groups respectively, birth intervals were consistently lower in P (see Table 3).

The difference between C and P in parity 1 was highly significant. The incidence of stillbirths and live-birth losses were lower in P but these differences were not significant (see Table 4).

Fostering practice was efficient on this farm, and at the first signs of piglets failing to compete within a litter, with body condition loss, such piglets were fostered on to newly farrowed non-experimental sows with spare rearing capacity. The great majority of these fostered piglets survived.

Thus, there were consistent indications in the results that the P treatment had desirable influences in reducing fear of humans, on the ease of handling and on the physiology of the sow, as indicated by the reduced intervals between successive piglet births. Mortality in terms of stillbirths and live-birth losses was also marginally but not significantly lower on P.

Discussion

There were indications from this study that the pleasant or 'befriending' treatment applied reduced fear of humans, improved ease of handling, reduced birth intervals and the incidence of savaging during parturition, while there were marginal reductions in the incidence of both stillbirths and live-birth losses. Only some of these differences were significant but all the trends were entirely consistent in terms of indicating positive responses from the pleasant treatment.

Although the pigs were, in general, well handled on this farm, it is likely that the pregnant gilts and sows involved in the study could be classified up to the time the pleasant treatment was applied as being on a 'minimal' handling treatment as described by Hemsworth et al. (1986). They were given food once daily from outside the pen or stall but had not been handled (tactile contact with humans) since they were served at the start of their pregnancy. Since it is the nature and number of the interactions (and particularly those of a tactile nature) which determine the quality of the human-animal relationship for the animal (Hemsworth and Coleman, 1998), it could be argued that the sows and gilts in this study had been subjected to no positive or negative tactile interactions with humans for approximately 100 days since mating, and therefore their human treatment up to this time was neither pleasant nor aversive, but was 'minimal' . Barnett et al. (1994) with poultry and Gonyou et al. (1986) and Grandin et al. (1987) with pigs, found that a high level of fear can result from reduced human contact. While such contact can be of a visual, auditory, olfactory, gustatory and tactile nature, it appears that the fear and stress responses of the animal to the human is particularly affected by the tactile interactions (Hemsworth et al., 1981; Gonyou et al., 1986; Pearce et al., 1989).

That the sows in the present study appeared to be fearful of humans at the start of treatment is indicated by their very low initial response to befriending. Thus, 94·3% of the gilts and 66·7% of the sows were classified as being very nervous in response to the initial attempts at befriending by the experimenter. In other words, a high proportion of these gilts and sows were demonstrating a fear response. However, the proportion of sows responding to the daily befriending increased quickly, indicating a rapid reduction in fear responses. The rapid response to befriending with a daily time input of only 1 min per animal is surprising at first sight, although in the studies of Hemsworth et al. (1981), Gonyou et al. (1986) and Pearce et al. (1989), pleasant handling treatments applied for only 15 to 30 s per animal daily were effective in reducing fear responses and alleviating chronic stress.

In the current study, while sows received direct befriending for only 1 min daily, it is likely that each gilt in the pen groups of six to eight was, in fact, inadvertently receiving this treatment for 6 to 8 min/ day. With the experimenter in the pen of gilts handling and stroking each one gently in turn and speaking quietly at the same time, all the gilts in the pen had comprehensive visual, auditory and olfactory and often also tactile contact with the experimenter. The fact that the responses to pleasant handling obtained from the gilts appeared to be slightly greater than those obtained from older sows may have been due to this factor of the duration of effective 'befriending' per day, or it may have been that the gilts, with less experience of previous handling by humans, had higher fear and chronic stress levels at the start of the treatment. This may have accentuated the differences between the pleasant and control treatments in gilts relative to the differences found in the sows.

In the process of moving the gilts and sows from the pregnancy pens to the farrowing pens, the befriended animals had higher 'ease of handling' and approach behaviour scores which were consistent, but were not significantly different from the controls. The isolation of individual gilts from their pregnancy pen group, herding along strange passage ways and eventually into the confinement of a farrowing crate, is likely to be a fear-provoking experience for many animals which is likely to result in acute and chronic stress responses. After transfer to the farrowing house, if gilts have not developed trust in their human carers as a result of reduced fear levels, then each time the stockperson enters the house and the farrowing pen and handles the gilt, e.g. to test for the present of colostrum and the imminence of farrowing, this is likely to induce acute stress responses until such regular pleasant daily handling results in reduction of fear levels and stress responses. In the absence of regular pleasant handling, the isolation and restraint within the farrowing crate, combined with pain and fear induced by the onset of parturition and contractions, are factors which are likely to increase acute and chronic stress levels. It is possible that the higher incidence of savaging of piglets, the significantly higher intervals between births and the marginally higher stillbirth rate in the control treatment are the outcomes of such stress responses.

Thus, the indications are that the parity 1 gilts on the pleasant treatment were less fearful and easier to handle than controls as they were guided from their original pregnancy pen to their farrowing accommodation. Kiley-Worthington (1990), in describing the handling of circus animals to reduce their fear of humans, has found that when a trusting animal-human relationship is developed, the animal will 'go places and do things with the handler that it would be otherwise frightened to do'.

Therefore, the parity 1 gilts on the pleasant treatment may have suffered less acute stress than the controls as they were being transferred from pregnancy to farrowing accommodation and less chronic stress when they were confined in the farrowing pen. The alternative interpretation is that the chronic stress associated with minimal human handling during pregnancy was alleviated more by the pleasant handling than on the control treatment in late pregnancy and during parturition.

A complication in interpreting the outcome of this study was that, while the experimenter applied the pleasant handling treatment and was involved in transferring all sows from pregnancy to farrowing accommodation, farm staff assisted with this transfer and were also involved in the normal commercial checks on testing for the presence of milk and imminence of parturition, and for monitoring the progress of farrowing as their other duties allowed. Thus, the independent influences of the experimenter and the farm staff cannot be determined.

It is possible that the gilts subjected to pleasant handling demonstrated stimulus generalization (Hemsworth et al., 1993). This is where the animal generalizes about humans in general from their experience with the most influential human in their lives or the most recent period in their life. So that, if they had been handled pleasantly by their main human contact and have had low fear and stress responses to this contact and handling, then they will show similar responses to other humans. However, there is some evidence that if animals have been subjected to pleasant treatment by one human contact and to aversive treatment of the same degree by another human, then fear responses to humans in general are likely to be more influenced by their responses to the more aversive of the two handlers (Hemsworth et al., 1994; de Passille et al., 1996).

However, since the gilts and sows on this farm appeared to be subjected to 'minimal' rather than aversive treatment during pregnancy, it is possible that the responses of the pleasant treatment sows to the farm staff in late pregnancy and during parturition were similar to those exhibited in response to the experimenter. Thus, in the case of the pleasant treatment, the presence of, and tactile contact with, any of the farm staff and the experimenter in the farrowing pen before and during farrowing might have been effective in helping to alleviate a chronic stress response relative to the sows on the control treatment.

While the outcome of this study tends to pose more questions than it answers, the results were generally promising, and there is a need to extend the studies to larger numbers of sows per treatment and to replicate the studies over a range of commercial conditions involving different housing systems, personnel and physiological status of sows, especially in terms of chronic stress levels.

References

Barnett, J. L., Hemsworth, P. H., Hennessy, D. P., McCallum, T. M. and Newman, E. A. 1994. The effects of modifying the amount of human contact on the behavioural, physiological and production responses of laying hens. *Applied Animal Behaviour Science* **41**: 87-100.

Cronin, G. M., Barnett, J. L., Hodge, F. M., Smith, J. A. and McCallum, T. H. 1991. The welfare of pigs in two farrowing/lactation environments: cortisol responses of sows. *Applied Animal Behaviour Science* **32**: 117-127.

Gonyou, H. W., Hemsworth, P. H. and Barnett, J. L. 1986. Effects of frequent interactions with humans on growing pigs. *Applied Animal Behaviour Science* **16**: 269-278.

Grandin, T., Curtis, S. E. and Taylor, I. A. 1987. Toys, mingling and driving reduce excitability in pigs. *Journal Animal Science* **65**: (Suppl. 1), 230 (abstr.).

Hemsworth, P. H., Barnett, J. L. and Hansen, C. 1981. The influence of handling by humans on the behaviour, growth and corticosteriods in the juvenile female pig. *Hormones and Behaviour* **15**: 395-403.

Hemsworth, P. H., Barnett, J. L. and Hansen, C. 1986. The influence of handling by humans on the behaviour, reproduction and corticosteriods of male and female pigs. *Applied Animal Behaviour Science* **15**: 303-314.

Hemsworth, P. H., Barnett, J. L. and Hansen, C. 1987. The influence of inconsistent handling by humans on the behaviour, growth and corticosteriods of young pigs. *Applied Animal Behaviour Science* **17**: 245-252.

Hemsworth, P. H., Barnett, J. L. and Coleman, G. J. 1993. The human-animal relationship in agriculture and its consequences for the animal. *Animal Welfare* **2**: 33-51.

Hemsworth, P. H., Coleman, G. J., Cox, M. and Barnett, J. L. 1994. Stimulus generalisation: the inability of pigs to discriminate between humans on the basis of their previous handling experience. *Applied Animal Behaviour Science* **40**: 129-142.

Hemsworth, P. H. and Coleman, G. J. 1998. *Human-livestock interactions: the stockperson and the productivity and welfare of intensively farmed animals.* CAB International, Wallingford.

Kiley-Worthington, M. 1990. *Animals in circuses and zoos.* Chiron's World, Little Eco-Farms Publishing, Basildon, Essex.

Lawrence, A. B., Petherick, J. C., McLean, K. A., Deans, L. A., Chirnside, J. and Vaughan, A. 1993. The effect of the environment on plasma cortisol in parturient sows. *Animal Production* **56**: 476 (abstr.).

Passille, A. M. de, Rushen, J., Ladewig, J. and Petherick, C. 1996. Dairy calves' discrimination of people based on previous handling. *Journal of Animal Science* **74**: 969-974.

Pearce, G. P., Paterson, A. M. and Pearce, A. N. 1989. The influence of pleasant and unpleasant handling and the provision of toys on the growth and behaviour of male pigs. *Applied Animal Behaviour Science* **23**: 27-37.

Pedersen, V., Barnett, J. L., Hemsworth, P. H., Newman, E. A. and Schirmer, B. 1999. The effects of handling on behavioural and physiological responses to housing in tether-stalls in pregnant sows. *Animal Welfare* In press.

Farm animal welfare — who writes the rules?
Occasional Publication No. 23 — British Society of Animal Science 1999
edited by A. J. F. Russel, C. A. Morgan, C. J. Savory, M. C. Appleby and T. L. J. Lawrence

Evaluation of the effects of training methodologies, motivational influences and staff and enterprise development initiatives for livestock industry workers in Scotland, Greece, Spain, Italy and Norway on livestock performance and indices of animal welfare

P. R. English[1], O. McPherson[1], S. G. Deligeorgis[2], J. M. Vidal[3], C. Tarocco[4], F. Bertaccini[4] and H. Sterten[5]

[1]Department of Agriculture, University of Aberdeen, MacRobert Building, 581 King Street, Aberdeen AB24 5UA
[2]Agricultural University of Athens, Greece
[3]Inatega SA, Leon, Spain
[4]University of Bologna, Italy
[5]Felleskjopet Forutvikling, Trondheim, Norway

Introduction

Performance recording schemes in livestock production have always highlighted the very large differences in livestock performance and financial margins between participating farms in all sectors e.g. Meat and Livestock Commission (MLC, 1998) for the pig, sheep and beef sectors and Milkminder Axient: Genus (1998) for the milk production sector. In any specific sector, under similar conditions of climate and other influential variables, some of this between-farm variation is due to different genotypes, food resources and building facilities but it is likely that a very large part of this variation is caused by the quality of the human resources — the management and the stockpeople (English, 1996). Each individual has an important influence and how well the stockpeople and managers combine as a team is likely to have an even greater influence. Seabrook (1974) was among the first to quantify the large independent influence of the stockman on the milk production of dairy cows. Hemsworth *et al.* (1981) also demonstrated large effects of the stockperson on the reproductive performance in pig herds in Holland. Ravel *et al.* (1996) quantified similar positive influences of good stockpeople on piglet survival in herds in Quebec. These workers found that the influences of the stockpeople were related to personality differences (Seabrook, 1974, Ravel *et al.*, 1996) and to the quality of the relationship between the stockman and the animals in his care as measured by the degree of fear responses of the animal towards the stockman or the absence of such responses (Seabrook 1974, Hemsworth *et al.*, 1981).

After establishing that a high level of fear in animals was the result of negative handling behaviour of stockpeople, Hemsworth *et al.* (1994) used a comprehensive training scheme designed to change the attitudes, beliefs and behaviour of the individual stockman responsible for the breeding management of sows on each of 35 farms in Australia. This scheme, which involved on-farm training using instructive guidance on pig behaviour, encouragement to change aversive behaviour towards pigs, training leaflets, videos, posters and regular newsletters, proved to be effective in changing the attitude of these stockmen towards using a much lower percentage of negative behaviours (mild, moderate and forceful hits, slaps, kicks and pushes) and a much higher proportion of positive behaviours (pats, strokes and one hand resting on the back) when moving and handling sows for detection of oestrus and mating. This training scheme resulted in an improvement in pigs born per sow per year of 7% on average, on these farms. The sows also became easier to handle which had a positive influence on job satisfaction and job turn-over rate declined.

Thus, the study of Hemsworth *et al.* (1994) focused on one stockman on each farm who had displayed in the past a high proportion of negative behaviours towards his pigs. There do not appear to be any reports of studies in the relevant literature on comprehensive on-farm training programmes involving the entire team of workers and the impact of training on farm performance. Muirhead (1983) did report increased performance in pig herds following on-farm training but the claimed improvements were not quantified. Many large livestock industry companies operate their own in-house training schemes and some of these are undoubtedly very effective. However, the details and impact of such schemes have not been publicized.

Despite the lack of quantitative data on the impact of on-farm training of the whole team of management and employees, both Segundo (1989) and English *et al.* (1992) presented firm hypotheses on the likely significant positive impact of well designed and appropriately delivered on-farm training for livestock industry workers. These hypotheses were based on the merits of 'purpose-built' training and concepts of team-working, partnership, motivation, and job satisfaction, and working in unison towards the business objectives of the livestock enterprise. Bennett (1989) claimed that effective in-house training of the workforce can improve the morale of the workers, create better interpersonal relationships and instil in employees a sense of loyalty to the company. Hemsworth and Coleman (1998) have also emphasized the importance and value of 'purpose-built' on-farm training to meet educational and training needs, as well as providing other dividends for livestock industry workers. Thus, on-farm training was the approach employed in the present study.

Material and methods

The details of training materials developed, the training approaches, the courses conducted, the associated motivational initiatives and the evaluation methods used have been described in the previous paper (English *et al.*, 1999). The measurement of on-farm performance in the 12 months before and after

the training and motivational initiatives were applied was monitored using the comprehensive recording systems in operation on each farm. There were no major changes to the farm facilities or to the systems operating on any of the four farms studied in the 12 months after the training initiatives were applied, relative to the prior 12-month period. Neither were there staffing changes apart from the departure from the dairy farm of one senior worker 6 months after the training initiatives were carried out.

Results

The farm performance data before and after the initiatives were applied are summarized in Table 1 (pig herds) and Table 2 (dairy herd).

Thus there were increased annual sales of pigs on farms A, B and C of 307 (+12·6%), 866 (+11·7%) and 726 (+13·4%) respectively in the year after the training/educational/certification/motivational initiatives had been applied because of improved sow reproductive performance and reduced mortality. The improvements in performance were achieved with minimal additional capital investment and almost entirely by (1) additional care (hypothermia prevention and sensitive fostering) of new-born piglets, (2) improved care of smaller, less

Table 1 *Farm results for 1 year before and 1 year after the training/education/certification/motivational initiatives were applied*

	Before	After	Additional pigs sold per year
Farm A (120) sows)			
Pigs weaned per litter	9·25	9·96	
Conception rate (%)	84	92	307
Litters per sow per year	2·2	2·3	(+12·6%)
Pigs reared per sow per year	20·35	22·91	
Farm B (520 sows)			
Litters per sow per year	2·03	2·10	
Stillbirths per litter	0·71	0·52	
Pigs reared per litter	8·84	9·12	1010
Pigs reared per sow per year	17·94	19·15	(+11·7%)
Rearing herd mortality (%)	4·0	2·4	
Finishing herd mortality (%)	4·0	3·2	
			Other dividends
Food per sow per year (kg)	1058	985	Reduced sow
Sow food cost per tonne (M.Lira)	0·44	0·43	food costs
Daily live-weight gain (g)			
Weaning to 30 kg	299	338	Increased growth
30 kg to slaughter	516	647	rate
Farm C (350 sows)			
Litters per sow per year	1·91	2·08	
Stillbirths per litter	0·80	0·53	
Pigs reared per litter	8·82	9·01	726
Pigs reared per sow per year	16·85	18·74	(+13·4%)
Rearing herd mortality (%)	4·0	3·0	
Finishing herd mortality (%)	4·5	3·6	
Daily live-weight gain (g)			Other dividends
Weaning to 30 kg	307	357	Increased growth
30 kg to slaughter	508	585	rate

competitive pigs, (3) earlier detection of disease and other problems combined with prompt application of remedial treatment and (4) better AI/service management through having a better understanding of the pig's needs and providing for these needs through enhanced stockmanship care. As well as reductions in mortality and enhanced reproductive performance, some economies were achieved in sow food usage on farm B, while pig growth rate from weaning to slaughter was increased substantially on both farms B and C. Thus considerable dividends in terms of enhanced pig survival, reproduction, growth and efficiency of production resulted from the training/educational/motivational/staff and enterprise development initiatives applied.

The main change noticeable in dairy herd performance in the 12-month period after training, relative to the previous 12 months, was substantial improvement in reproductive performance. Pregnancy rate to first insemination increased by 18 percentage points while number of inseminations per pregnancy was reduced by 0·35 per pregnancy. The most likely reasons for these improvements were considered to be more efficient and more timely detection of oestrus, possibly more careful handling of the cows before, during and after artificial insemination, and more timely inseminations so that more cows were inseminated closer to the optimum stage in relation to the timing of ovulation. The improved pregnancy rate to first insemination was expected to reduce calving interval but the main improvement in this parameter was expected in year 2 after the initiatives were applied. A marked reduction was achieved in bacterial count, which

management attributed to improved hygiene both during milking and in the lying areas. The increase in both protein and fat content of milk were considered to be due to dietary improvements.

Discussion

The improvement of livestock performance associated with the initiatives

These results are based on only four farms, three in the pig sector and one in the dairy sector. Such 'before' and 'after' comparisons are currently in progress on many pig, dairy and sheep milk and lamb production enterprises in all participating countries.

On all four farms for which data are available to date, substantial improvements were achieved in production parameters. These were attributed to the education/training/motivational initiatives applied because no other major changes took place on these farms over this 2-year period.

While all stockpeople demonstrated great interest in education and training and in the motivational initiatives, achieved substantial increases in post-course test scores relative to pre-course tests scores and in general were extremely positive about all the initiatives, (see previous paper: English *et al*, 1999), the magnitude of some of the improvements achieved in year 2 were none the less surprising.

On the basis of the earlier supposition (see **Introduction**) that a large proportion of the variation in performance between livestock enterprises of the same type under similar conditions is largely due to differences in the 'quality' of the management-stockpeople team, it is interesting to examine the differences between pig herd performance categories in the MLC recording scheme (MLC, 1998) (see Table 3).

When the differences in a commonly accepted major efficiency parameter such as 'pigs weaned per sow

Table 2 *Farm results for 1 year before and 1 year after the training/education/certification/motivational initatives were applied*

Farm D (340 dairy cows)	Before	After
Milk yield per cow (l)	7097	7127
Milk protein (g/kg)	33·0	33·5
Butter fat (g/kg)	36·2	39·1
Hygienic quality		
Cell count (,000)	260	272
Bacterial count (,000)	6	4
Pregancy rate to first insemination (%)	33	51
No. of inseminations per pregnancy	2·65	2·3
Lactation length (days)	310	310
Calving interval (days)	409	403
Calf mortality (livebirths) (%)	1·0	0·3

Table 3 *UK breeding herd results (MLC, 1997)*

	Bottom third	Average	Top third	Top 10%
Herds	85	254	85	25
Sows per herd	217	277	338	249
Weaning (days)	26	25	24	24
Pigs reared per sow per year	19·2	21·7	23·4	25·0
	Base	+13·0%	+21·9%	+30·2%
		Base	+7·8%	+15·2%
			Base	+6·8%

per year' is examined, it can be seen that the top 10 per cent is 6·8% better than the top third, the top third is 7·8% better than the 'average' while the average is 13·0% better than the bottom third. The difference between the average and the bottom third is similar to the 'before' and 'after' differences between the farms in the present study. This helps to put the 'before' and 'after' differences in the present study into perspective and the percentage differences between the categories in Table 3 help to make the point that the poorer the initial performance level, the easier it is to make substantial improvements. Apart from herd A (Table 1), which was on a small family farm in Spain, the other two pig herds had fairly low performance levels in year 1. In addition the reproductive performance in the dairy herd was also relatively poor.

The enhancement of the knowledge and understanding of the stockpeople, the improved basis of their skills (including handling), their enhanced motivation and team working, or some combination of these and other associated factors, appeared to be effective in achieving substantial improvements in important performance parameters.

As more 'before' and 'after' data are collected from other herds and flocks, it is likely that the improvements achieved on some farms will be much smaller than in the four farms monitored to date. On other farms, perhaps those with very high levels of performance and which already have a very knowledgeable, highly skilled and very motivated management-stockpeople team operating the enterprise, no improvements may be noticeable. A small proportion of farms may well suffer depressed livestock performance following a training-motivation exercise for reasons which may be obvious, such as an unexpected outbreak of disease, or for reasons which are less obvious.

It will be important, therefore, that as this study proceeds and data are obtained from more farms, an increased awareness is acquired of the factors which influence the variable responses which may be obtained from different farm situations. This may help to predict in advance the farm situations in which similar educational/training/motivational initiatives to those employed in this study may be cost-effective and those farms in which these approaches are unlikely to be cost-effective.

At this stage one can only speculate on the most influential components of the current initiatives which are contributing to improvements in animal performance. Among these possible influences are (1) enhanced knowledge and understanding of the animals' requirements and of how best to provide for these needs on the farm in focus, (2) an improved basis for skills including correct handling procedures (maximizing the positive and minimizing the negative or aversive influences as described by Hemsworth and Coleman (1998), (3) better team working, (4) enhanced motivation and (5) better job satisfaction. Undoubtedly the synergistic influence of these complementary components is greater than the sum of the individual influences. In other words, the combined 'package' is likely to be the influential element in the improvements monitored to date.

Positive interactions of the elements of the overall initiatives

Several human psychologists, animal scientists and experienced livestock managers have contributed to our understanding of the interaction of the elements contained in the current package. Lloyd (1975), in highlighting the lack of training and of trained staff in the poultry industry, contended that training to improve understanding of the birds' needs and associated skills would not only enhance animal care but would also have positive influences on job satisfaction, work performance and employment stability, thus reducing staff turn-over and helping to keep a good working team together. On the basis of experience, Bennett (1989) claimed that training can improve workers' morale, create better interpersonal relationships, instil in employees a sense of loyalty to the organization as well as providing other intangible benefits. Grusenmeyer (1992) reported similar associated influences of well designed training in the USA dairy industry. Hemsworth *et al.* (1994), in using appropriate training to change faulty attitudes of stockpeople towards using more positive behaviours and fewer negative behaviours when handling breeding sows, succeeded in this objective. This was shown to result in better reproductive performance and in the ease of handling of the animals. This enhanced behaviour and performance of the animals in their care proved to have a motivating influence on the stockpeople and enhanced job satisfaction and also appeared to reduce job turn-over.

Vroom (1964), in the non-agricultural sector, found significant correlations between job satisfaction and the incidence of on the job accidents, absenteeism, staff turn-over and even better mental and physical health. Thus, a combination of influences from the application of the entire education/training/ motivation package in the present work are likely to have contributed to the enhanced performance in the livestock enterprises in the study. The feeling of achievement in reducing mortality and improving breeding performance, in turn, is likely to provide further motivation and job satisfaction.

Improvement in indices of animal welfare
Among the major objectives of these initiatives are the enhancement of livestock performance and business efficiency through improving animal health and welfare. It is clear from the results to date that some obvious indices of welfare, such as survival of piglets and older pigs, have been enhanced through meeting needs more effectively, including earlier diagnosis and remedying of problems. However, it is important to establish whether or not higher overall productivity in terms of enhanced reproductive performance, survival and growth can be equated with enhancement of animal welfare.

Enhanced animal productivity and animal welfare
The concept of 'biological fitness' which can be defined as the basic ability to survive, grow and reproduce has been discussed by Fraser and Broom (1990), Broom and Johnson (1993) and Hemsworth *et al.* (1996) as being potentially a useful index of welfare. The concept is based on the premise that if the animal is suffering from acute or chronic stress there can be undesirable behavioural responses in terms of fear and the development of vices, as well as physiological responses associated with prolonged activation of the hypothalamus-pituitary-adrenal axis. This in turn can lead to suppression of the immune system leading to increased disease susceptibility and higher mortality, as well as depressions in growth, reproduction and milk production. Such stress induced depressions in growth and reproductive performance stem from the disruption of protein metabolism and key reproductive endocrine events (Klasing 1985; Moberg, 1985; Clarke *et al.*, 1992).

Thus, there are strong arguments for using overall animal performance in terms of reproduction, lactation, survival and growth as a useful index of welfare (Beilharz and Zeeb, 1981; Beilharz, 1982). However, Broom and Johnston (1993) have urged rightful caution regarding generalizing about the closeness of this association, indicating that a high level of animal performance might be achieved with the support of procedures and products which are not consistent with welfare enhancement. Such examples include the force feeding of geese to enhance growth and liver weight, the use of bovine and porcine somatotropin to enhance milk yield in dairy cows and growth in pigs respectively and the use of in-food antibiotics to suppress endemic disease conditions induced by faulty husbandry and facilities.

However, in the case of animal performance increases (reproduction, survival and growth) in the current study which result from the application of the educational, training and motivational initiatives,

these are likely to reflect improvements in both overall welfare within the system and that of the individuals which were most disadvantaged before the initiatives were implemented.

The basis of the educational and training initiatives is in enhancing awareness of the basic needs of the livestock, on how best to provide for these needs, on behavioural indices of well being, on the ability to detect problems earlier and rectify them more promptly and effectively, and the importance of stockperson-animal relationships to the animal, its well being and performance. The further emphasis is on enhancing motivation and job satisfaction and the stimulation to improve animal care through better understanding, attention to detail and good husbandry in general.

Thus the improvements in animal performance achieved in the livestock enterprises participating in the study very largely stem from these enhanced husbandry influences and not from artificial agents such as in-food antibiotics and exogenous hormones which are likely to compromise animal welfare.

Projected development of the initiatives
The projected further development of the educational / training / motivational initiatives being evaluated in the present study is summarized in Figure 1.

Part of the future strategy will be the training of trainers so that each farm will eventually have the opportunity to be responsible for its own regular and progressive training. Thus the owner, managers and senior stockpeople can gradually contribute increasing proportions of the training provision. It is

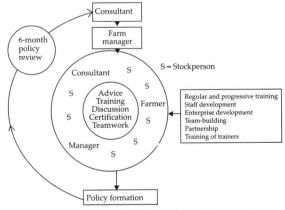

Figure 1 Projected development: a model for regular and progressive training, staff development, team building and enterprise development.

desirable that the main farm consultants (e.g. the veterinarian, nutritional consultant, the husbandry or business adviser) also become more involved in training. Up to the present, it is likely that these consultants communicate almost exclusively with management. This communication at management level should continue but should also be extended to include the stockpeople during the regular and progressive training which is envisaged. With all personnel involved in training, trouble shooting, and problem solving together, the talents and ideas of the stockpeople can contribute to the policy making of the management team. Thus, progressively, the stockpeople themselves have the opportunity to contribute to policy making. This is effective team working as well as training and the stockpeople feel an increasing sense of partnership in the business. Conferring such increased problem solving and policy making responsibility has been found to contribute substantially to employee motivation and enhanced job satisfaction (Herzberg *et al*, 1959; Bowen, 1992; Grusenmeyer, 1992; Umphrey, 1992). These workers found that farm policies which had the 'handprint' of the entire management-stockpeople team on them were much more likely to succeed. Grusenmeyer (1992) established on the basis of experience in large dairy herds in the USA that good stockpeople need leadership and not management, and further asserted that such good employees should not be over managed and under lead.

Conclusions
Thus, while the on-farm educational, training and motivational approaches deployed in this study have been successful to date in a small number of farms in enhancing livestock performance, the initiatives are still in their early developmental stages. However, the interim results are promising and making the most of human resources on farms, both individually and collectively, in effective teams of animal carers, trouble shooters, problem solvers and policy makers, is likely to be the most cost-effective way in the future to ensure high standards of animal welfare, livestock performance and business efficiency in livestock enterprises.

Acknowledgements
We are grateful to the European Union for the award of a grant for this work under the Leonardo da Vinci programme.

References
Beilharz, R. G. 1982. Genetic adaptation in relation to animal welfare. *International Journal of the Study of Animal Problems* **3**: 117-124.

Beilharz, R. G. and Zeeb, K. 1981. Applied ethology and animal welfare. *Applied Animal Ethology* **7**: 3-10.

Bennett, R. 1989. *Managing people.* Richard Clay, Great Britain.

Bowen, M. K. 1992. The role of the dairy manager in human resource management. In *Large dairy herd management* (ed. H. H. van Horn, and C. J. Wilcox), pp. 757-763. American Dairy Science Association.

Broom, D. M. and Johnson, K. G. 1993. *Stress and animal welfare.* Chapman and Hall, London.

Clarke, I. J., Hemsworth, P. H., Barnett, J. L. and Tilbrook, A. J. 1992. Stress and reproduction in farm animals. In *Stress and reproduction* (ed. K. E. Sheppard, J. H. Boublik and J. W. Funder), pp. 239-251. Serono Symposium Publications, vol. 86. Raven Press, New York.

English, P. R. 1996. Stockmanship: improving this valuable resource. *Proceedings of the Saskatchewan Park Industry Symposium. Saskatoon, November 1996*, pp. 111-125.

English, P. R., Burgess, G., Segundo, R. and Dunne, J. H. 1992. *Stockmanship: improving the care of the pig and other livestock.* Farming Press, Ipswich, Suffolk, England.

English, P. R., McPherson, O., Deligeorgis, S. G., Vidal, J. M., Tarocco, C., Bertaccini, F. and Sterten, H. 1999. Evaluation of training, certification and career development strategies for livestock industry workers in Scotland, Greece, Spain, Italy and Norway. In *Farm animal welfare. Who writes the rules?* (ed. A. J. F. Russel, C. A. Morgan, C. J. Savory, M. C. Appleby, and T. L. J. Lawrence), pp. 144-149. British Society of Animal Science, occasional publication no. 23.

Fraser, A. F. and Broom, D. M. 1990. *Farm animal behaviour and welfare.* CAB International, Wallingford, UK.

Grusenmeyer, D. 1992. Maximising human resource output. In *Large dairy herd maangement* (ed. H. H. Van Horn and C. J. Wilcox), pp. 764-771. American Dairy Science Association.

Hemsworth, P. H., Barnett, J. L. and Campbell, R. G. 1996. A study of the relative aversiveness of a new daily injection procedure for pigs. *Applied Animal Behaviour Science* **49**: 389-401.

Hemsworth, P. H., Barnett, J. L. and Hansen, C. 1981. The influence of handling by humans on the behaviour, growth and corticosteroids in the juvenile female pig. *Hormones and Behaviour* **15**: 396-403.

Hemsworth, P. H. and Coleman, G. J. 1998. *Human-livestock interactions: the stockperson and the productivity and welfare of intensively farmed animals.* CAB International, Wallingford.

Hemsworth, P. H., Coleman, G. J., and Barnett, J. L. 1994. Improving the attitude and behaviour of stockpeople towards pigs and the consequences on the behavioural and reproductive performance of commercial pigs. *Applied Animal Behaviour Science* **39**: 349-362.

Herzberg, F., Mausner, B. and Snyderman, B. 1959. *The motivation to work.* J. Wiley, London.

Klasing, K. C. 1985. Influence of stress on protein metabolism. In *Animal stress* (ed. G. P. Moberg), pp. 268-280. American Physiological Society, Baltimore, USA.

Lloyd, D. H. 1975. Effective staff management. In *Economic factors affecting egg production.* (ed. B. M. Freeman and K. N. Boorman), pp. 221-251. British Poultry Science, Edinburgh.

Meat and Livestock Commission. 1998. *Meat and Livestock Commission pig year book.* MLC, PO Box 44, Milton Keynes.

Milkminder Axient: Genus. 1998. *Axient Milkminder annual report 1997-98.* Genus PLC, Westmere Drive, Crewe.

Moberg, G. P. 1985. Influence of stress on reproduction: measure of wellbeing. In *Animal stress* (ed. G. P. Moberg), pp. 245-267. American Physiological Society, Bethesda, Maryland.

Muirhead, M. 1983. The veterinary surgeon's role as an advisor in pig production. *International Swine Update. SQUIBB. March 1983.*

Ravel, A., D'Allaire, S. and Bigras-Poulin, M. 1996. Survey of management and housing in farrowing quarters among independent and integrated swine farms in Quebec. *Canadian Journal of Veterinary Research* **60:** 21-28.

Seabrook, M. 1974. A study of some elements of the cowman's skills as influencing the milk yield of dairy cows. *Ph.D. thesis, University of Reading.*

Segundo, R. C. 1989. A study of stockpeople and managers in the pig industry with special emphasis on the factors affecting their job satisfaction. *M.Sc. thesis, University of Aberdeen.*

Umphrey, J. E. 1992. Understanding employee motivation. In *Large dairy herd management* (ed. H. H. Van Horn and C. J. Wilcox), pp. 786-792. American Dairy Science Association.

Vroom, V. H. 1964. *Work and motivation.* J. Wiley, London.

Farm animal welfare — who writes the rules?
Occasional Publication No. 23 — British Society of Animal Science 1999
edited by A. J. F. Russel, C. A. Morgan, C. J. Savory, M. C. Appleby and T. L. J. Lawrence

Evaluation of training, certification and career development strategies for livestock industry workers in Scotland, Greece, Spain, Italy and Norway

P. R. English[1], O. McPherson[1], S. G. Deligeorgis[2], J. M. Vidal[3], C. Tarocco[4], F. Bertaccini[4] and H. Sterten[5]

[1]*Department of Agriculture, University of Aberdeen, MacRobert Building, 581 King Street, Aberdeen AB24 5UA*
[2]*Agricultural University of Athens, Greece*
[3]*Inatega SA, Leon, Spain*
[4]*University of Bologna, Italy*
[5]*Felleskjopet Forutvikling, Trondheim, Norway*

Introduction

The studies of Seabrook (1974 and 1984) with dairy cows and Hemsworth *et al.* (1981 and 1986) and Ravel *et al.* (1996 and 1999) with pigs, demonstrated significant influences of the stockperson on animal performance and indices of welfare. Despite this important influence in the livestock industries, comparatively little research has been carried out to establish the scientific basis of stockmanship so that the components of this resource could be measured and improved (English *et al.*, 1992; Hemsworth and Coleman, 1998).

English *et al.* (1992), Erven (1992) and Hemsworth and Coleman (1998) have drawn attention to the complexity of livestock care jobs, since they demand a comprehensive understanding of the needs of the animals and a high level of skills in providing for these needs and in handling the animals generally. This emphasizes the need for suitable education and training. In addition, other livestock industry researchers have drawn attention to the needs of workers in any job for motivation, job satisfaction and good team spirit/team working in any management-employee group (Maslow, 1954; Bowen, 1992; Grusenmeyer, 1992; Umphrey, 1992). The well established principle of regular and progressive training as motivating influences contributing to job satisfaction and job performance in non-agricultural industries has been emphasized (Lloyd, 1975; English *et al.*, 1992). Other positive influences on motivation, job satisfaction and job performance established in the livestock industries include a progressive career structure (Erven, 1992; Umphrey, 1992), status enhancing job titles (Bray, 1992; Umphrey, 1992), and team working including a sense of partnership in the business with an influence on 'trouble shooting', working out

solutions, setting targets and policy making in general (Bowen, 1992; Grusenmeyer, 1992).

Therefore, the theoretical ingredients of high quality stockmanship including careful selection of employees, ensuring good working conditions, regular and progressive provision of relevant education and training, a dynamic career structure to recognize achievements, team working, motivation and job satisfaction, appear to be well established. However, the available evidence indicates that stockpeople in general are not well provided for in terms of essential provisions which would help them to be more competent in, and satisfied with, their work and also to make a much larger contribution to the care of their animals, animal welfare and productivity, the efficiency of the livestock enterprise and the success of the business.

One syndrome of this general lack of provision for stockpeople is high job turn-over in the livestock industries (Segundo, 1989; Cleary, 1990; Goodman, 1990; English *et al.*, 1992; Howard *et al.*, 1996) Hemsworth and Coleman, 1998). A job turn-over rate varying from 2 to 5 years has been reported in these studies. Howard *et al.* (1990) described job turn-over as 'a disruptive, costly process' on the running of the enterprise, especially in relation to team working. The main causes of job dissatisfaction leading to employee turn-over have been found to be autocratic management style, poor communication opportunities with management, sub-optimal provisions for animal care and the lack of both training provisions and recognition of achievements (Segundo, 1989; Howard *et al.*, 1990). The great majority of studies have shown that pay rewards appear to be acceptable. In this latter context, Howard *et al.* (1990), in their studies in Canada, have drawn attention to the fact that pay scales in the agricultural sector in general are considerably below those in other equivalent industry sectors. They allude to the non-pay attractions of working in the agricultural sector. Therefore, it would appear that the high turn-over of staff in the livestock sector could be reduced if more attention was paid to non-pay related provisions which are important to stockpeople. Therefore, in the present study, the provision of on-farm education and training, the concept of a dynamic career structure, recognition of achievements by way of certification and the attitude of stockpeople to status-enhancing job titles, were evaluated.

Material and methods

Training materials

Educational and training materials were developed which were designed to meet the training needs of the stockpeople and management staff in different livestock industry sectors: pigs; dairy cows and calves; milk sheep and lambs. These materials took the form of educational training manuals, slide sets, videos, skills exercise, knowledge tests and questionnaires to evaluate the courses and the other initiatives.

Training approaches

An on-farm training approach was adopted so that the entire working team — owner, managers and stockpeople could be together for training. The owner and/or the manager of the farm was approached with regard to their willingness to participate and the number of farm staff attending each course varied from four to 20. The timing of training was selected to suit the farm staff, the least busy day of the week for the staff being selected. The preferred course timings in the dairy and pig sectors were 9.00 to 11.30 h and 13.00 to 17.00 h respectively. Before the course, the livestock enterprise was inspected by the trainers along with the owner and/ or the manager, to see the stockpeople at their work and to assess the strengths and weaknesses of the system and the specific problem areas which should be a particular focus for education, training and discussion within the training group. The training took place either in the farm office on in a room in the farm house.

Course procedure

The course was initiated by the introduction of all participants to each other in an attempt to form an atmosphere conducive to good team-working. The objectives of the project were outlined and particularly the rôle of the course tests. Since the aims of these tests could be misinterpreted and be intimidating to some participants, it was explained that the 'knowledge tests' before and after the course were designed to evaluate the course content and the delivery and not to test individual participants. Thereafter, the pre-course test was conducted and this involved approximately 20 short answer 'true-false' or 'tick the correct answer' type of questions. The course then proceeded with slide and video presentations and skills exercises (e.g. piglet fostering practices) conducted using paper exercises. In these presentations, particular focus was placed on principles and practices pertaining to problem areas on the farm. Full opportunity was afforded for intervening discussion, for clarifying misunderstandings, focusing on problem areas and working out the best and most cost-effective solutions. At the completion of this session, the post course test was conducted. Thereafter, all course participants completed a 'course evaluation form' in which they were asked to evaluate all aspects of the course. In addition, they were asked to indicate their desire for regular training and desired frequency of training. Their opinions were also sought on a dynamic career structure and, if they favoured such, they were asked to state their main reasons for such interest. They were also asked to examine a list of alternative job titles and to select the title which most appealed to them. Finally, they were asked to answer questions on their career aspirations.

At the end of the course, all participants were given a copy of the training manual which had been produced as part of the project and invited to study it prior to the next training session. They were also invited to borrow video material, when available, so as to provide the opportunity for self-learning. Finally, course certificates were presented to each participant, the grading being decided in advance by the owner and/or the manager to reflect the competence in the workplace of each employee.

Following the completion of the course, a 'consultancy report to management' was produced. This report was based on (a) observations made of strengths and weaknesses during the pre-course visit to the livestock enterprise, (b) the farm records to date and (c) the comments/suggestions of the owner (and manager) and also those of the stockpeople made during the course. This report was designed to guide farm policy in the subsequent months before the next training course/'policy formulation exercise'.

All courses conducted in Scotland and Italy in both the pig and dairy sectors were conducted on farm. All courses conducted in Spain, Greece and Norway in the pig, sheep milk and lamb sectors involved small family farms and were conducted on a group basis at a central location.

Table 1 *Responses to post-course questionnaires*

Sector	Degree of satisfaction with course materials and course delivery — Classification of very useful/useful†	Acceptability of course duration of 2 to 5h	Optimum course length (h) 2	3	4	Desired course frequency (months) 1	2	6	12
	% participants	% participants	% participants			% participants			
Pig	98·8	94·9	25	44	31	24	35	35	6
Dairy	94·3	88·9	26	55	19	22	33	37	7
Sheep	92·1	76·3	37	29	34	42	36	15	7

† Relative to 'moderately useful/waste of time'.

Results

A total of 111 'test courses' (56, 23 and 32 in the pig, dairy and sheep milk and lamb sectors respectively), involving 1386 participants and 7289 person training hours were conducted and evaluated. Of these courses, 47, 21, 23, 9 and 11 were conducted in Scotland, Spain, Greece, Italy and Norway respectively. In Scotland and Italy there was universal support for on-farm training in the pig and dairy sectors as it could be 'purpose built' to the specific needs of each farm. The results of the course evaluations and responses to related questions regarding the preferred duration and frequency of courses are summarized in Table 1.

Thus, a very high proportion of course participants (92·1 to 98·8%) found the courses, the course materials and delivery methods to be 'very useful/

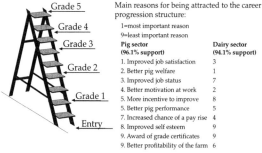

	Main reasons for being attracted to the career progression structure:
Grade 5	1=most important reason
Grade 4	9=least important reason
Grade 3	
Grade 2	
Grade 1	
Entry	

	Pig sector (96.1% support)		Dairy sector (94.1% support)
1. Improved job satisfaction		3
2. Better pig welfare		1
3. Improved job status		7
4. Better motivation at work		2
5. More incentive to improve		8
5. Better pig performance		5
7. Increased chance of a pay rise	4
8. Improved self esteem		9
9. Award of grade certificates		9
9. Better profitability of the farm	6

Figure 1 Concept of a career progression ladder.

useful'. The preferred duration of individual courses varied between 2 and 4 h with most support for 3-h courses and almost as much support for 4-h as for 2-h courses. Participants expressed a strong wish for very regular training — at 6-monthly intervals or even more frequently in the majority of cases.

The results of pre- and post-course knowledge tests are presented in Table 2. The post-course test scores were 20·7, 9·5 and 25·4% higher than the pre-course test scores in the pig, dairy and sheep sectors respectively.

In the pig and dairy sectors, respectively, 96·1 and 94·1% of course participants were attracted to the idea of a career progression structure, going from basic entry grade through grades 1 to 5. (see Figure 1).

The main reasons for being attracted to such a career progression structure in the pig sector were (in order of priority): (1) improved job satisfaction; (2) the attainment of better pig welfare; (3) improved job status; (4) better motivation at work; (5) greater incentive to improve. 'Increased chance of a pay rise'

Table 2 *Pre- and post-course test scores*

Country	No. of courses	Test scores Pre	Post	Increase %
A. Pig Sector				
Scotland	26	71·9	82·0	14·0
Spain	5	60·8	80·8	32·9
Italy	7	60·2	77·4	28·6
Greece	3	59·0	89·0	50·8
Weighted mean		67·6	81·6	20·7
B. Dairy cow and calf sector				
Scotland	19	88·0	94·5	7·4
Spain	4	53·0	67·0	26·4
Weighted mean		81·9	89·7	9·5
C. Sheep milk and lamb sector				
Spain	6	54·5	58·7	7·7
Greece	6	51·8	74·8	44·4
Mean		53·2	66·7	25·4

came well down the priorities in the reasons for being attracted to the structure, which surprised many employers and managers. It appeared that many employers did not understand the aspirations of their employees. In the dairy sector, the main reasons for being attracted to such a career ladder were: (1) the attainment of better animal welfare; (2) better motivation at work; (3) improved job satisfaction and (4) increased chance of a pay rise.

Alternative job titles
Course participants were provided with a list of alternative job titles and asked to select the one which they preferred. The job titles incorporated a list of component terms in the pig sector such as pig, animal, livestock, stock (as in 'stockman'), care or carer and technician or specialist, and equivalent terms in the dairy sector. In the list of job titles in the pig and dairy sectors there were as many titles incorporating general terms such as 'animal', 'livestock', and 'stock' as there were specific 'pig' or 'cow'/'dairy' terms in the choices provided. The breakdown of preferred components of a job title for 70 pig and 17 dairy stockpeople are summarised in Table 3

Table 3 *Preferred component terms in job title*

Pig sector	Pig	Animal/Stock /Livestock	Technician Specialist	Care Carer
Stockpeople				
No.	30	40	43	28
%	42·9	57·1	61·4	40·0

Dairy sector	Cow/Cattle /Dairy	Animal/Stock /Livestock	Technician Specialist	Care Carer
Stockpeople				
No.	3	14	10	10
%	17·6	82·4	58·8	58·8

Thus, in the pig sector, a majority of stockpeople (57·1 %) expressed a preference not to have the prefix 'pig' in their job title. Sixty-one per cent were attracted to the terms 'technician' or 'specialist' in their job title and 40% to the terms 'care' or 'carer'. Dairy stockpeople provided similar responses. If the title of the pig and dairy stockpeople was changed to 'animal care specialist', 93·2 and 76·5% in the pig and dairy sectors respectively indicated that they would support such a change.

Discussion

The results provide considerable encouragement that with (1) the provision of training packages carefully designed in relation to educational/training needs and appropriate delivery methods, (2) regular and progressive training, (3) additional motivational influences such as a career ladder and (4) selection of more descriptive and status-enhancing job titles, livestock industry posts would become more attractive to personnel already in post and also to potential recruits to the livestock care profession. Some of these aspects will be discussed in turn.

Alternative education/training provisions and their impact
Existing training provisions for stockpeople include instruction from the owner, manager or senior stockpeople, vocational training at colleges, training agency courses on specific skills and techniques, and lectures on technical topics organized by ancillary industry sectors such as animal food and breeding companies or veterinary groups. While these provisions all play an important rôle in the education and training of farm staff, it is not usually possible for more than a small proportion of employees to attend outside training courses and lectures. In addition, these alternative training provisions do not constitute a specifically designed 'package' to meet the specific training needs of each farm, in which the entire farm team can participate. In a survey in Scotland carried out by Wright (1985) on alternative training provisions, a clear preference was expressed by stockpeople for on-farm training. In addition, Grusenmeyer (1992) has emphasized the importance of the team-building, motivational and job satisfaction aspects of on-farm training in which the owner, manager and all staff are involved. Grusenmeyer (1992) also referred to the excellent opportunity provided by 'on-farm' training for the entire team to be involved together in trouble shooting, the identification and solution of problems and for policy formation. Good stockpeople value the opportunity to become involved in such problem solving and forward planning. This provides them with a greater sense of belonging and partnership in the business. Such involvement has been demonstrated to be a strong motivator of staff and to contribute substantially to job satisfaction (Bowen, 1992).

The involvement of the owner and manager with staff in regular training sessions, in which problems of livestock care and productivity are addressed and solutions worked out together, would be likely to remove most of the causes of job dissatisfaction found by Segundo (1989) in pig herds in Scotland. Many of these related to poor communication and inadequate time for discussion on livestock related problems between management and stockpeople.

Attitude of stockpeople to training

What was extremely encouraging in the current project was the very positive attitude of stockpeople to training, the concentration and interest which they demonstrated, their enthusiastic participation in discussion and their desire to address and solve problem areas in the enterprise. As indicated earlier, they expressed a wish to have regular training of this nature (at 2 to 6 monthly intervals) and for training sessions to last for an average of 3 h with more than 25% of stockpeople expressing a wish for continuous 4-h training sessions fitted into a normal working day! This is indicative of a craving for education and training along with the associated discussion, troubleshooting and problem solving elements.

In conducting the training, many training sessions in the pig sector did last for a continuous period of 4 h usually from 13.00 to 17.00 h, with only a very short half-time break for refreshments. When these training sessions had been completed and as the 'trainers' were preparing to leave, the stockpeople sought to ask further questions and to continue the discussion. This was despite the fact that they had their animal care work to complete for the day and none of the stockpeople involved sought extra overtime payments for their prolonged day. This reflects their great thirst for learning and training and their attitude towards understanding their animals and to caring for them more effectively.

Career structures and certification

Regarding the concept of a dynamic career structure, this was accorded a very high level of support (96·1 and 94·1% in the pig and dairy sectors respectively). The main reasons for their interest in such a career ladder related to improved job status and self-esteem, greater motivation to improve their understanding and animal care (welfare) and better job satisfaction. Their linking of career ladder advancement with increased pay came well down the list of their priorities for being attracted to such a career structure. These responses surprised many owners and managers who anticipated that the linking of advancement up the career ladder to pay would be at the top of the priorities for their stockpeople. This is a common misconception among industry leaders, for in most studies on the job satisfaction/dissatisfaction of livestock industry employees, many non-pay factors feature much more highly in causes of dissatisfaction than does low pay (Segundo, 1989; Grusenmeyer, 1992).

The apparent indifference of stock people to the award of a grade certificate was surprising. This may reflect the fact that material things such as pay and certificates were less important to them than non material factors such as self-esteem. It must be pointed out that stockpeople had completed their questionnaires before they were awarded with their 'animal care specialist' grade certificate. On further reflection, perhaps influenced by their family's responses, they may value their attainment certificate more highly.

Alternative job titles and the profession of animal care

Regarding job titles, it is important to most people that the title of the job they do reflects the standing and nature of the job as well as the knowledge and skills required. Job titles such as 'pigman' or 'cowman' for very knowledgeable, high skilled and caring stockpeople do not give any impression of such qualities. A marked preference was expressed in both the pig and dairy sectors for 'non-pig' and 'non-cow/non-dairy' job title components to be replaced by more general 'animal/stock/livestock' prefixes. Strong support was also expressed for the inclusion of the terms specialist or technician and care or carer in the job title. The preferred title of the authors to reflect the knowledge, skills and animal caring attitude of good stockpeople was 'animal care specialist'. If their current job title was changed to this, a high proportion of the stockpeople (93·2 and 76·5% in the pig and dairy sectors respectively) indicated their support for such a change. Bray (1992), in the USA dairy sector, has also placed emphasis on the importance of job titles in relation to the image of the job and the self esteem and status of good stockpeople. Bray (1992) claimed that a more worthy job title in keeping with the knowledge, skills and animal caring attitude of the employee was an important factor which increased the chances of obtaining, for example, a bank loan and credit facilities.

English *et al.* (1992) and Hemsworth and Coleman (1998) have emphasized the importance of recognizing livestock care as a profession in relation to the self esteem of good stockpeople already in post and the attractiveness of the job to prospective employees. It would seam logical that there should be one general title for all livestock carers rather than a range of titles according to the species concerned. Bray (1992) has referred to the challenge of obtaining a bank loan or credit facilities in a store with some current job titles. Because of the distorted attitude of some sectors of society to those who care for animals as a 'cowman' or 'pigman' or a 'henwife', stockpeople will almost certainly have higher status in the eyes of others and may perhaps also be more credit worthy if they are a member of the very worthy profession of 'animal care specialists'.

Aspirations of the stockpeople

The pig stockpeople participants in the current study were asked about their future job aspirations if a dynamic career structure was in place. Over 90% wished to remain in the pig industry as a career, and all aspired to move progressively up the career ladder. Half of these aimed to progress into section or unit management, while the other half wished to remain as a stockperson and to become progressively more knowledgeable, skilled and competent in the workplace. This was a very encouraging commitment to the pig industry.

This constituted the last question in the questionnaire. Prior questions covered their evaluation of the course and course materials, their desire for regular and progressive 'on-farm' training, the duration and frequency of such training, their attitude to a dynamic career structure and to status-enhancing job titles. It is possible that the answers regarding job aspirations were influenced by their vision of better times ahead involving regular training, an exciting career structure, better self-esteem and status, team working, greater sense of partnership in the business and generally better motivation and job satisfaction.

These possible effects of the initiatives, as well as the job turn-over rate, the attractiveness of the job to new applicants, the number of applicants for jobs, the quality of animal care, animal performance, enterprise efficiency and business success, have yet to be evaluated.

Acknowledgements

We are grateful to the European Union for the award of a grant for this work under the Leonardo da Vinci programme.

References

Bowen, M. K. 1992. The role of the dairy manager in human resource management. In *Large dairy herd management* (ed. H. H. Van Horn and C. J. Wilcox), pp. 757-763. American Dairy Science Association.

Bray, D. R. 1992. Job descriptions and job images. In *Large dairy herd management* (ed. H. H. Van Horn and C. J. Wilcox), pp. 772-776. American Dairy Science Association.

Cleary, G. V. 1990. Personnel management and record keeping. In *Pig production in Australia* (ed. J. A. A. Gardner, A. C. Dunkin, and L. C. Lloyd), pp. 284-291. Australian Pig Research Council, Canberra. Butterworths.

English, P. R., Burgess, G., Segundo, R. and Dunne, J. H. 1992. *Stockmanship: improving the care of the pig and other livestock.* Farming Press, Ipswich, Suffolk, England.

Erven, B. L. 1992. Recruiting, selecting and training dairy farm employees. In *Large dairy herd management* (ed. H. H.

Van Horn and C. J. Wilcox), pp. 777-785. American Dairy Science Association.

Goodman, S. 1990. Effective staff management. In *Proceedings of Conference and Trade Fair 'Pigs North East', York Racecourse. (MLC/ADAS/NFU/Farmers Guardian) March 1990.* Meat and Livestock Commission, Milton Keynes.

Grusenmeyer, D. 1992. Maximising human resource output. In *Large dairy herd management* (ed. H. H. Van Horn and C. J. Wilcox), pp. 764-770. American Dairy Science Association.

Hemsworth, P. H., Barnett, J. L. and Hansen, C. 1981. The influence of handling by humans on the behaviour, growth and corticosteroids in the juvenile female pig. *Hormones and Behaviour* **15**: 396-403.

Hemsworth, P. H., Barnett, J. L. and Hansen, C. 1986. The influence of handling by humans on the behaviour, reproduction and corticosteriods of male and female pigs. *Applied Animal Behavioural Science* **15**: 303-314.

Hemsworth, P. H. and Coleman, G. J. 1998. *Human livestock interactions: the stockperson and the productivity and welfare of intensively farmed animals.* CAB International, Wallingford.

Howard, W. H., McEwan, K. A., Brinkman, G. L. and Christenson, J. 1990. *Human resource management on the farm: attracting, keeping and motivating labour on Ontario swine farms.* Department of Agricultural Economics and Business, University of Guelph, Guelph, Ontario, Canada.

Lloyd, D. H. 1975. Effective staff management. In *Economic factors affecting egg production.* (ed. B. M. Freeman and K. N. Boorman), pp. 221-231. British Poultry Science, Edinburgh.

Maslow, A. M. 1954. *Motivation and personality.* Harper & Brothers, New York.

Ravel, A., D'Allaire, S. and Bigras-Poulin, M. 1996. Survey of management and housing in farrowing quarters among independent and integrated swine farms in Québec. *Canadian Journal of Veterinary Research* **60**: 21-28.

Ravel, A., D'Allaire, S., Bigras-Poulin, M. and Ward, R. 1999. Psychodemographic profile of stockpeople working on independent and integrated swine breeding farms in Québec. *Canadian Journal of Veterinary Research* In press.

Seabrook, M. 1974. A study of some elements of the cowman's skills as influencing the milk yield of dairy cows. *Ph.D. thesis, University of Reading.*

Seabrook, M. F. 1984. The psychological interaction between the stockman and his animals and its influence on performance of pigs and dairy cows. *Veterinary Record* **115**: 84-87.

Segundo, R. C. 1989. A study of stockpeople and managers in the pig industry with special emphasis on the factors affecting their job satisfaction. *M.Sc. thesis, University of Aberdeen, Aberdeen.*

Umphrey, J. E. 1992. Understanding employee motivation. In *Large dairy herd management* (ed. H. H. Van Horn and C. J. Wilcox), pp. 786-792. American Dairy Science Association.

Wright, D. 1985. *Training investigation: pig production in Scotland.* Agricultural Training Board, West Wickham, Kent.

Farm animal welfare — who writes the rules?
Occasional Publication No. 23 — British Society of Animal Science 1999
edited by A. J. F. Russel, C. A. Morgan, C. J. Savory, M. C. Appleby and T. L. J. Lawrence

The specification of stocking density in relation to the welfare of finishing pigs

H. A. M. Spoolder[1], S. Corning[1] and S. A. Edwards[2]

[1]ADAS Terrington, Terrington St Clement, King's Lynn PE34 4PW
[2]Scottish Agricultural College, Craibstone Estate, Bucksburn, Aberdeen AB2 9YA

Introduction

The Welfare of Livestock Regulations (Great Britain Parliament, 1994) specify a system of increasing space allowance for finishing pigs based on a series of weight bands (Figure 1). However, the width of the bands in the Regulations impose a great degree of inflexibility on the management of finishing pig accommodation. By law, a producer with fully slatted flatdeck facilities designed to house second stage weaners from 17 to 35 kg live weight, would have to house pigs at 0.4 m^2 per pig. A 2×4 m pen would therefore house 20 animals.

An alternative approach to specifying space allowance is to use the equation suggested by Edwards *et al.* (1988), which continuously relates total space requirements (A) to average pig live weight M: $A (m^2) = 0.030 \times M^{0.67}$ (kg) (see Figure 1). Using this equation in the above example, a producer would need to allow 0.32 m^2 per 35-kg pig and be able to house 24 pigs in the same pen. However, before the use of this equation can be considered, its welfare advantages and disadvantages relative to existing legislation will have to be investigated in a worst-case scenario: a hypothetical one in which a producer would offer the minimum level of space per pig based on either the equation or the banded system.

The type of flooring (solid or slatted) and the presence of bedding may well affect the outcome of any stocking density experiment. Both the space allowance methods described above, ignore the quality of the floor and only relate pig weight to 'total unobstructed floor area'. Previous recommendations in the 1983 Welfare Codes specified a precise lying area but did not indicate the amount of extra space needed for other functions.

The present study therefore looked at the effects on pig welfare of providing space at the minimum stocking densities described by the bands of the Regulations, compared with those calculated using the equation by Edwards *et al.* (1988), in fully slatted accommodation as well as on solid floors with and without straw.

Material and methods

Eighteen groups of 12 pigs (weight 29.1 (s.d. 4.2) kg) were allocated to a 2×3 factorial experiment. It compared space allowance, increasing according to the above equation (E) or to the banded system (B) and floor type: fully slatted (F), solid sloping floor without straw (N) or solid sloping floor with straw bedding (S). Each of the six treatments had three replicate pens, giving a total of 18 pens (216 animals). Groups remained on treatment until an average weight of 110 kg was reached. Concentrate food and water were provided *ad libitum*. Straw was available to animals on the S treatments from a straw hopper, which was topped up daily.

All pigs were weighed every fortnight. E pens were adjusted to a size determined by the anticipated average weight of the pigs a week from the date of weighing, using the equation. B pens were adjusted on the day the predicted average weight of the pigs reached the next band (i.e. at 50 kg or at 85 kg). Floor area of the pen was increased whilst maintaining the same ratio between length and width of the pen.

Data were collected on a wide range of parameters, such as performance (weight gain, food intake), behaviour (time budgets, skin damage), pen cleanliness post-slaughter pathology (stomach lesions, heart lesions, weight of adrenal glands) and health records.

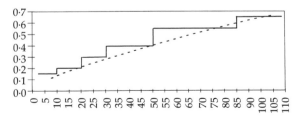

Figure 1 The relationship between stocking density and average weight of pigs per pen according to the equation $A(m^2) = 0.030 \times M^{0.67}$ (kg) (- - -) and according to the Welfare of Livestock Regulations 1994 (———).

Results

Performance

The only significant effect of stocking density treatment was found on the hot weight at slaughter (78·4 $v.$ 81·1 kg for B $v.$ E respectively; $P < 0·05$), although related variables (such as sale weight and killing-out proportion) were not different. There was a tendency for backfat levels to be lower at slaughter in F pigs compared with N pigs (9·53 $v.$ 10·17 mm, for F $v.$ N respectively; $P < 0·1$). Daily live-weight gain was not affected by any of the treatments.

Behaviour

A total of 10 250 lines of data were collected with information on the behaviour, substrate used and posture of 72 focal pigs (two males and two females in each of the 18 pens). No effects at all of the stocking density treatment were found on any of the behavioural parameters measured. Manipulation of pen components (straw, floor, walls, etc.) was lowest in N pigs (52, 47 and 57% of active time for F, N and S respectively; $P < 0·05$), of which in S pigs about 45% of active time was spent manipulating straw. There was an indication that oral behaviours (tongue sucking, sham chewing) occurred more frequently in F than in N pens (1·5 $v.$ 0·4%, F $v.$ N; $P < 0·1$), but pen mate manipulation did not differ. The average skin lesions scores were not different between the stocking density treatments but a smaller number of lesions were found on pigs of the non-straw treatment (8·5, 4·8 and 8·3 lesions on average for F, N and S respectively; $P < 0·05$). However, this may have been confounded by pen cleanliness.

Cleanliness

Strawed pens had a smaller proportion of the floor area soiled than pens with barren floors (58·8 $v.$ 76·5% clean floor area for without straw and with straw respectively; $P < 0·001$). There was no relationship between the proportion of pen area soiled and the stocking density treatment (68·7 $v.$ 66·6% clean floor area, for the E and the B method respectively; $P > 0·05$).

Health records and post-slaughter measurements

Health records showed rectal prolapses to be the main reason for taking pigs off trial (seven animals, 3·3%). Ten out of the 11 pigs removed came from unstrawed pens (either N or F). There was no effect of treatments on the incidence of heart abnormalities or parakeratosis of the pars oesophagus of the stomach.

Discussion

It was concluded that straw provision may provide welfare benefits in terms of pen cleanliness and its properties as a foraging substrate. However, the results of the space allowance treatments suggest that there is no difference in level of welfare offered to finishing pigs between a system which increases space allowance according to the equation suggested by Edwards et al. (1988) and the banded system described in the Welfare Regulations.

The initial publication of the above results (Spoolder et al., 1997) was followed by MAFF's Guidelines on Schedule 3 of the Welfare of Livestock Regulations. The Guidelines reinforce the 1994 Regulations but in addition suggest a 'line A' (very similar to the Edwards et al. (1988) equation). Providing space allowances below this line is a direct infringement of the Regulations. Space allowances between line A and the banded line of the Regulations will be the subject of discussions with the producer, who will have to provide an action plan to improve the situation. The report of the EU Scientific Veterinary Committee (1997) recognizes the findings of the above study in part. Conclusion 33 states 'The necessary space for a pig to lie down in lateral recumbancy can be calculated by the formula $0·047 \times$ weight$^{0·67}$ m^2. When the available space has been $0·03 \times$ weight$^{0·67}$ m^2 per animal, no negative effects on performance have been detected'. These recommendations may form the basis for future EU welfare legislation.

Acknowledgements

The authors gratefully acknowledge the support received from MAFF. They would also like to thank Dr Tony Lawrence of the University of Liverpool for providing visual aids for scoring stomach lesions, and Mr Edwin Lunn of Geo. Adams for his expertise and skill in collecting the post-slaughter data. Finally, the work of ADAS Terrington's technical staff is also gratefully acknowledged.

References

Edwards, S. A., Armsby, A. W. and Spechter, H. H. 1988. Effects of floor area allowance on performance of growing pigs kept on fully slatted floors. *Animal Production* **46:** 453-459.

Great Britain Parliament. 1994. *Welfare of livestock regulations. Statutory instrument no. 2126.* Her Majesty's Stationery Office, London.

Ministry of Agriculture, Fisheries and Food. 1997. *Pig space requirements.* Her Majesty's Stationery Office, London.

Scientific Veterinary Committee. 1997. The welfare of intensively kept pigs. *DOC XXIV/B3/ScVC/0005/1997,* European Commission, Brussels.

Spoolder, H. A. M., Corning, S. and Edwards, S. A. 1997. A comparison of methods of specifying stocking density for welfare and performance of finishing pigs on different floor types. *Proceedings of the British Society of Animal Science* p. 43.

Farm animal welfare — who writes the rules?
Occasional Publication No. 23 — British Society of Animal Science 1999
edited by A. J. F. Russel, C. A. Morgan, C. J. Savory, M. C. Appleby and T. L. J. Lawrence

Methods of assessing adequacy of drinker provision in group-housed pigs

S. P. Turner and S. A. Edwards

Scottish Agricultural College, Ferguson Building, Craibstone Estate, Bucksburn, Aberdeen AB21 9YA

Introduction

Competition for resources accounts for the greater part of animal aggression and access may be prioritized in favour of those of highest social rank. Consequently, under commercial conditions, provision of resources to a group of pigs must be adequate to allow all animals sufficient access, regardless of social status.

Although the volume of drinking water offered to growing pigs is generally not restricted, the ability of pigs to gain access to the drinking points themselves has received little attention. The current Welfare Codes have adopted caution in advising the provision of one nipple drinker per 10 growing pigs fed a dry diet. Producers have frequently extended this ratio to one drinker per 20 animals without encountering problems.

Furthermore, the advent of large straw court housing demands a reassessment of current resource provision. Extrapolating the drinker allocation of a small group of pigs to a larger group situation would be unwise.

Thus the purpose of this investigation was to describe the effects of drinker allocation and group size, in isolation and their interaction, on the drinking behaviour, aggression and performance of heavy, medium and light weight pigs.

Material and methods

Over the period January to July, 640 Large White × Landrace growing pigs (start weight 36 ± 5·0 kg) were allocated to one of four treatments for 5 weeks. The experiment comprised of four replicates of a 2 × 2 factorial design of two nipple drinker to pig ratios (1 : 10 *v.* 1 : 20) and two group sizes (20 *v.* 60). Space allowance and feeding space per pig remained constant. The groups of 20 were selected from three smaller commercial pens, and the groups of 60 from nine pens.

The nipple drinkers were of standard commercial type (Arato, '80 Pig Drinker', Clacton-on-Sea, UK). A flow meter, which was calibrated regularly, recorded daily water use per pen. The flow rate of the individual drinkers was noted at the beginning of each replicate. Ambient temperature was recorded daily 1 m above floor height.

Two males and one female of each of three weight classes, heavy (41·9 (s.e. 0·57) kg), medium (35·7 (s.e. 0·51) kg) and light (30·9 (s.e. 0·63) kg), were selected from each pen on which to concentrate observations.

Daily water use per pen was used to calculate mean water use per pig. Time-lapse video recordings were made during the 4th week on trial. Alternate 30 min blocks throughout the 24-h period were analysed using continuous sampling to describe the frequency and duration of drinking bouts. The number of fresh cuts, scratches and abrasions of the focal animals were counted, by a single observer, at 3 days post mixing, and at the end of the 1st and subsequent weeks, up to week 4.

Average daily gain (ADG) was calculated from live-weight measurements made on the day of mixing and at the end of weeks 2 and 4. Average daily food intake (ADFI) and the food conversion ratio (FCR) were calculated on a per pen basis.

All values were corrected for the number of animals on trial. The influence of replicate was examined in each case. All parameters were analysed using a randomized block analysis of variance or two-way ANOVA.

Results

Considering all members of the pen, individuals in larger groups used more water than those in smaller groups, irrespective of drinker allocation (5·04 *v.* 3·66 (s.e.d. 0·230) l per pig per day, $P < 0.001$). Heavy, medium and light weight pigs visited the drinkers a similar number of times (1·16, 1·31 and 1·14 (s.e.d. 0·161) visits per pig per h, respectively), performed drinking bouts of similar duration (26·6, 23·5 and 24·9 (s.e.d. 2·55) s per visit), and consequently spent a similar amount of time drinking per day (722, 762

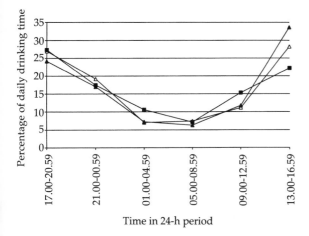

Figure 1 Percentage of daily drinking time occuring during 4-h blocks for each weight class when treatment was pooled: —△— heavy; —■— medium; —▲— light.

and 701 (s.e.d. 90·6) s per pig per day). Weight class and treatment did not interact to significantly affect these parameters.

The 24-h period of video analysis of each pen was divided into six blocks of 4 h. Plotting the percentage of daily drinking time occurring during each block revealed no effect of treatment on the diurnal pattern of drinking in any weight class (Figure 1).

Treatment, in isolation, or in interaction with weight class, did not significantly affect the lesion score during either the whole period, or at 3 days post mixing alone (11·1, 9·3, 11·0 and 12·2 (s.e.d. 1·36) lesions per pig for pooled focal pigs in 60 pigs — three drinkers, 20 pigs — one drinker, 60 pigs — six drinkers and 20 pigs — two drinkers respectively over the whole trial period).

The mean ADG, ADFI, and FCR of the pen was not affected by treatment. The interaction between treatment and focal pig weight class did not affect

ADG. Pigs beginning the experiment with a lower inter-quartile start weight gained more slowly in a group of 60 with three drinkers (Table 1). This pattern was repeated by the pigs with an upper inter-quartile start weight and the interaction between start weight and treatment was not significant.

Discussion

The drinking behaviour of the lightest animals in the pen closely matched that of the heaviest, indicating that weight (and possibly, by inference, rank) was not correlated with drinker access. Alternatively, the resource was not sufficiently limited to encourage the necessary degree of competition. This may account for the similarity in diurnal use of the drinkers for heavy, medium and light weight animals in each treatment. From the results of various workers (Gonyou and Stricklin (1981), Stricklin and Gonyou (1981) in beef cattle and Morrow and Walker (1994) in pigs), sub-optimal feeder allocation caused subordinate animals to make frequent visits to the feeder at night. The lack of an interaction between weight and treatment on lesion score further suggests that the intensity of competition was similar in each treatment.

The lower ADG of the upper-interquartile start weight animals in a group of 60 pigs with three drinkers indicated that the low weight pigs were not being selected against specifically by this treatment. The absence of an interaction between weight and treatment on performance in our trial, suggests that the competition pressure was not sufficient to highlight a weight effect on resource access, should one exist.

Preferential access of heavier animals to resources was not observed, and, moreover, light-weight animals were not selectively penalized with respect to their drinking behaviour, the aggression they received, or their ADG in any treatment. It is probable that the restrictions imposed by each of the

Table 1 *Average daily gain (kg) of the pen, focal pigs and pigs of lower and upper inter-quartile start weight in the four combinations of group size and drinker allocation*

	Treatment					Significance† of drinkers × group size
	60 pigs, 3 drinkers	20 pigs, 1 drinker	60 pigs, 6 drinkers	20 pigs, 2 drinkers	s.e.d.	
Pen mean	0·69	0·68	0·66	0·67	0·029	
Pooled focal pigs	0·70	0·70	0·65	0·67	0·034	
Lower quartile	0·53	0·68	0·68	0·59	0·059	*
Upper quartile	0·63	0·80	0·70	0·64	0·046	**

† Drinker effects and group size effects were not significant ($P > 0.05$).

treatments was not adequate to cause an affect of weight on these parameters. Thus, in a large group of 60 pigs, with one drinker per 20 animals, the welfare and performance of the lightest individuals did not suffer.

Acknowledgements

SPT gratefully acknowledges the support of the Cruden Foundation. SAC receives financial support from SOAEFD. The authors wish to thank all of the staff at Tillycorthie Farm for their assistance.

References

Gonyou, H. W. and Stricklin, W. R. 1981. Eating behavior of beef cattle groups fed from a single stall or trough. *Applied Animal Ethology* **7:** 123-133.

Morrow, A. T. S. and Walker, N. 1994. Effects of number and siting of single space feeders on performance and feeding behaviour of growing pigs. *Journal of Agricultural Science, Cambridge* **122:** 465-470.

Stricklin, W. R. and Gonyou, H. W. 1981. Dominance and eating behavior of beef cattle fed from a single stall. *Applied Animal Ethology* **7:** 135-140.

Farm animal welfare — who writes the rules?
Occasional Publication No. 23 — British Society of Animal Science 1999
edited by A. J. F. Russel, C. A. Morgan, C. J. Savory, M. C. Appleby and T. L. J. Lawrence

Plantar pododermatitis in turkeys: results of a preliminary study looking at incidence and severity in the UK

J. H. Guy and J. Jeffery†

Department of Agriculture, University of Newcastle, Newcastle upon Tyne NE1 7RU

Introduction

The *Codes of recommendations for the welfare of livestock — turkeys* (Ministry of Agriculture, Fisheries and Food, 1991) state that one of the five basic welfare needs of turkeys is the prevention, or rapid diagnosis and treatment of, injury, disease and infestation. Plantar pododermatitis is one of a number of non-infectious causes of lameness in turkeys (Farm Animal Welfare Council, 1995), a condition believed to be common in the UK and therefore not unique to any single producer. Previous studies have reported an incidence of plantar pododermatitis of between 10 and 40% in turkey poults (Nairn and Watson, 1972) and as much as 88% in broilers (Greene *et al.*, 1985). It is an ulcerative condition of the skin over the plantar surface of the feet, causing suffering, particularly if the lesions become infected (Hancock, 1996). In addition to lameness, plantar pododermatitis has been found to cause reduced growth rate in turkeys (Martland, 1984) and, in broilers, to predispose birds to hock ulceration and subsequent breast lesions (Greene, *et al.*, 1985). According to Pattison (1989), unsightly breast and hock lesions may result in carcass downgrading and are of serious economic loss to the poultry industry. Wet or poor quality litter is a common cause of plantar pododermatitis, although a diet deficient in biotin can also lead to the condition developing, even with good litter quality (Thorp, 1996).

The aims of this study were (1) to determine the incidence and severity of plantar pododermatitis within the UK turkey industry, and (2) to investigate whether this condition was likely to cause pain and suffering in affected birds.

Material and methods

Four different abattoirs across the UK were selected for this study, each of them processing turkeys which had been reared intensively in conventional, enclosed housing. Each abattoir was sampled on just

one occasion, measuring both the incidence (% of birds affected) and severity of plantar pododermatitis at abattoirs 1, 2 and 4 and incidence only at abattoir 3. Severity of lesions on the metatarsal and digital foot pads was assessed using a graded scoring system, from 0 to 3 (Table 1), adapted from Martland (1984). A mean lesion score was subsequently calculated for each abattoir. The sample size was 43, 64, 100 and 100 feet for abattoirs 1, 2, 3 and 4 respectively.

A further 10 feet from abattoir 4, showing a range in severity of ulceration, were selected for histological analysis. Each foot was labelled and submerged in neutral buffered formalin saline for 12 days. On day 13, the feet were individually wrapped in cotton wool which had been soaked beforehand in neutral buffered formalin saline, then transported in sealed plastic bags to the Veterinary Investigation Centre, Langford, Bristol. A single sagittal section was taken through the centre of each foot pad and examined histologically.

Results

Across the four abattoirs, the incidence of plantar pododermatitis was 100% (Table 2), with a mean lesion score of 2·23. There was no significant difference ($P > 0.05$) between abattoirs for the mean lesion scores.

Histological examination showed that, at the site of the lesion, the dermis had been completely ulcerated and replaced by a zone of granulation tissue and a

† Present address: 2 Sisters Food Products Ltd, Alpha Business Park, Smethwick, Warley, West Midlands, B66 1AW.

Table 1 *Scoring system for plantar pododermatitis (adapted from Martland, 1984)*

Score	Classification
0	No plantar pododermatitis present
1	Small caps present (maximum cover $\frac{1}{4}$ of pad area)
2	Larger scabs present (occupying between $\frac{1}{4}$ and $\frac{1}{2}$ of pad area)
3	Majority of pad covered with large, deep ulcers

Table 2 *Incidence of plantar pododermatitis and mean lesion score for four abbatoirs*

Parameter	Abattoir				
	1	2	3	4	s.e.d.
No. of feet	43	64	100	100	-
Incidence (%)	100	100	100	100	-
Mean lesion score	2·14	2·34	-	2·20	0·127

fibrino-cellular exudate, the latter merging into a thick highly cellular crust. In the superficial dermis there was diffuse infiltration by granulocytes and some oedema.

Conclusions

With an incidence of 100% across four different abattoirs, and most feet showing a moderate level of ulceration, plantar pododermatitis is clearly of major concern to the UK turkey industry. It is likely that the inflammatory response seen in cells of the dermis of affected feet would have been associated with some discomfort to the bird. As such, plantar pododermatitis can be considered as detrimental to the welfare of turkeys and research should now be instigated to determine both the exact causes of this condition and effective management practices to eliminate its occurrence.

Acknowledgements

The authors would like to thank Ms Judith Abrehart, Technical Manager-Agricultural, Tesco Stores Ltd, Cheshunt for advice and considerable assistance given in collecting the samples, and Mr Roger Hancock, Senior Veterinary Investigation Officer and Mr Roger Gunning, Veterinary Investigation Officer, both of the Veterinary Investigation Centre, Langford, Bristol, for conducting the histological analysis. We are also grateful to Dr Mark Pattison, Veterinary Services Director, Sun Valley Foods, Hereford for kindly supplying photographs for the scoring system. Funding for this work from Tesco Stores Ltd is gratefully acknowledged.

References

Farm Animal Welfare Council. 1995. *Report on the welfare of turkeys.* PB 2033. Farm Animal Welfare Council, MAFF Publications, London.

Greene, J. A., McCracken, R. M. and Evans, R. T. 1985. A contact dermatitis of broilers — clinical and pathological findings. *Avian Pathology* **14:** 23-38.

Hancock, R. 1996. Legislation and poultry welfare in the UK. In *Poultry diseases, fourth edition* (ed. F. T. W. Jordan and M. Pattison), pp. 495-502. W. B. Saunders Company Ltd, London.

Martland, M. F. 1984. Wet litter as a cause of plantar pododermatitis, leading to foot ulceration and lameness in fattening turkeys. *Avian Pathology* **13:** 241-252.

Ministry of Agriculture, Fisheries and Food. 1991. *Codes of recommendations for the welfare of livestock — turkeys.* PB 0077. MAFF Publications, London.

Nairn, M. E. and Watson, A. R. A. 1972. Leg weakness of poultry: a clinical and pathological characterisation. *Australian Veterinary Journal* **48:** 645-656.

Pattison, M. 1989. Problems of diahorrea and wet litter in meat poultry. In *Recent developments in poultry nutrition* (ed. D. J. A. Cole and W. Haresign). Butterworths, London.

Thorp, B. H. 1996. Diseases of the musculoskeletal system. In *Poultry diseases, fourth edition* (ed. F. T. W. Jordan and M. Pattison), pp. 290-305. W. B. Saunders Company Ltd, London.

Farm animal welfare — who writes the rules?
Occasional Publication No. 23 — British Society of Animal Science 1999
edited by A. J. F. Russel, C. A. Morgan, C. J. Savory, M. C. Appleby and T. L. J. Lawrence

Does separate housing of newly calved heifers influence social behaviour and lessen claw horn lesion development?

D. E. Cross[1], D. N. Logue[2], J. E. Offer[2], L. M. Birnie[1] and M. A. Lomax[1]

[1]*University of Aberdeen, MacRobert Building, 581 King Street, Aberdeen, AB24 5UA*
[2]*Dairy Health Unit, SAC Veterinary Services, Auchincruive, Ayr KA6 5AE*

Introduction

Minimizing exposure of the newly calved heifer to environmental stress at its introduction into the dairy herd would have benefits in terms of production and animal welfare. Fordham *et al.* (1991) suggested that housing environment changes were more stressful than previously assumed. Observations of increased behavioural activity after environmental changes over periods of several weeks were suggested to be a mechanism for greater stress levels of the animals at key periods in the life cycle. Increased first lactation yields would bring considerable economic benefits associated with higher returns (Phelps, 1992). Behavioural stresses may lower animal reproductive efficiency, expressed as a longer return time to service and thus an increased calving interval (Moberg, 1991). Changes in management around the calving period in dairy heifers was observed to predispose heifers to *pododermatitis aseptica* (PDAS), often loosely called 'subclinical laminitis', leading to solar ulceration (Bazeley and Pinsent, 1984). Abnormal behavioural patterns are also associated with lameness (Colam-Ainsworth *et al.*, 1989). The importance of reducing incidence of lameness in order to improve dairy cattle welfare is well recognized. Recent work in Ireland and Scotland indicated that behaviour should be considered as a factor in foot lesion and lameness development (Logue, 1996). This study examined the hypothesis that separate housing of first calving heifers from the adult herd would have a beneficial effect upon claw horn lesion development and the extent to which behavioural changes may be associated with this effect.

Material and methods

Animals and treatments

Twenty-four heifers were allocated by calving date into two groups of 12, separate (S) and mixed (M) at calving. The S group was housed with a further 15 heifers in Cantilever style cubicles (2·1 × 1·25 m) and the M group was housed with 47 cows in a section of the same house with a mixture of Cantilever and Auchincruive style cubicles (2·2 × 1·3 m). The cubicle house had concrete floors with sawdust bedding and automatic scrapers. Passageways were level-floored and scraped seven times daily. All animals had access to a cubicle each. Both groups were given a silage-based complete diet supplemented with concentrates (0·4 kg/l at 25 kg milk) in the milking parlour. Three cows were lost from lesion studies and five from behavioural studies, all from group M due to health problems unrelated to the present report.

Lesion data

In the lesion study, data were obtained for each hind claw, assessing foot angle, foot length and foot lesions for severity and extent. These data were collected in the manner described by Leach *et al.* (1997), approximately 1 month pre-calving and 1, 3 and 5 months post calving. Lesion data used were obtained from a simultaneous study on the heifers (Logue *et al.*, 1998).

Behavioural study

Behavioural data were collected 4 months post calving. Activity was recorded every 20 min over 24 h to characterize the daily time budget, based on the modification of a method previously described by Singh *et al.* (1993). A novel object approach test, based on modification of a method by Boissy and Bouissou (1995), measurement of parlour docility (Dickson *et al.* 1969) and parlour rank order entry were also undertaken. These tests provided a range of behavioural parameters in normal husbandry situations and conditions which could then be analysed for potential stress situations.

Statistical analyses

Data from the lesion studies were analysed as log transformed sum of lesions across all eight claws. All behavioural data sections were analysed using SPSS package for UNIX release 6.0 using Pearsons square analysis, analysis of variance tests and GLM (least maximum likelihood) tests. Students *t* tests were effected using Minitab 7.2 package.

Results

There was a significant difference ($P < 0.05$) in total lesion score between groups (means 1·96 and 2·16, s.e.d. 0·2), for S and M groups respectively. In terms of behaviour, total time standing was not significantly different. However, S tended to spend less of total passageway time ruminating (27·8% compared with M group at 40%; $P > 0.05$). S group heifers spent significantly less time standing in passageways relative to M group heifers and more time standing in cubicles ($P < 0.001$). In the novel object test, S spent significantly longer (107·73 (s.e.d. 28·1) s) close to the object than M (79·23 (s.e.d. 20·25) s, $P < 0.05$). S heifers also had a corrected parlour entry order average of 12·51 (s.e.d. 1·88), compared to 34·69 (s.e.d. 2·47) for M ($P < 0.001$). However, M heifers were more docile than S heifers (average score 2 to 3 and 1 respectively). Total feeding time was not significantly different between groups although M heifers tended to feed later during late night and early morning.

Table 1 *Number of observations of standing in each specific location site for each treatment group*

Activity	Separate	Mixed	Significance
Standing in passage	97 (41·1%)	75 (59·5%)	$\chi^2 = 20.23$ d.f. = 2
Standing in cubicle	72 (30·5%)	13 (10·3%)	***
Total	169	88	

Discussion

Separate housing of first calving heifers reduced claw horn lesions particularly due to PDAS after calving and for this reason, is likely to reduce herd lameness in the longer term (Logue, 1996). The longer times spent standing in dirty passages was associated with increased claw lesions in the M group. Although not significantly different, the increased rumination time while standing in these passageways may have a biological importance in relation to the development of these lesions. In addition, there were subtle differences in behaviour of the S group compared with the M group. M group heifers were less inquisitive than those of the S group and rated lower in herd dominance order, with entry order into the parlour. Parlour entry order was corrected statistically by random pairing of animals as far as possible as the group sizes were different. The M group also had a more docile parlour temperament. Accommodation used to conduct this study employed the same management regime and used the same building, only containing cubicles of differing design — Cantilever and Auchincruive. As cubicle dimensions were similar and provided similar accommodation, we have considered carefully whether treatment effects may have been due to this factor. Observations revealed that group M heifers

had a choice between style of cubicle but showed no preference for one over the other. Interpretation of results was complicated by the different size of groups but this was accounted for by using the generalized linear model in the statistical analysis. However, these results suggest that a management system involving separate heifer housing will reduce feet problems and the behavioural analysis supported that M group heifers were displaced by older cows. As a result, it is concluded that separate housing and feeding systems may be of value to limit dairy lameness and PDAS or 'subclinical laminitis'.

Acknowledgements

D. Cross is grateful to the involvement of O. McPherson in statistical analysis. SAC receives funding from SOAEFD.

References

Bazeley, K. and Pinsent, P. J. N. 1984. Preliminary observations on a series of outbreaks of acute laminitis in dairy cattle. *Veterinary Record* 115: 619-622.

Boissy, A. and Bouissou, M. F. 1995. Assessment of individual differences in behavioural reactions of heifers exposed to various fear-eliciting situations. *Applied Animal Behaviour Science* 46: 17-31.

Colam-Ainsworth, P., Lunn, G. A., Thomas, R. C. and Eddy, R. G. 1989. Behaviour of cows in cubicles and its relationship with laminitis in replacement dairy heifers. *Veterinary Record* 125: 573-575.

Dickson, D. P., Barr, G. R, Johnson, L. P and Wiecker, D. A. 1969. Social dominance and temperament in Holstein cows. *Journal of Dairy Science* 53: 904-907.

Fordham, D. P., Al-Gahtani, S., Dunotoye, L. A. and Rodway, R. G. 1991. Changes in plasma cortisol and β-endorphin concentrations and behaviour in sheep. *Animal Production* 52: 287-296.

Leach, K. A., Logue, D. N., Kempson, S. A., Offer, J. E., Ternent, H. E. and Randall, J. M. 1997. Claw lesions in dairy cattle: development of sole and white line haemorrhages during the first lactation. *The Veterinary Journal* 154: 215-225.

Logue, D. N. 1996. Productivity, management and disease in dairy cattle. *XIX World Buiatric Congress, Edinburgh 8th-12th July 1996*, pp. 83-88.

Logue, D. N., Offer, J. E. and McGovern, R. E. 1998. The housing effects of first calving Holstein Friesian heifers separately or with the adult herd on claw conformation and lesion development. In *Proceedings of the 10th international symposium on lameness in ruminants, 7-19th September 1988, Lucerne* (ed. C. J. Lischer and P. Ossent), pp. 60-62. University of Zurich.

Moberg, Gary P. 1991. How behavioural stress disrupts the endocrine control of reproduction in domestic animals. *Journal of Dairy Science* 74: 304-311.

Phelps, A. 1992. Vastly superior first lactations when heifers fed separately. *Feedstuffs* 64: 11.

Singh, S. S., Ward, W. R., Lautenbach, K. and Murray, R. D. 1993. Behaviour of lame and normal dairy cows in cubicles and a straw yard. *Veterinary Record* 133: 204-208.

Farm animal welfare — who writes the rules?
Occasional Publication No. 23 — British Society of Animal Science 1999
edited by A. J. F. Russel, C. A. Morgan, C. J. Savory, M. C. Appleby and T. L. J. Lawrence

The stunning monitor for cattle, sheep and pigs

J. Heal

Meat and Livestock Commission. Winterhill House, Snowdon Drive, Milton Keynes, MK6 1AX

Introduction

A survey conducted by the Division of Food Animal Science (DFAS) of Bristol University on behalf of the Ministry of Agriculture Fisheries and Food (MAFF) looked at the electrical stunning of pigs in British abattoirs. The survey concluded that most abattoirs were using equipment with low voltage capabilities and that many were unable to meet the minimum current requirements required by EU legislation. MAFF was therefore reluctant to implement legislation within Great Britain (GB) before equipment was available to allow the industry to meet the minimum requirements.

Following the results of the survey, the Meat and Livestock Commission (MLC) sponsored a research project to develop a system of controlling, monitoring and recording the delivery of stuns to pigs. The system would be designed to calculate, by checking the voltage available and measuring the impedance of the animals head, if an effective stun could be delivered. The system would only allow the operator to proceed with the stun if predetermined parameters were met and would therefore provide a fail-safe function as its primary rôle.

Stunning monitor development

Extensive field testing with prototypes resulted in the development of a unit that incorporates an effective fail-safe function. Additionally, a visual display of each stun profile provides an on-line monitoring capability for abattoir personnel, Meat Hygiene Service (MHS) and MAFF State Veterinary Service (SVS) staff. A further feature is a record of the profile of every stun to allow plant management and officials to view stuns retrospectively ensuring requirements are met throughout all operational periods.

The stunning monitor is now commercially available, manufactured by Hellenic Systems Ltd (HSL) and marketed by the MLC. The unit is compatible with all existing stunning equipment and therefore allows an abattoir to provide quickly this important element to monitor operations on the slaughter line. MAFF is considering the draft GB legislation for all three species as the stunning monitor is designed to be used for cattle and sheep as well as pigs. A legislative implementation date will be set to allow abattoirs a reasonable lead time to install the monitoring equipment.

The installation of the stunning monitor will ensure that only effective stuns are delivered to each animal through the fail-safe mechanism. This control will act as a training tool for stunner operatives, raising performance standards. The recording of all stun profiles will provide visibility of operations to MHS and MAFF personnel who have responsibility to ensure welfare standards are met. The equipment will make a significant contribution in providing reassurance to retailers and consumers that welfare standards are maintained at the highest level in a most critical area of the processing chain.

Farm animal welfare — who writes the rules?
Occasional Publication No. 23 — British Society of Animal Science 1999
edited by A. J. F. Russel, C. A. Morgan, C. J. Savory, M. C. Appleby and T. L. J. Lawrence

Chronic inflammatory responses of lambs to rubber ring castration: are there any effects of age or size of lamb at treatment?

J. E. Kent[1], V. Molony[1], R. E. Jackson[1] and B. D. Hosie[2]

[1]*Department of Preclinical Veterinary Sciences, University of Edinburgh, Royal (Dick) School of Veterinary Studies, Summerhall, Edinburgh EH9 1QH*
[2]*Scottish Agricultural College, Veterinary Investigation Services, Bush Estate, Penicuik, Midlothian EH26 OQE*

Introduction

In the United Kingdom (UK), rubber rings can only be used to castrate and/or tail dock lambs under 1 week of age. Some hill sheep farmers find it impractical to carry out these procedures at this age. Small differences occur in the behavioural and plasma cortisol response to the acute pain caused by the rubber ring in lambs under a week of age compared with those at 6 weeks old (Kent *et al.*, 1993; Molony *et al.*, 1993) and the Farm Animal Welfare Council (FAWC, 1994) recommended that use of the rubber ring method should be permitted on lambs up to 6 weeks of age. However, we have shown previously that the rubber ring acts as a foreign body at the neck of the scrotum and can, for 4 to 6 weeks after application, produce septic lesions in calves (Molony *et al.*, 1995) and 6-week-old lambs (Kent *et al.*, 1997). These lesions are accompanied by behavioural changes considered to be indicative of chronic pain. This paper brings together three studies in order to compare the chronic inflammatory effects of rubber ring castration in 2-day (the current practice of many lowland sheep farmers), 28-day (an age which might be practical for hill sheep farmers) and 42-day-old housed lambs.

Material and methods

Suffolk or Dorset cross Dorset/Finn lambs, less than 2 days of age, were castrated and tail docked using the standard elastrator rings (Paragon), half using local anaesthetic applied by needleless injection (1·2 ml total) (RR) (no. = 10). A further 10 lambs acted as non-castrated/tail docked control lambs (H) for behavioural observations only. Two groups of eight 28-day-old lambs of the same breed were castrated using standard rubber rings. Each group was subjected to a different method for the reduction of acute pain as part of another study. The groups were castration using local anaesthetic, applied by multishot injector (2 ml) (RRms) or Panjet needleless injector (1·2 ml) (Rrpan). The results of this study will be published elsewhere. Only the chronic effects are considered here. Only eight lambs castrated by

rubber ring (RR) with local anaesthetic (50% from each method) were observed for behaviour, together with their uncastrated twin (H). Results from 2-day and 28-day-old lambs are compared with the values obtained previously from 42-day-old Scottish Blackface (SBF) lambs (Kent *et al.*, 1997).

The rubber ring acted as a foreign body at the neck of the scrotum, causing a lesion that, twice weekly after treatment, was measured (lateral width (mm)) and scored for the presence of swelling (0 to 2·0), inflammation (2·5 to 3·0) and infection (3·5 to 5·0).

Behavioural observations were carried out by four persons for two 3-h periods (between 14.00 h and 21.00 h) weekly for the 28-day-old lambs and after 10, 20, 31 and 42 days for the 2-day-old lambs. A 'playbox' for the lambs to jump on was placed in the pens for the second 3-h period. The frequency of occurrence of tail wagging, easing quarters, foot stamping, kicking, itching quarters, head turning, particularly to the scrotum and inside hindleg, lying down, standing up and playing on the box were recorded continuously and the lambs' posture was

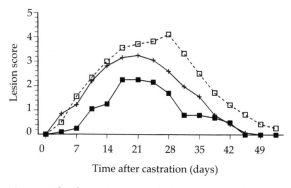

Figure 1 The change in average lesion score with time after rubber ring castration of lambs at 2 days (■), 28 days (+) and 42 days (❑) of age.

Table 1 *The effect of age at castration using elastrator rings on the mean time of the scrotum to drop off and the mean maximum lesion size and clinical score*

Age at castration (days)	Breed†	no.	Time for scrotum to drop off (days)	Percentage of lambs with scrotum 'off' 28 days after treatment	Lesion score	Lateral with (mm)
2	Dorx	10	31	60	3·1[a]	18[a]
28	Dorx	16	34	69	3·6[a]	21[a]
42	SBF	16	35	94	4·2[b]	27[b]
	F-value‡		1·6 ($P > 0.05$)	2·4 ($P > 0.05$)	11·8 ($P < 0.001$)	18·6 ($P < 0.001$)

† Dorx: Dorset or Suffolk × Dorest-Finn lambs; SBF: pure Scottish Blackface or Greyface lambs.
‡ F-value from the analysis of variance and the probability of a significant difference between groups: different superscripts within columns represent values significantly different from each other ($P < 0.05$).

recorded every 6 min (Noldus Observer program). A one-way analysis of variance was used to analyse the lesion parameters.

Results and discussion
The average clinical score of the lesion increased less in 2-day-old lambs than either in 28-day-old lambs or in 42-day-old Scottish Blackface lambs (Figure 1). In 2-day and 28-day-old lambs there was no significant difference between the mean time taken for the scrotum to drop-off, the mean maximum lesion score or the mean maximum width of the lesion (Table 1). In 42-day-old lambs the lesion was larger as was the mean maximum width of the lesion (Table 1). In 42-day-old lambs the lesion was larger (Figure 2 and Table 1) and more likely to become infected although the scrotum did not take much longer to drop off. For Dorset lambs only, there was a correlation ($r = +0.51$) between the maximum lesion width recorded (y) and the weight (kg) of lamb (x) at castration $y = 15.8 + 0.44x$.

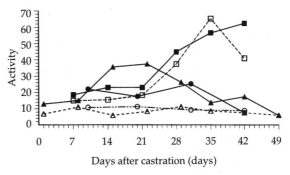

Figure 3 The change in the average behavioural activity (food stamping, kicking, itching quarters, easing quarters and tail wagging summed) recorded in a 6-h period after rubber-ring castration of lambs at 2 days (○,●), 28 days (□,■) and 42 days (△,▲) of age: H — handled control lambs (open symbols); RR — rubber-ring castrated lambs (closed symbols).

The only behaviours which significantly ($P < 0.05$) increased in 2-day-old castrated lambs were head turning to the scrotum and inside hindleg (medians for an average 6-h period 0·3 v. 1·8, H v. RR) and the combined frequency of foot stamping, kicking, easing quarters, itching quarters and tail wagging (medians 9 v. 16·3), though none of these activities was significantly increased on their own. The only active behaviour significantly increased ($P < 0.05$), in 28-day-old treated lambs (RR) was the incidence of head turning, particularly to the scrotal region (medians 0 v. 0·3 for H v. RR treated lambs). In both 2-day and 28-day-old lambs there was no clear relationship between the active behaviours and the change with time in the clinical score and size of lesion as seen for 6-week-old castrated lambs (Figure 3). The increase in active behaviours in the 28-day-old lambs also occurred in the control lambs and was related to a change in the source of the straw bedding.

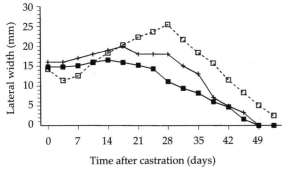

Figure 2 The change in average width of scrotal lesion after rubber ring castration of lambs at 2 days (■), 28 days (+) and 42 days (□) of age.

In lambs of all ages studied, the rubber ring at the neck of the scrotum acted as a 'foreign body', resulting in an inflammatory lesion which was larger and more likely to become septic in the older lambs. There was no significant difference between 2-day and 28-day-old lambs in the time taken for the scrotum to drop off, the size or clinical score of the lesion. There was a weaker relationship between the behaviours and the changing lesion score in 2-day and 28-day-old Dorset cross lambs compared with that found for 42-day-old SBF lambs suggesting that the smaller lesion may be a less aversive stimulus than the larger, infected lesion found in the older SBF lambs or that the measuring system was insufficiently sensitive. Further investigation of the sensitivity of the measuring system and of the effects of age, breed and size of lamb at castration will be necessary to resolve this issue.

Acknowledgements

Our thanks go to the Ministry of Agriculture, Fisheries and Food, Scottish Office Agriculture, Fisheries and Environment Department and the Meat and Livestock Commission for financial support and the Moredun Research Institute who provided facilities.

References

Farm Animal Welfare Council. 1994. *Report on the welfare of sheep*. Ministry of Agriculture, Fisheries and Food. Tolworth Tower, Surbiton, UK.

Kent, J. E., Molony, V. and Robertson, I. S. 1993. Changes in plasma concentrations of cortisol in lambs of three ages in the first three hours after three methods of castration and tail docking. *Research in Veterinary Science* **55:** 246-251.

Kent, J. E., Moloney, V., Hosie, B. and Sheppard, B. 1997. Assessment of chronic inflammatory pain after rubber ring castration of six week old lambs. *Proceedings of the Sheep Veterinary Society* **21:** 93.

Molony, V., Kent, J. E. and Robertson, I. S. 1993. Behavioural responses of lambs of three ages in the first three hours after three methods of castration and tail docking. *Research in Veterinary Science* **55:** 246-251.

Molony, V., Kent, J. E. and Robertson, I. S. 1995. Assessment of acute and chronic pain after different methods of castration of calves. *Applied Animal Behavioural Sciences* **46:** 33-48.

Farm animal welfare — who writes the rules?
Occasional Publication No. 23 — British Society of Animal Science 1999
edited by A. J. F. Russel, C. A. Morgan, C. J. Savory, M. C. Appleby and T. L. J. Lawrence

Aggression in pigs: an example of using basic research in an applied context

H. W. Erhard†, M. Mendl[1]‡, and D. D. Ashley[2]

[1]*Scottish Agricultural College, Edinburgh, West Mains Road, Edinburgh EH9 3JG*
[2]*Veterinary School, University of Glasgow, Glasgow G61 1QH*

Introduction

Most animal welfare researchers agree that a mixture of applied and basic research is required to address the complex problems in this area. However, basic research is sometimes more difficult to justify, particularly in the current climate where the public, politicians and media often measure the importance of research primarily in terms of the economic benefits it can deliver. Basic research may thus be dismissed as pointless by the public at large. Here we provide an example of basic research in animal behaviour and welfare which, by addressing a fundamental question about behavioural organization in animals, has resulted in an applied research programme partly funded by commercial organizations, which may in the long-term have important economic and welfare consequences for the pig industry.

The study presented here was part of a 3-year project on the extent to which individual behavioural differences in pigs can be interpreted as characteristics of animal 'personality'. 'Do pigs have personality?' is a good example of a basic research project which at first sight might appear to have no applications. However, this research may in fact provide an important approach to tackling the welfare problems caused by high levels of aggression between pigs.

The aim of this project was to determine whether attack latency of individual pigs as recorded in a controlled test situation predicts elements of aggressive behaviour in a different situation, namely when groups of unfamiliar pigs were mixed. If this was the case, it was suggested that aggressiveness could be regarded as a personality trait.

Present addresses:
† Macaulay Land Use Research Institute, Craigiebuckler, Aberdeen AB15 8QH.
‡ Department of Clinical Veterinary Science, University of Bristol, Bristol BS40 5DU.

Material and methods

The attack latency test

In this test, an intruder pig is introduced into the test pig's home pen, and the time from when the test pig first makes contact with the intruder to when it attacks is recorded. Immediately after an attack, the intruder is removed from the pens and returned to its own home pen. If no attack occurred within 3·5 min after introduction of the intruder, the test is terminated and an attack latency of 3·5 min assigned to the test pig. This test was carried out on 2 days consecutively with 85 and on 78 pigs in 2 years consecutively (age 11 weeks), and with 53 pigs 4 weeks apart (age 7 and 11 weeks).

The mixing

One hundered and fifteen pigs were categorized according to their average attack latency into high and low aggressive pigs (H and L; $20·6 \pm 2·9$ and $156·5 \pm 8·5$ s respectively). Eighty-eight of these pigs were then mixed into new groups of eight pigs per group. Each new group contained four pigs from each of two litters. The new groups contained 4H + 4H (four groups), 4H + 4L (four groups) and 4L + 4L (three groups). The groups were observed and their behaviour recorded on days 0, 1, 2, 6 and 7 after mixing. Behaviours recorded were number, duration and intensity of fights (as measured by the number of skin lesions on the pigs from the winner litter in each group) and their lying preference (whether pigs avoided lying down next to a pig from the unfamiliar litter or not). The lying preference score ranges from '+1' (unfamiliar pigs were always avoided) to '−1' (unfamiliar pigs were never avoided). A score of '0' indicated that both happened equally often.

Results

Attack latencies were consistent across time (Spearman rank order correlations between tests on consecutive days (two replicates): $r_s = 0·56$ (no. = 85, $P < 0·001$) and $r_s = 0·73$ (no. = 78, $P < 0·001$) and across 4 weeks: $r_s = 0·57$ (no. = 53, $P < 0·001$; for more information see Erhard and Mendl, 1997).

When the pigs were categorized into high and low aggression pigs (H and L) according to their attack latency, and mixed into new groups, we found that attack latency predicted the time spent fighting (time (s) spent fighting per pig in the 2 h post mixing: H/H: 443·6, s.e. 168·0; H/L: 82·8, s.e. 54·5; L/L: 144·0, s.e. 7·75; ANOVA, $F_{2,8}$ = 3·12, $P < 0·10$) as well as the intensity of fighting (number of skin lesions on pigs from winner litter: H/H: 84·5, s.e. 3·95; H/L: 20·5, s.e. 5·67; L/L: 36·1, s.e. 10·67; ANOVA, $F_{2,8}$ = 28·27, $P < 0·001$) and the speed of group integration (lying preference score: H/H: 0·41, s.e. 0·12; $t = 3·44$, no. = 4, $P < 0·05$; H/L: 0·45, s.e. 0·12; $t = 3·70$, no. = 4, $P < 0·05$; L/L: 0·09, s.e. 0·16; $t = 0·53$, no. = 3, $P > 0·05$; for more detail see Erhard et al. 1997).

Discussion

The results show that attack latency was consistent across time and predictive of other elements of aggressive behaviour in a different situation (elements of fighting behaviour and group integration after mixing in a group environment). Aggressiveness may therefore be considered a personality trait in pigs.

These results have a value beyond the basic understanding of pig behaviour. Many studies which aimed at finding ways of reducing aggression after mixing, found considerable individual difference in the performance of aggressive behaviour (e.g. Kelley et al., 1980; McGlone and Morrow, 1988; Mount and Seabrook, 1993), which increases the number of animals needed to detect significant treatment differences. If the variation within treatment can be reduced by prior assessment of the individuals and by including this information in the experimental design, the number of individuals required to detect treatment differences can be reduced. Thus the number of pigs undergoing experimental mixing will be reduced, which is of importance, since mixing aggression poses serious welfare problems (e.g. Petherick and Blackshaw, 1987).

Erhard et al. (1997) reported that a major part of the problems occurring at mixing was due to the presence of pigs with short attack (SA) latencies. They fought more vigorously when mixed with other SA pigs and performed more biting/chasing behaviour when mixed with long attack latency pigs. Groups containing SA pigs were also slower to integrate, which was reflected in their lying preference. We therefore suggested that it may be beneficial for the welfare of pigs, if the proportion of SA pigs in the population could be reduced (Erhard et al., 1997).

Information on individual aggressiveness in pigs may thus be used in breeding programmes to reduce the proportion of high aggressive pigs in the population and thereby the suffering and economic losses caused by aggression in the pig industry as a whole. This possibility is now the subject of research funded jointly by government, pig industry companies and animal welfare charities.

Thus, a project which appeared not to have any applications has resulted in information which can be applied to improve animal welfare, with consequent economic implications.

Acknowledgements
The initial study was funded by the BBSRC, UFAW and SOAEFD.

References

Erhard, H. W. and Mendl, M. 1997. Measuring aggressiveness in growing pigs in a resident-intruder situation. *Applied Animal Behaviour Science* 54: 123-136

Erhard, H. W., Mendl, M., and Ashley, D. D. 1997. Individual aggressiveness can be measured and used to reduce aggression after mixing. *Applied Animal Behaviour Science* 54: 137-151

Kelley, K. W., McGlone, J. J., and Gaskins, C. T. 1980. Porcine aggression: measurements and effects of crowding and fasting. *Journal of Animal Science* 50: 336-341

McGlone, J. J. and Morrow, J. 1988. Reduction of pig agonistic behavior by androstenone. *Journal of Animal Science* 66: 880-884

Mount, N. C. and Seabrook, M. F. 1993. A study of aggression when group housed sows are mixed. *Applied Animal Behaviour Science* 36: 377-383

Petherick, J. C. and Blackshaw, J. K. 1987. A review of the factors influencing the aggressive and agonistic behaviour of the domestic pig. *Australian Journal of Experimental Agriculture* 27: 605-611

Farm animal welfare — who writes the rules?
Occasional Publication No. 23 — British Society of Animal Science 1999
edited by A. J. F. Russel, C. A. Morgan, C. J. Savory, M. C. Appleby and T. L. J. Lawrence

Summary and conclusions

R. C. Roberts

Institute of Cell, Animal and Population Biology, University of Edinburgh, West Mains Road, Edinburgh EH9 3JN

This is a highly personal view of the proceedings of the meeting. I shall not attempt to summarize the individual papers, if only because the authors have more than adequately done so themselves. Instead, I shall concentrate on drawing together some general themes that emerged from the discussions of a very heterogeneous audience, comprising as it did representatives of welfare organizations, the agricultural and allied industries, research and advisory organizations and finally, a sprinkling of people whose rôle in animal welfare is best described as administrative. Given such a potential diversity of viewpoints, it is perhaps remarkable that considerable unanimity was achieved on a number of topics.

It was generally agreed that much has already been achieved in areas of animal welfare. There is a much greater awareness of welfare issues, among producers and consumers alike, than was the case even a decade ago. It was also to be noted that in general, there is now much better communication between the welfare lobbies and the livestock industry. While the industry could claim, with some justification, that it has always been pro-welfare, it is anxious to improve its practices and welcomes constructive comment. If nothing more, industry is fully aware of the commercial implications of welfare issues, and is very intolerant of any malpractices that damage its image. All this emerged very clearly from the meeting and is the context in which much of the discussion is to be interpreted.

It was strongly asserted by more than one speaker, and never seriously disputed, that while improved welfare is technically feasible, it can seldom be done without incurring additional costs. These costs inevitably feed through to the consumer and it was suggested by some speakers that an increasing proportion of consumers is increasingly willing to pay more for welfare-friendly products. There are some encouraging suggestions that this may be so, to some extent, but in my view, the case was not fully made. The data are very difficult to obtain and even more difficult to interpret rigorously. What people say they would pay and what they actually choose to pay, given a choice, are far from perfectly correlated. Also, several branded animal products incorporate welfare friendliness but whether consumers buy these because of the welfare or whether they are persuaded by other features of the brand — labelling, packaging, reliability — is not always clear. These are only examples from a complex array of factors that determine consumer choices but there is doubt in my mind that the willingness-to-pay claim has not yet been resolved. I do not know for sure, but I suspect, that sales of paté de foie gras have not declined much as awareness of welfare issues have increased.

In any case, we have a problem about increasing the price of food. It may not matter, or matter very much, to well paid people in employment. But it could matter a great deal to people on income support. Cheap food has been one feature of agricultural policy in the United Kingdom (UK) since World War II. Agricultural systems have evolved to be what they are in order to put the most competitively priced product on the market. It therefore follows inexorably that any change to the system, for welfare or other purposes, is almost bound to put up the price. Animal welfare, in common with the whole range of environmental issues that engage our attention, tend to be the luxuries of a well fed, affluent society. In parts of the world where there are intolerable levels of infant and child mortality, people seem to worry less about the welfare of their domestic livestock. We need not approve of their attitude but we can still view it with some compassion

While the willingness-to-pay issue was not resolved at the meeting, it will over time inevitably resolve itself. On one point, there was complete agreement: it would be totally wrong to direct welfare-friendly products at a niche market. That would contravene the principle that improved welfare of farm animals is a necessary goal in its own right. It would be unethical to relegate it to a marketing ploy to develop high-priced products; it must develop on a wider base and for its own sake. The point was also made, and accepted with sympathy, that the current

(September 1998) financial plight of the livestock industry had potentially disastrous consequences for animal welfare. You cannot have good stockmanship if you have no stockmen to carry it out.

While these and many other aspects of welfare were vented at the meeting, its main theme was: who writes the rules? On this, there was virtual agreement: the consumer does. The ways in which the consumer does this are varied, and the individual papers go into different aspects. There are two main avenues by which the consumer directly and indirectly sets welfare standards: (i) via the legislators, for whom consumers vote (or not), and (ii) via the retailers, whom they keep in business (or not).

Consumers, in total form what we call society and there is no member of that society who does not consume. While individuals select what precisely they will consume, more generally society at large decides what is acceptable or unacceptable. Governments and politicians, in framing legislation, will react to the wishes of the electorate. They may offer leadership or guidance but they tend to be less proactive in many areas than they would sometimes have us believe, especially as elections are approached. Animal welfare is no exception; governments reflect the will of society. That said, it is not always an easy task for them to interpret what society wants. In the UK they are formally advised on welfare matters by the Farm Animal Welfare Council. This is an independent, broad-based body that seeks a comprehensive and balanced view of welfare, which usually forms the basis of government's further thinking on the matter. Other bodies can also influence government action, not least producer organizations and the welfare lobbies. As mentioned earlier, there is an increasing willingness by the producers and the welfarists to work in tandem. However, probably the most important influence on government, among all the advice and consultation, is the will of the electorate. The consumers will, in the end, decide what legislation is necessary and acceptable.

Government legislation is all very well, but as pointed out clearly by two speakers, there are increasing difficulties about harmonizing UK legislation with those of the European Union (EU) and World Trade Organization (WTO). The thinking on animal welfare may be converging among members of the EU, though there may still be some way to go. However, WTO regulations may open up trade with countries whose welfare standards fall short of local aspirations. As things stand, this problem is insoluble, except in so far as the consumer, again, may exercise influence through the retail sector. But this would require the consumer to be informed about welfare standards throughout the world and then act on them. This does not seem to be a realistic prospect.

Nearer home, the consumer can have enormous influence through the retailers, and that is undoubtedly the most direct way of setting the rules on welfare. Veal crates were banned largely through consumer resistance of the product. The sale of free-range eggs is said to be increasing, albeit slowly. And there has certainly been an increase in the labelling of animal products that imply improved welfare, e.g. 'outdoor pork'. These trends will continue, though the standards may be set by consumers prepared to discriminate on perceptions of welfare, rather than on any detailed knowledge of the means of production.

An interesting point of view was expressed during one of the discussions of the rôle of the consumer. When buying a washing machine or a cotton garment, the purchase is made on grounds of affordability and value for money. The consumer does not worry whether the article was produced under conditions of sweated labour, or child labour, or in defiance of health and safety at work. And so, the argument ran, it should be with food products; the consumer should be able to assume that welfare standards were up to scratch, as enshrined in legislation and adequately monitored by whoever. While this view has merit in a local context, it only underscores the difficulty of applying local standards world-wide.

Although well over half of those attending the meeting were scientists, it was interesting to note the general agreement, even among the scientists themselves, that scientists could not and should not write the rules. There are reasons for this, not least that the science itself is seldom precise enough to be definitive. But more importantly, everyone accepted that the decisions on welfare must reside with society at large. The scientists have an important rôle in supplying information and in seeking a better understanding of the issues involved and in suggesting solutions. But beyond that, they simply wear a consumer hat, like everyone else. The issues go beyond, often well beyond, the domain of science.

It goes without saying that any rules must be enforced, if they are to be of any use. This means monitoring, often difficult and always expensive. And if anyone breaks the rules there must be effective sanctions. There are in place, and have been for a long time, legal sanctions with severe penalties for some offences. These laws undoubtedly are effective but the fact that we can still read about serious offences, from time to time, illustrates the difficulty of enforcement. While legal sanctions are the most reassuring, we need not dismiss the power of self-regulation, if exercised properly. To kick someone out of the club, if he misbehaves, can be a very effective sanction. But the will must be there to use it, if need be.

In summary, my impressions of the main points to emerge from the meeting were as follows. (a) The consumer, quite properly, writes the rules, with various bodies helping. (b) Much has already been achieved, both in terms of scientific rigour and the adoption by industry of improved welfare practices. (c) Further improvements will doubtless be achieved; we are in fact unlikely to reach a steady state where no one wants more welfare. (d) There is a remarkable and widespread desire by industry to continue to improve welfare standards.

While the general picture is therefore encouraging, there are still difficulties. (e) There are problems, not fully addressed at this meeting, about the methods and the costs of effective monitoring, and about the application of proper sanctions should the need arise. (f) There is the much bigger problem of international acceptance of common standards; if any country rejects a food product on welfare grounds, it is no solution to export bad welfare to more distant areas where the consumer has little influence and no control, and probably little knowledge of the conditions under which imported foods are produced.